CAPABILITIES IN A JUST SOCIETY

What sort of entitlements should citizens have in a just society? In this book, Rutger Claassen sets out a theory of what he terms 'navigational agency', whereby citizens should be able to navigate freely between social practices. This shows how individuals can be at the same time free and autonomous in striving for their own goals in life, but also embedded in social practices in which they have to cooperate with others. He argues that for navigational agency people need three sets of core capabilities: those that allow human empowerment in civil society, a decent level of socio-economic subsistence and political participation in democratic decision-making procedures. The idea of navigational agency, the book argues, provides an alternative to dominant versions of the capability approach to social justice, and strengthens its liberal foundations.

RUTGER CLAASSEN is an Associate Professor of Ethics and Political Philosophy at the Department of Philosophy and Religious Studies at Utrecht University. He has published in journals including *British Journal of Political Science, Economics & Philosophy, European Journal of Philosophy, Law & Philosophy* and *Politics, Philosophy & Economics.*

CAPABILITIES IN A JUST SOCIETY

A Theory of Navigational Agency

RUTGER CLAASSEN

Utrecht University

CAMBRIDGE
UNIVERSITY PRESS

CAMBRIDGE
UNIVERSITY PRESS

University Printing House, Cambridge CB2 8BS, United Kingdom

One Liberty Plaza, 20th Floor, New York, NY 10006, USA

477 Williamstown Road, Port Melbourne, VIC 3207, Australia

314–321, 3rd Floor, Plot 3, Splendor Forum, Jasola District Centre,
New Delhi – 110025, India

79 Anson Road, #06-04/06, Singapore 079906

Cambridge University Press is part of the University of Cambridge.

It furthers the University's mission by disseminating knowledge in the pursuit of education,
learning, and research at the highest international levels of excellence.

www.cambridge.org
Information on this title: www.cambridge.org/9781108473262
DOI: 10.1017/9781108561853

First published 2018

Printed and bound in Great Britain by Clays Ltd, Elcograf S.p.A.

A catalogue record for this publication is available from the British Library.

ISBN 978-1-108-47326-2 Hardback

To my father, Karel Claassen,
and to the memory of my mother,
Marlies Claassen-Vermunt

Contents

Figures

Tables

Acknowledgements

Work on this book has taken six years, and my engagement with the capability approach and the other themes integrated in the capability theory presented here goes back even further. I first used an agency-based capability framework in my dissertation (2008) on the moral limits of the market, with applications to the commodification of the media, care work and security services. After that, I also employed the capability approach as a normative theory in other applied contexts, from the rights of future generations to disputes within competition law. Those working on applied topics will recognize that the variety of normative considerations coming up when thinking about practical questions can be bewildering; and many prefer to work with loosely grounded, pluralist normative approaches to study such applied topics. I have always felt the urge to see how a plurality of normative considerations could be integrated into one consistent, and well-founded normative framework (I recognize that this urge – which I simply cannot suppress – is for better or worse: there are dangers to over-systematization too). At some point, this focused my attention on the general project of defending a capability theory to social justice. Being dissatisfied with the way the capability approach was developed thus far in political philosophy, I decided at some point to put down my own thoughts in a book. This was a much longer enterprise than expected and over the years I accumulated many debts.

First of all, I would like to thank Joel Anderson, Bert van den Brink, Marcus Düwell, Thomas Fossen and Ingrid Robeyns for commenting on draft chapters of the manuscript. The discussions with them about the themes of this book have been of great benefit to me over the course of the years. I have known each of them for a long time and their own philosophical commitments have been a continuous source of intellectual inspiration for me. Indeed, it is not unfair to say that this book would not have been the same without having been exposed for so many years to Joel's work on personal autonomy, Bert's work on liberal perfection-ism, Marcus's work on agency and human rights and Ingrid's work on the capability approach. Thomas's role is special given his enduring critical stance to *normativist* projects in political philosophy in general, but has been not less valuable for that in reminding me of the limits of what I try to achieve here.

Several other people sent me comments on draft chapters which were immensely helpful: Elizabeth Anderson, Florian Bekkers, Justin Bernstein, Deryck Beyleveld, Constanze Binder, Gerhard Bos, Morten Byskov, Robin Celikates, Dascha Düring, Fleur Jongepier, Marie Göbel, Lisa Herzog, Annemarie Kalis, Pietro Maffetone, Marco Meyer, Tim Meijers, Fabian Schuppert and Lieske Voget-Kleschin. I had the honour of subjecting the almost-finished book manuscript to the scrutiny of the Research Master students in the Core Readings session of 2016, and I would like to thank – without offense to the others – Suzanne Jacobi, Marin Kaufman, Dick Timmer and Leon van Rijsbergen for their intense engagement with the project. A special thanks to Sem de Maagt, who read and commented on more draft versions than is healthy for a normal human being. I often felt unable to do justice to the depth of all their comments, but I offer the finished book hoping it does justice to some of them.

The work has been presented at several occasions. In particular, I would like to thank audiences at the Practical Philosophy Colloquium of Groningen University, the Annual Conference of the Dutch Research School in Philosophy, the Working Group of Political Philosophy of the Dutch Research School for Practical Philosophy (especially Gijs van Donsselaar's incisive comments), the Conference of the Association for Social and Political Philosophy in Amsterdam, 2015, the Human Development and Capabilities Association Conference in Washington, DC, 2015 (especially the comments by Des Gasper and Mozaffar Qizilbash) and the Workshop on Development Ethics in Utrecht, 2016. Special thanks go to the audience at the Ethics Institute Colloquium in Utrecht which discussed parts of the manuscript on several occasions, to Huub Brouwer for organizing a Dutch Research School of Philosophy (Onderzoeksschool Wijsbegeerte, OZSW) 2017 book symposium on the manuscript and to Martin van Hees, Thomas Nys, Jojanneke Vanderveen and Huub himself for their challenging comments on that occasion.

The project benefited from financing by the Netherlands Organisation for Scientific Research (NWO), under VENI-grant no. 275-20-031 (2012–15), which is gratefully acknowledged. I thank the *European*

Journal of Philosophy for reprinting the paper 'An Agency-based Capability Theory of Justice'. It appears here as Chapter 2 with minor revisions except for one substantial addition of a new passage at the very end (from: 'This leaves open the question ...'). At Cambridge University Press, two anonymous reviewers provided supportive reviews as well as valuable critical suggestions. Hilary Gaskin has been enormously encouraging and supportive of the project as an editor and Marianne Nield has provided invaluable assistance.

Finally, I wish to thank my wife Carine for her comprehension and patience with me which, as always, is indispensable when working on a book. My children Eline, Casper and Stijn (now ten, eight and four years old) should be thanked for their lively presence which has always been a pleasurable distraction from the moment they would storm into my study room commanding their father's attention. The humorous dedication circulating on the internet – 'thanks to my wife and children, without whom this book would have been completed two years earlier' – does contain some truth, but this is not something I regret. Nonetheless, sometimes it was better to retreat from their company, and at these occasions several other family members have lent me their quiet rooms upstairs in their own homes: Karel Claassen, Christianne and Jan Verwoerd and Anna and Pieter Punt. For their loving support, I thank all of them.

The book is dedicated to my father, whose professional practice as a lawyer, and my late mother, whose loving hand during my childhood, have implicitly taught me more about justice than I am able to convey explicitly in these pages.

Introduction

In a just society, each citizen is equally entitled to a set of basic capabilities. This view is at the heart of the capability approach to social justice. Justice is not a matter of equalizing citizens' bundles of resources (exemplified by their income and wealth) or their level of subjective well-being. Rather, it is a matter of guaranteeing for them a set of basic capabilities – abilities or opportunities to function in specific ways. This is the starting point of any capability approach to justice, a view that I share. But there is a wide range of theories of social justice that are compatible with this basic commitment and the two main theories of social justice by proponents of the capability metric – that of Amartya Sen and that of Martha Nussbaum – have attracted numerous criticisms, many of which I share. This book, therefore, aims to provide a fundamentally different capability theory of justice that demonstrates the potential of the capability approach to give an attractive answer to the question of social justice.

Sen's approach is characterised by a staunch refusal to make substantive claims about the basic capabilities required for social justice, insisting that the determination of any list of requisite capabilities should be left to the democratic process. Nussbaum offers an elaborated capability theory of justice and I side with her ambition rather than Sen's reluctance. But in formulating its criterion for selecting basic capabilities, Nussbaum's theory is wedded to a neo-Aristotelian view of human flourishing. Like many critics, I find her approach too perfectionist and insufficiently liberal. Hence, in this book I propose to break new ground and offer a third route, according to which basic capabilities should be identified as those necessary to lead the life of what I call 'a free and autonomous agent'. On my approach, then, the notion of agency becomes the normative criterion for the selection of basic capabilities required for social justice.

A key challenge that arises when developing this new direction is that the notions of agency that we ordinarily find in liberalism are overly individualistic. This opens the door to the criticism that they present a parochial, Western way of life. To rebut these objections, I propose to embed the notion of agency into the social context of action to a much greater extent than is usually done. I, thus, develop a conception of free and autonomous agency as embedded in social practices and then distinguish 'participational agency' from 'navigational agency' as two types of social embeddedness. In these terms, we can be agents by participating as a member within social practices (like playing tennis or being a judge in a court) or we can be agents in a stronger sense by being able to navigate between social practices and to choose for ourselves which practices we want to participate in. This distinction allows us to more clearly articulate what justice should be about. I defend the view that justice should be understood in terms of (capabilities for) navigational agency; our real ability to choose the social practices in which we participate.

In a slogan, then, the book aims to 'liberalize the capability approach, while socializing liberalism'. The resulting theory I call an 'agency-based capability theory of justice'. This book aims to offer a new way to realise the potential of the capability approach to offer a theory of social justice and, hence, a new candidate for theorizing social justice more generally.

Justice is about giving people their due – this rough description implies that all individuals should somehow be treated with equal respect and concern. But how should this equality of individuals be understood? They somehow have an equal claim, but what should an equal, just distribution be about? Since Amartya Sen's paper 'Equality of What?' (Sen 1979) the debate about the metric suitable for formulating distributive principles has been framed in terms of the distribution of resources, capabilities or utility. The capability metric can be understood as intermediate between these other two metrics. On the input-side, economic systems of production create a bundle of resources (goods and services) which is then distributed in some way to individuals. These resources function as a means to realise a set of capabilities. On the output side, once people have a set of capabilities, they can choose for themselves how to function. This will lead to outcomes, which in the capability approach are called 'achieved functionings'. Individuals will derive a level of utility (satisfaction, happiness) from that level of functioning: a subjective state indicating the value of the achieved functionings to them.

Nussbaum, Sen and others have argued that, in conceptualizing justice, a capability metric is superior to both utilitarian and resourcist metrics.[1] If justice concentrates on resources, it confuses means with ends (Sen has argued this 'fetishizes' resources (Sen 1990)). This is problematic because it ignores inter-personal variations in the ability to convert resources into capabilities. If one person needs more resources than another to reach the same capability level, it would be perverse to think that equal treatment involves giving them the same bundle of resources. For example, a physically disabled person often requires more resources to be able to transport her/himself from home to work than a person not suffering this disability. Human diversity in the conversion of resources into capabilities needs to be taken into account. One response is to reformulate the demands of justice in terms of equality of utility. But if justice concentrates on utility, then it makes society responsible for the level of satisfaction people derive from their actions. This leads to the well-known problems of expensive tastes and adaptive preferences. If one person needs more capabilities to realise the same level of satisfaction, a utilitarian theory requires that society cater to these differences and offer the person with the expensive taste this more extensive set of capabilities. Similarly, if one person has adapted to misery and requires fewer capabilities to be as happy as other persons, society can do justice to them by offering this smaller set. These are perverse results, which deny people's responsibility for their own choices and the subjective well-being resulting from these choices.

I will not discuss these familiar arguments between the different metrics in this book and I will take the superiority of the capability metric for granted (R. Dworkin 2000; Pogge 2002; Pierik and Robeyns 2007; Sen 2009; E. Anderson 2010a; Brighouse and Robeyns 2010; Kelleher 2015). The intermediate position between resources and utility considers a person's potential – rather than actual – achievements normatively decisive and views this potential as a matter of a free choice on the basis of the resources she has at her disposal. The question then becomes: which potential achievements? If justice is to be conceptualised in terms of a person's set of capabilities, which capabilities are to be in that set? Obviously, the basic formula will involve each citizen being equally entitled to a set of basic capabilities. But which basic capabilities are these supposed to be?

---

[1] This book focuses on the capability approach's contribution to the field of theorizing about justice. The approach has also been applied in other areas (such as quality of life measurement, human development policies, project evaluations, etc.). It is multi-disciplinary with contributions from philosophers, social scientists, economists, etc. For overviews of work in the capability approach, see Robeyns (2005b, 2006, 2017b) and Deneulin and Shahani (2009).

This question has received two radically different answers. On the one hand, Sen has been reluctant or even opposed to presenting a canonical capability list, arguing that basic capabilities should be selected in a process of public reasoning (Sen 1999b, 2004a, 2009). He endorses the proceduralist approach that leaves capability selection up to democratic processes of public deliberation. This reluctance to theorize a list of basic capabilities has met with several criticisms (Pogge 2002; Nussbaum 2003a; Srinivasan 2007). It is a matter of some debate what exactly Sen's stance is; whether he is actively hostile to capability theories of justice or merely sees himself as offering a capability *approach* that leaves open (and remains agnostic) about the development of several types of capability *theories* (Robeyns 2016). To the extent that Sen and others actively hold that it is problematic when academics/philosophers try to propose fully specified capability theories of justice, theirs is an example of a wider 'displacement critique' (Baderin 2016a, 2016b) directed against theories of justice in political philosophy. My main problem with this position is that it dissolves theorizing about justice into democratic theory; it becomes impossible to give substantive input in the democratic process about what justice requires.[2] That, in a way, is a missed opportunity for democracy itself. Democracies thrive, not when political philosophers – or others – stop arguing for a specific conception of justice, but when they contribute to political debates by offering their theories as proposals in the public arena (Claassen 2011b; Byskov 2017). I will not focus on the debates with Sen's view about these matters in this book. Instead, I concentrate my critical attention on Martha Nussbaum's capability theory – she did work out a more-or-less complete capability theory of justice; as this work also wants to do.

In the course of a series of articles and books, Nussbaum has formulated her famous set of ten central capabilities for a good, flourishing life (Nussbaum 2000b, 2006, 2011b). This proposal was originally presented as a neo-Aristotelian theory of the good (Nussbaum 1990). It has attracted criticism from liberal philosophers who are worried about the perfectionist character of her theory. The core of their concern is that Nussbaum's theory prescribes, for all the major spheres in life, what it is to flourish in these spheres and then translates this theory of the good into specific constitutional entitlements to be protected by the state.

---

[2] Another problem is that democratic deliberators may be essentially as prone to adaptive preferences and other vices of subjectivist theories as the utilitarianism Sen set out to replace when introducing the capability metric. See Dowding (2006), Sugden (2006), Sumner (2006) and Qizilbash (2011).

I share these criticisms and will explain them in more detail in Chapter 1, where I also argue that Nussbaum's turn to a theory of 'political liberalism' has not – in my view – helped her capability theory escape these criticisms.

Most defenders of the capability approach to justice choose either a Nussbaum-style substantive, objectivist-list theory of well-being or a Sen-style proceduralist reliance on the democratic process.[3] This dichotomy reinforces the impression that one either has to go for a substantive (but largely perfectionist) theory or a procedural (but largely empty) theory. I believe this is a false dilemma. My theoretical inclination is to agree both with those who object that proceduralist theories miss the normative substance necessary for a full capability theory of justice and also with those who object that Nussbaum's capability theory is too perfectionist. The solution, as I see it, is to go for a substantive but thinner capability theory, based on a liberal conception of free and autonomous agency.

To position this proposal for an agency-based capability theory, the book will start by situating the capability approach in the debate about liberalism. It is, of course, not self-evident that a just society should be liberal. Communitarian critics of John Rawls and other liberals in the 1980s argued that liberalism uses an 'unencumbered' or 'atomist' view of the person that would insufficiently take into account the social or community-based aspects of the good human life. This criticism led to two competing liberal responses. Perfectionist liberals acknowledged the charge and defended liberalism as a theory based on a conception of the person as an autonomous chooser. Political liberals thought that the communitarian criticism gave us reasons to move in the opposite direction and show how a liberal theory could do without a conception of the person, or at least without a strong commitment to autonomy as an ethical ideal underlying one's political theory. The debate is often cast in terms of an ideal of political neutrality with respect to the good life (political liberals) versus a liberal theory of the good life as the autonomous life (perfectionist liberals). In Chapter 1 I argue that we do best to embrace a position in this debate which I call 'moderate perfectionist liberalism'. The thrust of this position is that liberalism – or indeed any political theory – cannot escape a commitment to an ideal of the good life, but should strive to minimise this commitment. A liberal view of the person as an autonomous agent

---

[3] For examples of objective list theories see Alkire (2002) and Qizilbash (1998), for proceduralist approaches see Robeyns (2005a) and Crocker (2008).

is trying to do exactly that. While the state, when using such an ideal as the justification of its policies, cannot remain neutral on the value of autonomy, it can try to stay neutral on all other matters that autonomous persons may decide upon for themselves. Using the capability theory of Nussbaum as a leading example, I argue that such a moderate perfectionist liberalism offers a more defensible understanding of the liberal aspiration to a just society than either more strongly perfectionist theories or political liberal theories. Working out this moderate perfectionist liberalism is the task of the remainder of this book.

We can agree with the communitarians that it is important to conceive of human agency as embedded in social practices. This is why it is important to emphasise that agency is always *participational agency* – agency embedded in social practices where humans coordinate their actions to achieve common and individual ends and play roles vis-à-vis each other. Even so, this does not take away the essential freedom and autonomy of agents. They still have their role to play and to determine for themselves how to do so. Liberalism becomes relevant at the point at which agents are able to expand their powers to act freely beyond the practices to which they happen – by birth, accident, or force – to belong. This is a special type of agency that I call *navigational agency* – the ability to move freely between social practices. In a just society, this is what individuals are genuinely able to do. The theory defending this type of agency is perfectionist in the sense that it contains a theory of the good; the good of free and autonomous agency. Nonetheless, this is a moderately perfectionist theory in that it remains limited to the value of free agency and does not extend to include other values. Showing that such a position can be sustained is the challenge I confront in the book as a whole. If my proposal works, it should provide an attractive position compared to strong perfectionists (such as Nussbaum's early neo-Aristotelian theory) and political liberals who (unsuccessfully, in my view) attempt to eschew reference to a theory of the good altogether.

The task of Chapter 2 is to present these conceptions of agency. First, I identify a conception of individual *agency* as consisting of a person's *autonomy* (i.e. their capacities to deliberate and choose their own ends) and a person's *freedom* (i.e. their capacities to realise their ends). Thus, agency as I will use the term comprises autonomy and freedom. Second, this conception of free and autonomous agency is to be understood as socially embedded in the sense that every action is a move in a social practice. Having defined social practices, I show how this leads us to accept two conceptions of agency, instead of one. *Participational agency* is the ability of an agent to make a move within a social practice – i.e. to be a participant in a specific social context. *Navigational agency* includes the abilities to: (1) entering and exiting social practices; (2) resolving conflicts between practices; (3) reforming existing practices; and (4) creating new practices. Liberalism's central claim to freedom can then be reformulated as a concern with a particular type of agency – i.e. navigational agency. These concepts are, in turn, specified in terms of capabilities so that justice emerges as a requirement to protect rights to the capabilities to navigational agency. I argue that agency itself is a (meta-)capability and that agency needs to be spelled out in terms of a list of basic capabilities, as agency's defining conditions.

The next step, in Chapter 3, is to justify this theory: why accept that justice is a matter of protecting for each citizen equal rights to navigational agency? The chapter first discusses how to introduce and understand such rights-claims. It shows how rights (and duties) are part and parcel of the deontic structure of social practices. Hence, agents always find themselves in social roles in which rights and duties are ascribed to them. The question is whether and how specific rights to navigational agency can be justified, even to those who understand themselves as what I call 'mere-participational agents' – those who have been socialized into the acceptance of specific social roles and who do not understand themselves as entitled to abdicate these roles and take on other ones instead. Examples of oppressed individuals in strongly hierarchical cultures would be typical examples of such agents. The chapter presents a long argument for the claim that even such agents, when engaging in their role-fulfilment, must inevitably critically assess the social purposes of the practices to which they have been bound. Moreover, such a critical scrutiny, where it is sufficiently rational, can be shown to issue in the conclusion that they should claim rights to become navigational agents. The method of justification here relies on transcendental argumentation – its conclusion is a rational implication of acceptance of the particular starting point in the self-understanding of participational agents. This is offered as an alternative type of justification compared to the normal appeals to reflective equilibrium in normative political philosophy.

Once we have a metric of justice, what is lacking is a specification of the distributive principle. This is the topic of Chapter 4. Here I will build upon Nussbaum's (and others') suggestion that the capability approach is *sufficientarian*; for each capability what is owed to citizens is a threshold level which specifies what is sufficient or enough. An 'equal entitlement to a set of basic capabilities', then, does not mean a strictly equal amount, but an equal right to a threshold amount which is the same for everyone. The sufficiency threshold, in my theory, is defined by what is sufficient to develop one's navigational agency. However, this sufficientarianism must be qualified in several ways. I argue in some detail for the incorporation of elements of the competing theories of prioritarianism (namely below the threshold), egalitarianism (namely for positional goods) and luck-egalitarianism (namely where choice is needed to develop agency). No short summary of these arguments is possible. The overall point is a nuanced yet consistent framework that does justice to the intuitions behind all these distributive schemes, yet justifies all of them by relating them to the development of agency as the central political task.

The three chapters in Part III elaborate the theory of Part II so as to establish which basic capabilities are required for navigational agency.[4] I argue for the inclusion of three sets of basic capabilities: empowerment capabilities (Chapter 5), subsistence capabilities (Chapter 6) and political capabilities (Chapter 7). The distinction is familiar from theories of basic rights into three types of rights – civil, socio-economic and political – and similar distinctions have also been proposed by other capability theorists (E. Anderson 1999, 316–18; Axelsen and Nielsen 2017).

First, *empowerment capabilities* empower individuals to make autonomous choices and lead free lives in civil society. This category makes participational agents into navigational agents, and it includes the main civil liberties as well as a capability to education. In Chapter 5 I concentrate on a particular challenge that these capabilities raise: can one specify these capabilities without falling back into a reliance upon perfectionist values? This question is discussed in two cases studies of the autonomy-side and the freedom-side of free and autonomous agency. On the autonomy-side the problem arises when we look at cases of adaptive preferences. To decide whether persons with adaptive preferences are to be subjected to paternalist interventions, requires a theory of autonomy that does not itself introduce perfectionist values through the back door. On the freedom-side, I take the freedom of association as a case study which raises the question whether we can specify rights to exit without relying on perfectionist values. In both cases, I argue, the challenge of avoiding perfectionism can be met.

Second, navigational agents need *subsistence capabilities*, such as basic health, housing and nourishment. Without these capabilities, one cannot

---

[4] The three sets of capabilities I think minimally belong on such a list. Whether there are basic capabilities which I have missed, I leave to readers to judge.

lead the life of a 'mere-participational agent', let alone that of a navigational agent. In Chapter 6 I specify what subsistence requires, by making the case for three principles for the distribution of subsistence capabilities. The first principle endorses a socially calibrated and upwardly adjustable subsistence threshold for these capabilities, the second principle makes this conditional upon certain demands of reciprocity and the third principle subjects this to a requirement of efficiency. While making the case for these principles, I also argue for the acceptance of positive duties (against libertarians and other opponents of such duties) which is vital if there is to be a right to subsistence in the first place; and I argue for a basic right to a system of property rights. In the final part of the chapter I discuss whether social justice should include a redistribution of income and wealth that goes beyond the subsistence threshold. I endorse a positive answer to this question, mainly (but not only) because of the detrimental effect of wealth inequalities upon the fair value of the political capabilities.

Finally, navigational agents also need *political capabilities*. These include capabilities that grant citizens opportunities for participation in the political sphere and also capabilities for legal standing. In this way we can ensure that the other capabilities are defined, protected and enforced by the political system. In Chapter 7 I focus on the question of whether democracy – defined as the political system which grants each citizen an equal right to participation – can be justified. I first explain the defects of existing liberal defences, which focus either on the instrumental value of democracy for implementing the other basic rights or its intrinsic contribution to citizens' freedom or autonomy. I then offer a new defence of democracy that is based on the equal duty citizens have to protect each other's basic (subsistence and empowerment) rights, which implies that they need equal rights to participation as a necessary means to fulfil that duty. The second half explains the implications of this stance for the issue of representative versus direct democracy, the always-present threat of a tyranny of majority rule and how to draw the boundaries of democratic political communities in a globalised world.

These three chapters cover a lot of terrain and, therefore, do so in a way which is necessarily broad-ranging and sketchy, whereas a book-length treatment would often be appropriate. The defence for presenting such a bird-eye's view of the issues surrounding empowerment, subsistence and political capabilities is my wish to give the reader a picture of what acceptance of the agency-based capability in the first half of the book would imply. The chapters of Part III offer what I consider to be the most convincing extensions from the theory developed in Part II. This should not be taken, however, as a simple matter of deduction from first principles to applications. It will undoubtedly be possible to reach some of the same 'applied' conclusions on the basis of other (competing) theoretical frameworks; and some may want to make forceful arguments for each of these issues that I should accept (slightly) other conclusions on the basis of the agency-based capability theory than I do here myself.[5] With these reservations in mind, the agency-based capability theory does provide a determinate lens on the issues of empowerment, subsistence and democracy – and in doing so constrains our range of options in how best to think about these issues. I have tried my best to fine-tune the spotlight as sharply as possible to show what picture emerges on the wall.[6]

Some final words of clarification about the overall status of the theory to be presented here. First, the theory is a *political theory*, more specifically a theory of 'political morality' (Raz 1986, 3). Such a theory is not a theory of morality overall, but focuses directly and exhaustively on the (moral) principles which can justify political action. The aim, then, is to describe which principles ought to be followed by those who have public authority. Such a theory is not a complete guide to political action, in two senses. One is that much of the specification of what public authorities ought to do needs to be done outside the theory and in its application. Principles do not determine their own application and hard work remains to be done through practical judgment in concrete circumstances

---

[5] The merits of a philosophical theory of justice, I think, lie not in reaching practical prescriptions about how to act that are, compared to rival already existing theories, completely distinctive and unique. While we can demand of a theory to have some action-guiding force (or at least to offer the normative principles which, when combined with suitable empirical data, would offer such guidance), the attractiveness of a theory of justice in my view should be judged by whether it is able to (1) offer a basis for defeating theories, which endorse different, competing prescriptions and (2) do so in a way which is better than 'fellow-travelers', i.e. theories which endorse similar (or even the same) prescriptions. The practical conclusions in Chapters 5, 6 and 7 therefore are not necessarily unique compared to every conceivable alternative theory, but they do try to show the added value (if not superiority) of using an argument from (navigational) agency instead of some other philosophical basis, to reach these conclusions. In the end, the primary value of philosophy is not in discovering completely new beliefs about the practical policies for a just society, however welcome that is as a by-product, now and then, on those rare occasions that it happens. Rather, it is in getting clear on 'why we ought (not) to believe what we currently believe', i.e. to increase and where necessary to criticize our present self-understanding.

[6] Elsewhere I used the capability approach for a range of applied topics: to evaluate the moral limits of the market (Claassen 2009a, 2011a, 2011c, 2011d), the justification of private property (Claassen 2015), the criteria for interpreting competition law (Claassen and Gerbrandy 2016), the existence of duties to future generations (Claassen 2016) and financial market regulation (Claassen 2017).

of political action. The other sense in which a theory of political morality is not complete is that it may allow for, but not require, certain types of political action. Some things that public authorities do may be prohibited by the theory, others required, but there may be a large area in between with actions that are permitted but not required by the theory. The theory may be morally indifferent in resolving some coordination issues – which do require public action – one way or the other (this distinction is familiar from moral theory more generally). I will here stay agnostic on the size and scope of this domain of the permitted-but-not-required (Claassen 2013).

The concept of public authority should be understood widely. I will repeatedly replace it by 'the state' since this is traditionally the main public authority. This equivocation is not meant to imply a belief that this is a realistic assumption. State power has been hollowed out at least in two ways: by international and supranational public organizations (like the UN, the WTO and the EU), and by private organizations fulfilling public functions (like associations and corporations). References to the state will be meant as a placeholder for whoever exercises public functions over a group of people. The defining attribute, then, is rather the *coercive powers* that come with public authority. Whoever is able to exercise powers over others which these cannot escape, has to justify these actions; political morality is meant to test these justifications. Coercive power needs to be exercised 'for the common good' or 'in the public interest' and the theory is to define that good/interest. This raises complicated questions about the nature of 'the political' which have to remain unaddressed here.

Second, a theory of political morality is here (as in much other philosophical work) given *in terms of social justice*. The task of politics is to ensure we live in a just society. This implies a specific conception of justice so that it covers the whole terrain of required political action, recalling Rawls's definition of justice as 'the first virtue of social institutions' (Rawls 1999a, 3). Some lament this association of social justice with the political sphere because so much of justice needs to be realised outside the political sphere. For example, the distribution of parental favours between children, the distribution of goods between friends or within private associations can be characterised as 'fair' or 'unfair', which implies that the concept of justice has application outside the political sphere. Also, many have rightly argued that informal social norms can be as unfair as government policies. Their dissolution will (besides possible political action) also require a change of attitude of private individuals. I do not – and need not – deny this, in order to maintain that justice, *to the extent that* it requires political action, covers the theory of political morality. But which matters of justice require political (i.e. potentially coercive) action? What institutional division of labour between public authorities and private actors should we accept when striving to realizing justice in a more encompassing sense? That is a substantive question and the split between the political and the non-political cannot be defined in advance of the theory itself.

Others may launch a complaint from the other side: doesn't politics cover many other moral norms besides – or beyond – those of justice? This I would deny. I confess being captivated by a somewhat hedgehog-like obsession with theoretical unity in the definition of political morality in terms of justice only (and even worse: with the definition of justice in terms of equality of agency). In defence of this I would reply that the concept of justice is defined not just through the concept of equality, but through the concepts of equality and freedom in tandem. A concept of equality refers to the formal aspect: people are to be treated equally. However, the theory also offers a substantive aspect, by specifying the respect with which people are treated as equals: as free and autonomous agents. Thus, under the banner of justice, a complex moral ideal of personhood can be included which offers the substance that others would want to juxtapose to a (probably slimmer) conception of justice. Moreover, such a substantive theory of justice can also make room for other moral/political ideals which are normally juxtaposed to justice: ideals like democracy and accountability, sustainability, economic welfare, physical and social security which in daily political life are used independently can best be understood as parts of the more comprehensive idea of a just society, as conditions for autonomous agency. This at least is the methodological rule of thumb I propose to follow before exploring the option of accepting a plurality of unrelated ideals of political morality. What is dearly needed in political matters is not just a list of political ideals but also insight in the relations between them, as parts of a whole.

Third, a final question is what the *concept* of justice is to which the agency-based capability theory stands as a *conception*. What is justice about? This question has gained increasing relevance in the debate about global justice where so-called 'non-relational' views argue that duties of justice are owed to anyone by virtue of being human, while 'relational' views restrict duties of justice to those with whom we stand in a certain relationship (for example, one of coercive authority). These two standpoints are then in a second step connected to a cosmopolitan and a nationalist stance, respectively. In my view, the opposition between 'being human' and 'being in a social/political relationship' as the trigger for moral duties is unsatisfactory. As will be argued in Chapter 2, one of the defining characteristics of being a human agent *is* to be embedded in social and ultimately also political relations. If we accept this, then whether this entails accepting duties of justice to those beyond our own borders, is a follow-up question that must be treated separately. The theory offered thus does work with the concepts of a 'political community' and of persons in their political role – i.e. as 'citizens' – but this does not commit it to a picture of a world of bounded political communities in which there are no transnational communities, forms of global coercive power and questions of social justice between nations. All of that will depend on the level of integration and globalization we face.

On my definition, then, justice – at least that part of it which informs the theory of political morality – is about the distribution of benefits and burdens amongst citizens in a political community. It defines what citizens owe each other qua citizens. This definition may seem close to Rawls's definition which ties justice to the 'benefits and burdens of social cooperation' and defines society as a 'cooperative venture for mutual advantage' (Rawls 1999a, 4). However, Rawls's definition has sometimes – rightly or wrongly – been interpreted as implying a compact between productive citizens only, who produce a surplus of goods and services when forming a society and must decide about the distribution of that surplus. This picture has been criticised for not including unproductive citizens, such as the severely disabled. Shouldn't every human being, in virtue of their humanity, be included in the circle of those who are owed certain rights in the name of justice? (Nussbaum 2006a). My theory answers this charge, not by tying justice to a conception of humanity in abstraction from social relations, but by relaxing the cooperative aspect of the political relation. It does not pre-suppose cooperation in a productive sense as a qualifier for membership in the political community; mere interactions with others in that community suffice, whether one is productive or dependent on the productivity of others. An agent is always an agent between others.

In writing this book, I have had to leave out of consideration several potentially important dialogues with other approaches. Utilitarians, libertarians, communitarians and others from a different normative persuasion would need more arguments to be convinced. Political realists, (radical) democratic theorists and some critical theorists and post-structuralists will probably (no, certainly) feel the theory remains too close to the kind of mainstream liberal theorizing they look upon with suspicion. Theoretical philosophers will want to know more about the use of conceptions of autonomy and agency and the problem of defending freedom of the will, while philosophers of technology will be wary of the possibilities for individual agency in a world dominated by technological artifacts. All of these deserve more than I can offer here. Nonetheless, my hope is that enough is being said to make this book interesting to a broad group of political philosophers as well as those interested in defining social justice for our world.

PART I

Positioning the Capability Approach in Political Theory

CHAPTER I

Liberalism: Combining Perfectionism and Neutrality

Liberal theorists have been divided over the issue of perfectionism. Given liberalism's preoccupation with individuals' freedom to pursue their own lives, some liberals have argued that liberalism should be understood as promoting an idea of the good: i.e. to live a free or autonomous life. Others, however, have argued that this claim itself restricts people's freedom – a liberal state should be neutral between different conceptions of the good life. I will address this debate between perfectionist and political liberals by focusing on Martha Nussbaum's capability theory as the leading example. The discussion between perfectionist and political liberals transcends capability theory, the latter being just one type of liberal theory. Nonetheless, given my overall purpose to reconstruct an attractive liberal capability theory of justice, it is useful to focus on Nussbaum's theory here. A critical discussion of her theory's problematic positioning as a perfectionist and (in a later phase) political liberal theory will clear the ground for the constructive chapters of Part II.

I will first propose a spectrum of four potential positions: political liberalism, two versions of perfectionist liberalism (moderate and strong) and non-liberal perfectionism. Given the latter's non-liberal credentials, liberals need to consider three positions: moderate and strong perfectionist liberalism, and political liberalism (Section 1.1). The rest of the chapter proceeds by elimination. Nussbaum's early Neo-Aristotelian capability theory, 'Nussbaum-I' (1988–95), is an example of strong perfectionist liberalism. This theory is objectionable, since it lacks the resources for dealing fairly with different groups' claims for having their preferred capabilities included in her list of central capabilities (Section 1.2). As a way to resolve this problem, Nussbaum from the end of the 1990s onwards presented her capability theory as a species of political liberalism. I argue that this political liberal turn fits badly with her continued endorsement of the same expansive, universally valid list of capabilities and is also otherwise problematic (Section 1.3). This leaves us with moderate perfectionist liberalism – the position I adopt in this book. I present two challenges which have been raised to this position: the 'balancing problem' and the 'incorporation problem' (Section 1.4). Answering these challenges will be a task for the rest of the book, where my aim is to show that the capability metric can still usefully be employed even if one accepts the objections to Nussbaum's early and late capability theories.

1.1   An Analysis of the Perfectionism/Neutrality Debate

To keep the discussion tractable, I present a scheme of four possible positions one can take about perfectionism, representing four points on a continuum, ranging from non-perfectionist to heavily perfectionist.[1] This section outlines the main features of these positions. They are all positions about perfectionism in the *justification* of state policies, not in the effect of such policies. Neutrality of justification does not prohibit a policy that has more favourable effects for a particular conception of the good, as long as the justification for doing so does not refer to the superiority of that conception over other conceptions (Wall and Klosko 2003, 8). Theories can then be classified as neutralist or perfectionist depending on whether in their justification they refer to a conception of the good life. A state policy is neutral if it is justified without any reference to a conception of the good life, while a state policy is perfectionist if its justification does make reference to such a conception.[2] The reference to the good in one's justification can be more or less strong (encompassing), so more or less perfectionist, hence we get a continuum (Table 1.1).

Neutralist positions hold that the state should stay neutral between any conceptions of the good citizens may hold (R. Dworkin 1978). Theories of political liberalism have become the dominant form this position has taken (Larmore 1987; Rawls 2005), and therefore I will use political liberalism as representative for the neutralist position. Within political liberalism, the idea of neutrality is reframed as the idea that liberal political theory should be 'political not metaphysical', a freestanding module that merely uses political conceptions of the person, society and justice which can be attached to different comprehensive moral and religious doctrines

---

[1] The scheme draws inspiration from Wall and Klosko (2003) who present a framework of three positions: neutralist, perfectionist and liberal perfectionist.

[2] These positions are best thought of as about the justification of all kinds of state policies, not merely about 'constitutional essentials'. This scope restriction, introduced by John Rawls, is unhelpful for me because of the wider purposes of the political theory later developed in this book. The distinction is also unstable, as Arneson has convincingly argued (Arneson 2003, 209–11).

Table 1.1. *Perfectionism versus neutrality: four positions*

	Least perfectionist ⟵————————————————⟶ Most perfectionist			
Name of doctrine	Neutralism/ political liberalism	Perfectionist liberalism		Non-liberal perfectionism
		Moderate variant	Strong variant	
Conception of the good	None	Freedom/ autonomy	Freedom/autonomy + non-liberal conception(s) of the good	Any non-liberal conception of the good
Aim of state action	Neutrality between different conceptions of the good	1. Promotion of freedom/ autonomy + 2. Neutrality as abstinence	1. Promotion of freedom/ autonomy + 2. Neutrality as even-handedness between non-liberal conceptions of the good	Promotion of the non-liberal conception of the good

(as long as they are 'reasonable'), and is justified to the extent that it is supported by an overlapping consensus of such doctrines. As we will see, Nussbaum-II is an example of this position: it proposes a list of capabilities that can form the object of an overlapping consensus.

The two intermediate positions are both forms of *perfectionist liberalism*. These do not abstain from a theory of the good, but proclaim that the animating justification for state policies is to ensure that each citizen is able to lead a free or autonomous life. This position is *less* perfectionist than non-liberal perfectionism, in that liberal lives can diverge widely in the range of values that free and autonomous individuals actually endorse and try to realize. By doing so, it leaves open which values to endorse in life, whereas non-liberal perfectionist theories tend to use the state to promote a specific set of values. On the other hand, perfectionist liberalism is *more* perfectionist than political liberalism since it explicitly endorses a (liberal) theory of the good, and so wants to condemn and discourage lives that are not freely or autonomously led. There are many different theories of freedom and autonomy, and therefore different variants of perfectionist liberalism. Most often, a conception of personal autonomy is put forward as the ideal of freedom animating perfectionist liberalism (Raz 1986; Wall 1998), but one could equally well imagine forms of perfectionist liberalism based on negative freedom, republican freedom or any other ideal of freedom.

The distinction between the moderate and strong variants can best be explained with reference to Joseph Raz's theory. He proposes that a state should focus on protecting personal autonomy, an ideal having three main conditions: (i) A person must have the inner mental abilities to make autonomous decisions; (ii) a person must have independence from others: this requirement rules out coercion and manipulation; and (iii) a person must have an adequate range of options from which to choose. A person who can only chose one option in a society (say, become a plumber) is not autonomous. The state has to ensure that citizens have access to an adequate range of options (Raz 1986, 372–8). The inclusion of the third condition has been the source of much criticism, since states would have to decide which options are valuable in order to decide which ones to subsidize and stimulate. Hence Raz's state is perfectionist in two senses. First, it adopts a liberal view of the good life as an autonomous life, which requires (non-controversially) autonomy-competences and non-interference from others. Second, its conception of autonomy requires the incorporation of non-liberal theories of the good in order to select valuable options.

Strong perfectionist liberalism can now be defined as the position that adopts all three Razian conditions, while moderate perfectionist liberalism adopts a conception of personal autonomy incorporating something like Raz's first two conditions only.[3] Moderate perfectionist liberals do not necessarily deny that persons need an adequate range of options to become autonomous, but their point is that the creation of these options should not be a matter of state action. Whether an adequate range of options is available should depend on the free play of social forces in a liberal society. Both positions are perfectionist on a first-order level (endorsing the value of freedom/autonomy as the central guiding ideal), but only the moderate position combines this with a certain neutrality between people's different conceptions of the good as a 'downstream value' (Patten 2012, 252), i.e. as a requirement on a second-order level (Colburn 2010a). Strong perfectionist liberals would, for example, want to support adequate choice in the religious sphere by using the state to ensure that a sufficient range of religious creeds is available (say, it actively

---

[3] Steven Wall calls these type (1) and type (2) perfectionism (Wall 1998, 197–8).

supports Protestantism, Buddhism and animistic religions, but not Catholicism, Judaism and Islam). Moderate perfectionist liberals would leave it up to the social life of autonomous individuals which religions they create and support themselves.

Moderate liberal perfectionists' endorsement of neutrality differs from the neutrality that political liberals claim in two senses. First, moderate perfectionist liberals value neutrality for different reasons: because they think this is warranted by respect for the autonomy of persons, not because this would be warranted by a freestanding political doctrine.[4] Second, the function of neutrality at the second level is different. For moderate perfectionist liberals, neutrality dictates that the state should only implement policies to realize those conditions necessary for the development of people's autonomy (Raz's first two conditions) and not go beyond that to *also* create a set of valuable options or discourage disvaluable options. By abstaining from doing more, it expresses neutrality towards the value of whatever way of life autonomous citizens choose. I will call this 'neutrality as abstinence'.[5]

Finally, there are various forms of *non-liberal perfectionism*. These positions hold that the state should endorse some conception(s) of the good *x*, where *x* can be everything except the liberal good of promoting freedom/autonomy. This formulation allows for two varieties, for the non-liberal good can be either illiberal or a-liberal. The general structure of an illiberal perfectionist theory is to prescribe a form of human excellence not all citizens are allowed to attain. Nussbaum has argued that Aristotle's position is illiberal in this sense for its lack of respect for women and slaves (Nussbaum 1988, 165, 2000b, 108). Such theories often accept a

---

[4] Wall and Klosko also distinguish between neutrality 'for neutralist' or for 'non-neutralist' reasons (Wall and Klosko 2003, 11).

[5] Some authors make a distinction between two levels. At the most general level, the point is whether liberalism is based on a comprehensive doctrine or not. Those who argue that liberalism is ultimately grounded in a comprehensive ideal of the autonomy of citizens are called 'comprehensive liberals'. Those who deny it are political liberals. At the second level, this fundamental first-order position might have two different consequences for one's view of acceptable state policies. One might either affirm or deny that the state may promote (stimulate, subsidize, etc.) valuable options and discourage disvaluable options. Those who affirm this are perfectionists about state action, while those who deny it are anti-perfectionists (or neutralists). One can affirm autonomy and either be perfectionist or neutralist at this second-order level. These positions are then referred to as 'comprehensive anti-perfectionism' and 'comprehensive perfectionism' (Mulhall and Swift 1996, 249–57; Quong 2011, 15–21). I find this way of putting things confusing. The 'comprehensive anti-perfectionist' position (comparable to my moderate perfectionism) can never be completely 'anti-perfectionist', for if it is truly 'comprehensive' (i.e. bringing in personal autonomy) then it has to commit itself to the promotion of personal autonomy in state policies. As I try to show, the real difference is whether one imports perfectionist considerations of a non-liberal kind in one's theory (through the options requirement).

hierarchy of different social classes which are treated unequally. The violation of the basic liberal principle of equal respect is then inscribed in the very theory because the ideal of the good refers directly to only a subset of the population. However, one could also imagine a state promoting an a-liberal good that, while not discriminating directly in this sense, is so demanding that not everybody will be able to attain it (say high levels of attainment in art, sport or science). Arguably most theocratic political theories are examples of non-liberal perfectionism; liberalism from John Locke onwards arose largely as a competitor to such theories which want to impose a specific religious way of life on the population as a whole.

Non-liberal perfectionism stands outside the *internal* debate between political and perfectionist liberalism. It is important to include it in our scheme for the sake of conceptual completeness, but also because it has a theoretical significance for the internal liberal debate. Remember that both non-liberal perfectionism and the strong variant of liberal perfectionism contain a reference to 'non-liberal goods' (Table 1.1). This raises the question whether strong liberal perfectionism can remain liberal. Raz's options requirement, at least as it is normally conceived,[6] requires a substantive non-liberal theory of the good so as to decide which options are valuable. If one plugs that theory into strong perfectionist liberalism, the theory threatens to collapse into non-liberal forms of perfectionism. One way to avoid this implication may be to emphasize the democratic legitimation of these state policies. If a majority endorses a particular conception of the good (and on condition that it merely stimulates this conception and does not coerce citizens to live according to it), then promotion of that conception may be legitimate. This still raises the question, however, whether such a policy is compatible with justice. Those with other conceptions of the good may have good reasons to feel unfairly disadvantaged. The most promising route for strong perfectionist liberalism seems to be to argue that the state should promote not one theory, but several theories, of the good — all of them in an *even-handed* way. This strategy of 'neutrality as even-handedness' reconciles the theory with liberalism by bringing in a form of neutrality, not by abstaining from

---

[6] In the chapters of Part II, I defend a form of moderate perfectionist liberalism in which a specific set of options is endorsed as a necessary condition for state policy, but this set is itself generated not by a non-liberal theory of the good, but by a (specific) conception of autonomous agency. Depending on how one frames the issue, my theory then is either moderate or strong perfectionist. I prefer to identify the strong variant with options generated by a non-liberal theory of the good, and call my own theory a form of moderate perfectionist liberalism.

endorsing any (non-liberal) conception of the good (the moderate's solution), but by endorsing all of them to an equal extent.

This finishes my overview. Let's now test the positions through a close engagement with Nussbaum's capability theory of justice.

1.2   Strong Perfectionist Liberalism (Nussbaum-I)

Nussbaum's early capability theory (hereafter: 'Nussbaum-I') was developed in a series of articles between 1988 and 1995. In this phase Nussbaum referred to her capability theory as a form of 'Aristotelian social democracy', or 'Aristotelian essentialism'. I will first present its main features and then evaluate it as a species of strong perfectionist liberalism.

Nussbaum's theory proposes a list of ten central capabilities essential to a flourishing human life. In one of her early articles, Nussbaum outlines the Aristotelian strategy she follows to construct that list:

> What he [Aristotle, author] does, in each case, is to isolate a sphere of human experience that figures in more or less any human life, and in which more or less any human being will have to make some choices rather than others, and act in some way rather than some other ... Aristotle then asks, what is it to choose and respond well within that sphere? And what is it to choose defectively? The 'thin account' of each virtue is that it is whatever being stably disposed to act appropriately in that sphere consists in. There may be, and usually are, various competing specifications of what acting well, in each case, in fact comes to. Aristotle goes on to defend in each case some specification, producing, at the end, a full or 'thick' definition of the virtue. (Nussbaum 1993, 245)

The identification of different spheres of human experience is vital. The idea of good or virtuous action is to be defined relative to each sphere. Examples of Aristotelian spheres are 'fear of important damages, especially death' (appropriate virtue for this sphere: courage), 'bodily appetites and their pleasures' (virtue: moderation), 'distribution of limited resources' (virtue: justice), etc. Nussbaum argues that a similar strategy can be used for her capability-oriented theory: it puts forwards conceptions of well-functioning in the most important spheres of human existence. Following this strategy, the central capabilities are constitutive parts of the good life – each capability with respect to another sphere of existence. Capabilities are 'not just instrumental to further pursuits: they are held to have value in themselves, in making the life that includes them fully human' (Nussbaum 2000b, 74). On the basis of this strategy, Nussbaum endorses a list of ten central capabilities, which together form the good life: capabilities to life, health and bodily integrity, the emotions and imagination, practical reason, etc.

When Nussbaum first presented her list, she referred to it as a 'thick, vague' conception of the good, rooted in the 'constitutive circumstances of the human being' (Nussbaum 1990, 219). While the capabilities are rooted in human existence, Nussbaum emphasizes that her list is evaluative from the start. To defend the evaluations underlying each capability, she presented a method called 'internalist essentialism'. Evaluative judgements are justified by a process of asking ourselves which capabilities we cannot do without, on pain of not recognizing our life as a fully human life: 'to find out what our nature is seems to be one and the same thing as to find out what we deeply believe to be most important and indispensable' (Nussbaum 1995, 106). Anyone who would try to defend the view that certain capabilities (like friendship, reasoning, health) can easily be given up, would have to live up to that position in his own life. That will turn out to be very difficult: 'the argument is claiming that the acceptance of a theoretical position entails a cost that the proponent of the position would be unwilling to pay' (Nussbaum 1995, 110).

Although Nussbaum-I's method is rooted in Aristotelian ethics and her list presents a view of the good life, Nussbaum offers her capability theory as a *political theory*, i.e. to provide a guide to political action, not to individual moral action. Nussbaum expects the state to guarantee the central capabilities to each citizen, as constitutionally guaranteed human rights (Nussbaum 1997, 2000b, 96–101, 2006, 284–91). This political theory is claimed to have *universal* validity. Nussbaum's universalism is closely related to her essentialism. It is because she believes to defend a view of the good human life that her theory is supposed to be applicable to all human beings, everywhere around the world.[7]

With this overview in hand, let's turn to the problem of perfectionism. Several authors have argued Nussbaum-I's theory is objectionably perfectionist (Qizilbash 1998; Arneson 2000b; Menon 2002; Barclay 2003; Okin 2003).[8] I will here take my lead from the version of the objection formulated by Eric Nelson. His argument proceeds in two steps. First, he argues that Nussbaum's theory is non-neutral:

> [T]here is certainly no sense in which it [Nussbaum's list] is neutral with respect to the good. It is not rational to want the things on the list

---

[7] This doesn't mean that she wants to impose the list on other countries: she merely recommends it to them as being 'a good idea' (Nussbaum 2000b, 103).

[8] For more favourable receptions of Nussbaum's perfectionism, see e.g. Arneson (2000b, 2010b); Richardson (2000); Hurka (2002) and Deneulin (2002, 2013). Serene Khader argues that identifying adaptive preferences requires a theory of the good (Khader 2011, 2012).

'whatever else one wants'. Suppose I am a celibate, and I believe sexual satisfaction is sinful; or suppose I am a misanthrope who does not see any value in associating with other human beings; or suppose I am one of those who thinks that laughter is a cruel expression of hatred ... or vainglory ...; or suppose I am a Christian Scientist who thinks it is illicit to employ many fundamental techniques of western medicine (such as blood transfusion). (Nelson 2008, 99)

All of these citizens, Nelson says, can reasonably complain that Nussbaum's capability list includes items that are offensive to them (capabilities to sexual satisfaction, affiliation, play and bodily integrity). Note that the distinction between neutral and non-neutral items follows the Rawlsian criterion for primary goods: things one wants whatever else one wants.[9]

Against this, a defender of Nussbaum's capability theory will probably say that citizens do not have to actually function in the way opened up by a capability. However, Nelson in a second step makes it clear that this move doesn't help Nussbaum:

It would be plausible enough if the list simply enumerated rights to non-interference, but the entire point of the exercise is to stress that what must be delivered (to the extent possible) is the *affirmative ability* to engage in the specified action. In the case of sexual satisfaction, it is not enough to ban the coercive denial of opportunities for sexual activity; rather, if person X is unable to experience sexual satisfaction for preventable reasons, Nussbaum is clear that X would be entitled to various available therapies in precisely the same sense that a crippled person would be entitled to costly measures designed to secure his freedom of movement. In other words, even if I myself consider sex to be sinful, I am required to fund somebody else's Viagra. How different is this from saying that one of the essential human capabilities is attending Roman Catholic mass every Sunday, and that, accordingly, although you yourself are not required to attend, you must pay for my communion wafers? (Nelson 2008, 100)

Let's be clear about why these citizens have a justified claim. The point is not in their being coerced into functioning, because they are not. A theory which legitimizes states to coerce citizens into functionings instead of capabilities is paternalist. This may be legitimate on certain occasions (see Section 5.3), but that is not the issue here. Paternalism is not the same as perfectionism (Claassen 2014a). The problem of perfectionism is that, even if a theory only provides capabilities (hence leaves choice to individuals as to their functionings), it still relies on a specific theory of the good to select these capabilities. Nelson leaves it somewhat

---

[9] Rawls later changed the criterion for primary goods to bring it in line with his political liberalism. Nussbaum follows this move as well (Nussbaum 2003b, 30).

implicit why this is problematic, so let's unpack his critique. I propose there are two problems.

1) Taxing non-users. First, citizens have to contribute to those state actions required to realize the contested capability. We do not have to agree with Robert Nozick's view of taxation as a form of theft to ask questions about the extent to which people can legitimately be coerced to contribute to things they do not want to consume. This subject has been extensively debated in the context of the so-called 'principle of fairness', which requires one to contribute to cooperative schemes which are just and to which one has voluntarily consented or from which one has reaped the benefits (Rawls 1999a, 96). Rawls is very demanding in requiring unanimity amongst all citizens for the state to legitimately implement measures from which only part of the population benefits. In his theory these measures (e.g. arts subsidies) are relegated to a separate exchange branch of government. Rawls motivates this explicitly with his anti-perfectionism. Normally the state shouldn't play a role in the promotion of perfectionist values (Rawls 1999a, 249–51, 291–2).[10]

Nussbaum replied to this problem, stating that '[i]f one ends up having a plan of life that does not make use of all of them [her ten central capabilities, R.C.], one has hardly been harmed by having the chance to choose a life that does' (Nussbaum 1998, 322, similarly 1997, 290). However, this remark only identifies the absence of harm at the receiving end of the state–citizen relation, i.e. the harm of the citizens as a recipient of state policies. It remains silent about the contributory side and thus unjustifiably ignores the harm being done by being coerced to pay taxes while not benefiting from them. This does not imply that one cannot legitimize taxation. However, the coercion involved needs to be legitimized through an argument that makes clear why the benefits of state action to some are allowed to outweigh the harm of taxation to others. Nussbaum's argument fails to convince with respect to the problem of taxing for perfectionist purposes.

2) Disrespecting non-users. Let's bracket the taxation problem by imagining a resource that falls like manna from heaven (say a newly

---

[10] When everyone consents, then the state could play a role, but this role is merely auxiliary: to help citizens organize their collectively agreed upon activities (Rawls' exchange branch). Such a unanimous agreement would amount to a perfectly executed strategy of even-handedness in promoting all conceptions of the good (discussed later in this section).

discovered natural resource that the state appropriates). Even if taxation is not necessary, is there really no harm, as Nussbaum claims, to providing capabilities to citizens who have no interest in using them? To be clear, we are not envisaging cases in which people would like to use an opportunity provided by the state, but cannot do so because of the presence of some obstacle (e.g. when they would like to apply for a college grant or a medical insurance program, but do not qualify under the existing rules). At stake are cases of non-use motivated by the fact that the state policy (paid by that resource) aims at the promotion of a capability that does not form a part of one's conception of the good. Then the state takes a partisan standpoint, while it should respect every conception of the good to the same extent. There is no immediate monetary setback for those whose conceptions do not get the same amount of support; but there is a failure of equal consideration of everyone's interests.

When Nussbaum discusses the usefulness of income and wealth to every citizen, she states an ascetic can support goods important to others even if she will not use them herself: 'she is happy to support an adequate distribution of them to others, given that she respects her fellow citizens who have different comprehensive doctrines' (Nussbaum 2003b, 30). Elsewhere she argues an Amish citizen 'who believes that it is wrong to participate in politics' will nonetheless support the inclusion of the right to vote on the capability list (Nussbaum 2006, 182–3). Nussbaum concedes that this creates some tension for the Amish believer in question, but nonetheless holds this person will agree to voting rights as a citizen of a democratic society. Indeed, 'it is not an implausible reconstruction of their thinking to ascribe to them the thought that a dignified life for a human being requires these capabilities – which include, of course, the right not to use them' (Nussbaum 2006, 184–5).

This reply doesn't address the underlying asymmetry in Nussbaum's capability theory. She treats two groups differentially who each can make a similar claim.[11] The first group consists of those who object to the *inclusion* of an item on the capability list because of their own non-use. Examples are Nussbaum's Amish citizen who doesn't vote and the ascetic who doesn't use income and wealth. But her reply to this group opens the

---

[11] A different problem is how a person can simultaneously believe voting is an intrinsically 'wrong' activity and that the opportunity to do so still is part of a dignified human life. The mental gymnastics that this asks of some citizens is a recurring problem for political liberalism, but I do not want to put argumentative weight on it here (see also Section 1.3).

door for a second group consisting of those who could object to the list because it *excludes* an item that they would want, given their conceptions of the good. Nussbaum remains silent on this group, but Nelson points to them where he mentions the Catholic who wants collective payments for his communion wafers. If Nussbaum requires the Amish and ascetic to support items of no value to them (even of disvalue, given their comprehensive doctrines), she has no argument to deny support to Catholics who can object that capabilities that are of exclusive use to them should be included. The Catholic can say: 'now it is your time to pay and support my conception of the good!'

Nussbaum's theory is stuck in an uncomfortable position: claiming fair treatment of all conceptions of the good, but delivering a capability list that doesn't live up to this promise. She can resolve this incongruence in two opposite directions. She can embrace the expansionary consequences of her argument and revise her list so that no group will have a reason for complaint. She would then adopt a capability version of the strategy of neutrality as *even-handedness*. Such a long list seems to fit well with the original motivation for her capability theory: to define for every sphere of human experience what is necessary for a good human life. Note the parallel here between Nussbaum's theory and Raz's adequate range of options requirement – while Nussbaum is after a flourishing life and Raz after an autonomous life, both are led to stipulate that this requires political support of a wide variety of different action-types. No citizen will spend his days in every sphere, but since every citizen will act in some sphere(s), each citizen will be fairly treated by state support to all spheres. A second alternative would be to remove all capabilities that give one or more groups a reason for complaint. That list should include only those capabilities that all citizens anticipate to use. This takes us back to the logic of Rawls's early theory in which primary goods figure as means for all purposes, whatever one's specific conception of the good.[12] It would lead to a list of 'primary capabilities' that gives people the means they need to explore (or even create) each sphere of existence themselves. This is neutrality by *abstinence*. These are the main two strategies by which perfectionist liberalism can incorporate a concern for neutrality, the former being exemplary for strong perfectionist liberalism, the latter for moderate perfectionist liberalism.

---

[12] One could object citizens never use all primary goods to the same extent. But the relevant fact is the *ex ante* expectation of use (in the Original Position), not actual use. Some public goods have an insurance character.

The ambition to even-handedness creates several problems. I want to single out three of them – infeasibility, intrusiveness and status quo bias – all familiar from the multiculturalism debate (Balint 2015).

First, even-handedness is likely to be *infeasible*. Once one starts to expand the list of capabilities to do justice to everyone's specific conceptions of the good, a truly even-handed capability list will have to become interminably long. State promotion of every conception of the good – however idiosyncratic and rare – would become the norm. It is highly questionable whether such a project could ever be carried out. The state would have to have detailed and up-to-date knowledge of everyone's conception of the good, which would stretch its epistemic capacities. In addition, it would have to have the means to cater to all these conceptions, which may be very costly. Whether this is feasible, of course, also depends on the level of concreteness on which one specifies conceptions of the good and their distribution in society. If the level of abstraction is high (say, complete religious systems) and the distribution is simple (only a handful of religions are adhered to), the problem is still relatively tractable. To the extent that one breaks down conceptions of the good more, so that they approach the level of the single life plans of individuals (say, flying to the moon, or climbing Mount Everest) and to the extent that the distribution of these conceptions is more heterogeneous (everyone wants to make something else of her life), the problem quickly becomes intractable.

Even-handedness cannot be only roughly or halfway successful, for then it would face increasingly bitter claims of those individuals and groups who saw their expectations of inclusion disappointed. The stakes are high, for in theoretical terms a not-completely even-handed policy would favour some conceptions of the good over others and thus collapse into a form of non-liberal perfectionism. But to the extent that it is more successful, even-handedness faces another problem: it becomes increasingly *intrusive*. The ideal requires a highly active state, deeply involved in the co-production of success in realizing people's private projects. Indeed, even-handedness stretches the limits of public involvement to such an extent that one can wonder whether the state would remain liberal in character, given liberalism's core commitment to the freedom of citizens to make their own choices in life. With public support (financial or otherwise) also comes public scrutiny and pressures for accountability.

Finally, all the previous considerations presume that we would restrict even-handedness to existing, actually held conceptions of the good. This however betrays a *status quo bias* which does not support possible, yet-to-be developed new conceptions of the good. If we want to eliminate this bias, we would need to second-guess which conceptions are going to be held in the future. Given the unpredictability of the future, this seems impossible. A milder form of tackling the bias seems to be to support currently existing conceptions of the good which have run out of favour (analogous to religions or languages that has become extinct). This, however, is highly impracticable if there are no currently existing persons wishing to pursue these conceptions. One cannot support something that isn't used by anyone today. One could, of course, argue that even-handed policies can legitimately be restricted to support for currently held conceptions, i.e. defend the status quo. This, however, makes it comparatively unattractive for people to try out and develop new conceptions of the good since they will have to fight for state recognition of these amid established contenders. Hence, they are put at a comparatively weaker position, which from the point of view of even-handedness itself is unfair.

Nussbaum's writings sometimes indicate a preference for the neutrality by abstinence strategy. While early on she was critical of the analogy between capabilities and primary goods (Nussbaum 1988, 150–2), later she argued that the two are very close (Nussbaum 2000b, 88). She also states: '[T]he basic point of the account is the same [as Rawls's, R.C.]: to put forward something that people from many different traditions, with many different fuller conceptions of the good, can agree on as the necessary basis for pursuing their good life' (Nussbaum 1997, 286). The problem is that this new presentation is not matched by any trimming down of her list of capabilities. As a consequence, Nussbaum's position remains stuck in the middle. She wants to have a list which is so thin that it looks like everyone needs the central capabilities (and will therefore agree upon them), but she continues to endorse a list of items too many of which are only useful (and hence acceptable) to some, but not all, specific conceptions of the good life. The change needed to create a truly abstinent capability theory is to select capabilities not because they are necessary components of a flourishing life, but as conditions for personal autonomy (or a similar liberal ideal of the good). While her list does include the capability for practical reasoning (which may be taken to overlap with personal autonomy), it also includes many other items that go beyond that. The reason Nussbaum has not moved in this direction seems to lie in her resistance to the ideal of personal autonomy, which will be discussed hereafter.

My rejection of strong perfectionist liberalism is only preliminary. The three objections presented above I consider strong, but one could nonetheless remain more hopeful of realizing even-handedness than I do. Also, one might think that abstinence is impossible anyway (see Section 1.4). The choice between the moderate and strong versions depends on their comparative (de)merits, hence on the way the moderate alternative is developed as well. The problems of even-handedness are only symptoms of the point which will be argued for in the chapters of Part II: that citizens do not *owe* each other state support for their particular conceptions of the good, because they only owe each other support for the protection of their autonomous agency.

1.3   Political Liberalism (Nussbaum-II)

In later work Nussbaum has substantially modified and defended her position against the earlier criticisms as to the perfectionism of her theory. We can speak of a new position, Nussbaum-II, most fully worked out in her books *Women and Human Development* (2000) and *Frontiers of Justice* (2006). The most important novelty, on which I focus here, is the introduction of political liberalism.[13] Nussbaum now offers her own

---

[13] Against criticisms of perfectionism, Nussbaum repeatedly stressed six features to convince readers her theory respects pluralism and choice (Nussbaum 2000b, 105, 2006, 78–80, 2011b, 108–11).

The first two features are modifications. The first one is the introduction of political liberalism, which I discuss in the main text. The second one is a modification of the capability list: basic political and civil liberties are now included, as well as a separate capability for practical reasoning. Both guarantee a power of making individual choices, fortifying citizens' ability to choose among all the other capabilities in forming and acting upon a plan of life. This, however, leaves untouched all her other capabilities which pretend to define flourishing in all spheres of human life. These capabilities remain on her list, causing the problems I noted.

The other four features are rather defences of Nussbaum-I. They are: (i) The goal of her theory is to realize capabilities, not functionings. Promoting functionings is the exception, promoting capabilities the rule. (ii) The capability list is only a proposal, open to revision in the future, if good arguments are put forward to do so. (iii) The central capabilities are deliberately formulated in an abstract way, leaving open space for specifications that fit the local context, or 'multiple realizability' (Nussbaum 2000b, 105). (iv) Issues of justification and implementation need to be separated. The fact that she considers her theory to be justified provides no basis for interfering with democratic processes in other countries, given their sovereign right to determine their own future.

These defences do not succeed in defusing the objection from perfectionism. Point (i) is merely a restatement of what is distinctive of capability theory. Its insufficiency has been pointed out in Section 1.2 (where I discussed Nelson's criticism). The final three replies seem to be directed not so much against an objection from perfectionism, but against an 'objection from universalism': that Nussbaum 'expresses no misgivings about the fact that, in taking control of the list, she assumes the prerogative not only of determining the philosophical import of others' contributions but also of assessing their moral worth, thus deciding whose opinions should be respected and whose should be rejected as mistaken or corrupt' (Jaggar 2006, 314; similarly, Okin 2003). Nussbaum decides which human capabilities are so important that they get a privileged status in the theory, as expressing our common humanity. This objection to Nussbaum's universalist ambitions would affect any capability theory. To counter it, changing the list won't help: the whole enterprise of list-making is problematic. This objection animates the 'debate about the list' between Nussbaum and

capabilities list as the object of an overlapping consensus, paralleling the move the later Rawls made by presenting his earlier theory of justice as fairness as justified through an overlapping consensus. Her list should be seen 'as a list that can be endorsed for political purposes, as the moral basis of central constitutional guarantees, by people who otherwise have very different views of what a complete good life for a human being would be' (Nussbaum 2000b, 74). We should not understand this move as a denial that the capability list represents a theory of the good life. It still does so. The crucial point is that Nussbaum now thinks it represents 'a partial, not a comprehensive, conception of the good life' (Nussbaum 2000b, 77). She provides elaborate defences of political liberalism against perfectionist forms of liberalism (Nussbaum 2003b, 2011c). Can the move to political liberalism save Nussbaum-II from the objection from perfectionism?[14]

A first answer is 'no', because this move is incomplete. We have to make a distinction between substance (content of the capability list) and method (strategy of justification). After Nussbaum's move to political liberalism, the substance of her capability theory remains largely the same. The list of central capabilities and the other theoretical elements,

---

Amartya Sen, who argues that list-making should be left to democratic debate (Sen 2004a). I consider the objection from universalism to be mistaken, and Nussbaum's replies (ii)–(iv) to be correct. She is right to emphasize that the list is only a proposal, and that it cannot be coercively implemented from the outside. The distinction between justification and implementation helps us to understand the idea of her theory being only a proposal. She understands her own work as offering something to public debate, nothing more, nothing less. As I have argued elsewhere, this expresses a particular view of the role of the philosopher in a democratic society (Claassen 2011b). Nussbaum is doing exactly the same thing as many others political philosophers who offer theories of justice. Nonetheless, all this doesn't take away the perfectionist critique.

Besides these six remarks she puts forward against critics to her perfectionism and universalism, we should note that Nussbaum-II makes two further modifications. First, she introduces two new methods of justification besides the earlier method of internalist essentialism (which is, however, not explicitly repudiated): an 'informed desire approach' and a role for 'narratives' and intuitions tested in 'reflective equilibrium'. Nussbaum now claims that we should see her theory as supported by a 'complex holistic method' (Nussbaum 2006, 355). I cannot possibly discuss the role of all these methods that are somehow to operate simultaneously. Given the dominance in her writings of the theme of political liberalism and her opposition to perfectionist liberalism, I will simply leave these other methods out of consideration. Second, Nussbaum has (without changing her list of capabilities) come to stress that they are capabilities, not merely for a fully human and flourishing life, but for a *dignified* human life. A concept of human dignity has become part of what the central capabilities are meant to express. I have discussed Nussbaum's concept of dignity elsewhere (Claassen 2014b). Moreover, an excellent analysis shows that Nussbaum's concept of dignity itself remains firmly Aristotelian and comprehensive, and does nothing to bring Nussbaum from the liberal perfectionist into the political liberal camp (Formosa and Mackenzie 2014).

[14] Criticisms of Nussbaum's political liberalism are given by Barclay (2003); Biondo (2008); Stark (2009); Katzer (2010) and Ferracioli and Terlazzo (2014). For further assessments of her theory as a whole, see Comim and Nussbaum (2014).

including her earlier essentialist method of justifying the capabilities are still present. Therefore, the same objections against the perfectionist character of her theory can still be addressed to Nussbaum-II.[15] This position remains an example of strong perfectionist liberalism in its content, even if its method of justification is now political liberal. Nussbaum-II is an unfinished project. To rebut the problem of perfectionism, the content of the capability theory itself would have to change. The problem cannot be taken away by an argument that the same list is now presented differently, as the result of an overlapping consensus.

While this conclusion makes a further investigation of Nussbaum-II redundant, it is still useful to enquire what Nussbaum's theory would be like if it were to complete the move to political liberalism. It seems to me such an attempt at a full move to political liberalism faces two challenges.

First, political liberalism was defended by Rawls as a method of justification within the context of modern democratic societies. Nussbaum's theory however has universalist aspirations. It is not supposed to merely elucidate the political values inherent in actually existing democratic societies. Instead it provides an interpretation of human nature that claims to have cross-cultural validity. These two elements are obviously at odds with each other (Barclay 2003, 12). This tension can be framed as one between her earlier internalist essentialist method of justification and the method of political liberalism. The capabilities list cannot simultaneously be created on the basis of a search for the truly human life *and* on the basis of an interpretation of the shared values of Western democracies. Different methods generate theories with a different normative status. The restriction to the liberal democratic context is integral to Rawls's political liberalism, and for good reason: finding an overlapping consensus is difficult enough in such societies. It becomes even more so once one extends the scope to all societies, democratic and non-democratic.

Second, on the level of substance a more thorough conversion to political liberalism would affect the capability list. For example, in Nussbaum's writings on the treatment of animals she offers a substantive argument about animal functioning which is an extension of Aristotle's conception of well-functioning (Nussbaum 2006). But, it is clear that this argument is not supported by an actual global overlapping

---

[15] Thus, I agree with Barclay that Nussbaum does not succeed in being a political liberal, but I disagree with her argument that Nussbaum already is a comprehensive liberal. She underestimates the perfectionism involved in formulating what is valuable for all spheres of life (Barclay 2003, 19). See also Terlazzo and Deneulin who argue that the character of Nussbaum-II's theory remains perfectionist (Deneulin 2002, 511–12; Terlazzo 2014, 188–91).

consensus, nor does it seem that such a consensus is forthcoming (Barclay 2003, 13–14). Similar conclusions will be reached for many other capabilities. If Nussbaum would really be a full and unqualified political liberal, any lack of consensus would have to make her scale back her capability claims. We should be reminded that Rawls did this by restricting political liberalism to the application to constitutional essentials only and removing the matters covered by the second (socio-economic) principle of justice from its range (Rawls 2005, 228–9). The fact that Nussbaum doesn't make similar moves is an indication of the continuing primacy of the non-political liberal commitments central to Nussbaum-I. As Nussbaum-II stands, there is more continuity than the move to political liberalism suggests.

One may, of course, wonder whether this scaling-back can be done at all: i.e. whether *any* form of political liberalism can remain true to its guiding method (overlapping consensus) and deliver an interesting theory of justice. As Jeremy Waldron argued, when discussing Rawls's political liberalism:

> A critical theory of justice has hard, critical work to do, on Rawls's original account ... The actual examples of overlapping consensus for a pluralist society provided in *Political Liberalism* are laughably easy by comparison. Both Kantians and non-Kantians might favour democracy, Rawls says, and both Christians and secularists may well oppose slavery (1993-122-5). The hard part comes when we try to establish an overlapping consensus among (say) Christian fundamentalists, Hindus, secular humanists, scientific determinists, and member of the dot-com generation on the definition of 'equal opportunity', the use of economic incentives, and the distinction between liberty and the worth of liberty. (Waldron 2004, 96)

This is as much a problem for Nussbaum as for Rawls. Nussbaum has stated that her theory is not a full, but only a partial theory of justice. However, she has remained open to the idea that a full capability theory of justice could be developed. To do this on the model of political liberalism seems a very tough challenge.[16]

We have, so far, reached the conclusions (i) that Nussbaum-II has not completed the move to political liberalism, (ii) if she would, a completely different capability theory would emerge, both in the scope of

---

[16] One way of integrating this problem in Rawls's theory is to say that *Political Liberalism* is not about justice at all, but about legitimacy (Estlund 1996). But then it becomes mysterious what can be said about justice from the point of view of a defender of political liberalism. Unsurprisingly, many defenders of political liberalism refrain from developing a theory of justice, e.g. Quong (2011, 15). But, as Waldron shows, this agnosticism renders their criticisms of perfectionist theories much less convincing.

its normative claims (non-universalist) and in its content (less expansive capability list), which (iii) arguably cannot fulfil the demands of a full theory of justice. Nussbaum herself comes to very different conclusions, and to understand why, we need to consider her explicit writings on the debate between comprehensive and political liberalism. She objects to comprehensive liberalism for two different reasons (in the following I adopt Nussbaum's term 'comprehensive liberalism', where elsewhere I prefer to use the label 'perfectionist liberalism').

First, Nussbaum objects to the inclusion of an ideal of autonomy. In one article she imagines a president visiting a campus of religious believers who hold that women are ethically subordinate. She claims a comprehensive liberal president would tell the believers that 'it is a deep metaphysical fact that men and women are equal and that this equality follows them wherever they are'. This president would tell the audience they hold an unreasonable doctrine. A political liberal president in contrast would say their doctrine is 'in the political sense unreasonable'. She would make clear to these believers that their doctrine can never be imposed upon the majority of the country, but nonetheless 'we will never say that it is second-class or an unreasonable doctrine'. Moreover, 'How you square your membership in the overlapping consensus with aspects of your comprehensive doctrine is your business' (Nussbaum 2003b, 36–7). Nussbaum is explicit that she does *not* believe that a comprehensive liberal would impose an autonomous lifestyle upon the believers. The problem she sees is only in the fact that comprehensive liberals engage in expressive injuries to religious groups by claiming that their doctrine is incorrect. Comprehensive liberals affirm an Enlightenment idea of autonomy, which is explicitly developed in contrast to the authority of the Christian religion: 'Autonomy thus means something positive, that one gives oneself laws and engages in critical reflection; but it also means something negative, that one denies that God is a necessary part of the justification of moral claims.' This is unacceptable to religious believers (Nussbaum 2003b, 39–42).[17]

Second, in her 2011 paper Nussbaum focuses on the doctrine of value pluralism. Raz believes that the state should create many valuable options, because an autonomous life is valuable only in pursuit of good options.

---

[17] She goes on to argue that she will require children from a religious background to have an education in which they will confront different views: 'children may not be held hostage to a single conception' (Nussbaum 2003b, 42). But she insists that this does not lead her to accept a comprehensive liberal view. However, the question remains what is left of the difference once such political demands on minorities are made.

This presupposes the truth of value pluralism: only because there are many (incompatible) good ways of living, do we need autonomy to be able to choose between them. But, Nussbaum maintains, value pluralism is controversial. Many religions, holding a monistic theory of value, would not accept it. Since the political tolerance of these religions is the hallmark of liberalism, Nussbaum argues that comprehensive liberalism is based on a doctrine that is too controversial (Nussbaum 2011b). Nussbaum takes her opposition to putatively disrespectful forms of liberalism to an altogether higher level, also criticizing Rawls's view of political liberalism itself as insufficiently disrespectful. Rawls relies on the idea of 'burdens of judgement' in distinguishing reasonable from unreasonable comprehensive doctrines. This epistemic criterion of reasonableness, Nussbaum argues, has the result that comprehensive doctrines which contain irrational elements (she mentions New Age and astrology, but also Christian belief in the Trinity) have to be judged unreasonable by fellow citizens. Instead, Nussbaum proposes, the unreasonableness of a doctrine should be an *ethical* matter: all comprehensive doctrines, however 'crazy' their beliefs, deserve equal respect. The only doctrines excepted from this are those denying a liberal political conception of justice, e.g. doctrines denigrating women or defending slavery (Nussbaum 2011b, 28–9).

How to respond? First, one may wonder about the consistency between Nussbaum's writings on political liberalism and on capability theorizing. In her latest book about the capability approach she states that the approach is itself 'pluralist about value: it holds that the capability achievements that are central for people are different in quality, not just in quantity; that they cannot without distortion be reduced to a single numerical scale' (Nussbaum 2011b, 18–19). This is not just a slip of the pen. The idea of several irreducible, qualitatively distinct capabilities is essential to her capability theory. But, if each individual's choice which capabilities to act upon is to be honoured because capabilities represent distinctly valuable life options, then Nussbaum de facto accepts the doctrine of value pluralism in her work on capabilities, while she rejects it in her work on political liberalism.

My second, more substantive response is that these attacks on autonomy and value pluralism backfire: Nussbaum cannot avoid relying on both autonomy and value pluralism herself. In my view, Nussbaum is much closer to Raz's position than she wants to admit. Let's start with value pluralism.

Nussbaum thinks perfectionist liberals' reliance on a controversial doctrine of value pluralism signals disrespect to those holding monist doctrines (such as all the major religions). However, Nussbaum's political liberalism relies on the acceptance between (religious) monists and pluralists of a 'reasonable disagreement' between them. How different is that from accepting pluralism? The reason for a political liberal to respect her neighbour's comprehensive doctrine lies not in the fact that she considers this doctrine true or rational, but in the fact that she recognizes the value of this doctrine *to her neighbour's life*. This, I would suggest, is exactly what the doctrine of value pluralism has been about all along. Unfortunately, Nussbaum focuses her presentation of value pluralism on Isaiah Berlin's work which associates value pluralism with the idea that there is a plurality of values which are all 'equally genuine, equally ultimate, above all equally objective' (Nussbaum 2011b, 8). In doing so, she fails to see the difference with Raz's understanding of value pluralism. For Raz, 'moral pluralism is the view that there are various forms and styles of life which exemplify different virtues which are incompatible' (Raz 1986, 395). A lifestyle has its value for us at least partly by virtue of our having chosen it. Our commitments (partly) create the value of the options we commit ourselves to (Raz 1986, 387–9). On Raz's understanding, the respect I owe to my neighbour's choices derives from the fact that she has chosen one out of a series of valuable comprehensive lifestyles. Both on Nussbaum's and on Raz's account citizens face a choice about respecting their neighbour's adherence to a comprehensive doctrine which is not their own. On both accounts, if we choose to respect our neighbour, this is because we affirm the value of the doctrine *to our neighbour*. We are not committed to it having objective value, or even stronger, to recognizing its value for us (that we should feel its pull and let ourselves be converted). Something very much like a belief in value pluralism must underlie the political liberal case as well. Nussbaum can only deny this fact by downplaying the similarities and mystifying the source of respect for all doctrines in political liberalism.

At this point, Nussbaum makes a two-fold move. She admits the 'moral' nature of political liberalism's adherence to a norm of 'equal respect' and even to 'autonomy' (Nussbaum 2011c, 16–18). However, the similarity to perfectionist liberalism this suggests is immediately denied by pointing to the fact that political liberalism relies on 'political autonomy' only (Nussbaum 2011b, 36). The political liberal presents his liberalism as a freestanding doctrine, a module which can be plugged into a variety of comprehensive doctrines and is not metaphysical, but political, in its origins. The remaining contrast would be that perfectionist liberals (i) want to extend the value of autonomy to one's personal life and say that only autonomously led lives are good lives and (ii) they do base this on a metaphysical doctrine about the good.

These differences seem overblown. First, perfectionist liberalism is as much a *political* theory as political liberalism. Raz's conception of autonomy is part of his theory of *political* morality. The purpose of the ideal of autonomy, in Raz and other perfectionists, is to justify political action and not to say something about moral life in general. Many things can make a life go well, but political authorities should focus on this one aspect: the autonomous quality of the choices made in such a life. Such a theory can be as 'freestanding', devised 'for political purposes only' as political liberalism is. Given the fact that the ideal of autonomy refers us for (the goodness of) any other aspect of our lives to our own choices, it is hard to see how this ideal can be 'comprehensive' in the way a theocracy would be. The autonomy-respecting state does not comprehensively dictate the details of its citizens' lives, but opens up a plurality of ways of living on condition that they are autonomously chosen. This leaves room for delegating decision-making power over part of one's life to third parties. For example, Raz explicitly distinguishes his conception of autonomy from self-realization views and rejects the latter as too demanding (Raz 1986, 375).

Second, whether such a perfectionist liberal theory is based on 'metaphysical' considerations depends on what one understands by this term. Both political liberalism and perfectionist liberalism need their conceptions of the person and society to be based on something. A theory constructed as purely political is no less in need of some form of grounding. Whether one calls this grounding 'metaphysical' is a secondary matter. Why would Rawls's political conception of the person as free and equal be less metaphysical in character than Raz's conception of autonomy? Both are conceptions of the person that can be qualified as 'ontological', 'anthropological' or 'metaphysical' – again depending on how one uses these terms. The fact that the conception of the person is constructed for the justification of political authority does not necessarily render these terms inapplicable. Here, again, there is no real difference between political and perfectionist liberalism.

The only remaining difference seems to be that political liberalism makes use of the justificatory device of an overlapping consensus and restricts its scope to democratic societies in which the ideals of liberalism already have a foothold. Actually, the repudiation of metaphysics may be meant to reflect nothing more than this: that the origin of the political liberal conception of the person and his autonomy is found in the overlapping consensus between reasonable doctrines of a democratic society. I will deal with the question of justification in Chapter 3. Here we should only remember that Nussbaum cannot accept such a restricted scope given the universalist ambitions of her theory. If liberal principles are judged attractive, it seems inconsistent to think these attractions stop at the borders of established constitutional-democratic societies. One might object that perfectionist liberal theories may be restricted in a similar sense. Raz's theory also derives the value of autonomy from the existing social practices of Western societies and has been criticized for doing so (Waldron 1989). This however, seems to be more an accidental feature of Raz's view than a necessary consequence of adhering to a conception of autonomy. Whereas political liberal theories are necessarily restricted in scope, perfectionist liberal theories can be worked out either in a more restricted or a more universalist direction.

In conclusion, it seems hard to accept a completely neutral position that denies, as a part of the normative case for neutralist state policies, a substantive commitment to autonomy and value pluralism.[18] Political liberalism is untenable if it is understood as guiding state policies without any such reference to the good. When these references are acknowledged and defended as 'for political purposes only', however, then in terms of justifying state policies (if not in terms of justifying the theory of the good itself) political liberalism collapses into its neighbour: moderate perfectionist liberalism.

1.4 Towards a Moderate Perfectionist Liberalism

Moderate perfectionist liberalism requires us to specify a conception of freedom/autonomy and show how this conception can be justified as a basis for political morality. This is the task of the chapters of Part II. As a preparation, here I discuss two particularly pervasive challenges that have risen to previous versions of perfectionist liberalism: the 'balancing problem' and the 'incorporation problem'.

Imagine that defenders of perfectionist liberalism bite the bullet against neutralists and roundly acknowledge the perfectionist character of their ideal of freedom (while simultaneously defending it as the most minimal form of perfectionism possible). They agree that having

---

[18] Similar arguments are made by Colburn (2010a, 254, 2010b) and Sadurski (1990, 124). For an interpretation of the whole history of political philosophy in light of the inevitability of relying on a 'normative anthropology', see M. White (2012).

freedom/autonomy makes a positive contribution to a good life: lives with more freedom/autonomy are *mutatis mutandis* better lives than lives with less of it. The problem is that the acknowledgment of freedom's value undermines its special status and makes it susceptible to *balancing* against other values. This undermines the freedom-view's claim that we can simultaneously commit ourselves to freedom as a value and bar other values from entering the calculation. Because of the importance of this problem, I will give two illustrations from different contexts.

A first illustration is from the human rights literature. James Griffin defends a human rights theory based on rights to free and autonomous agency. For his normative defence of agency he has endorsed the teleological defence of the value of agency just sketched: having agency makes the lives of individuals better (Griffin 2008, 66–80). But then John Tasioulas criticized Griffin at several occasions for his reliance on agency and proposed a pluralist theory of the good, instead, to justify a list of human rights. He states:

> [C]onsider now a paradigmatic right: the human right not to be tortured. For Griffin, its justification resides in the way in which the pain torture inflicts undermines one's agency by 'destroy[ing] one's capacity to decide and to stick to the decision' (Griffin 2001b 311). However, it is puzzling in the extreme that the evil of pain in itself, independently of its corrosive impact on one's agency, forms no part of the justification. For, as Griffin admits, the avoidance of pain is one of our basic interests (Griffin 2001b: 313). Similar observations apply to other rights. Certainly education is necessary for autonomy, but why deny that the value of understanding is also sufficiently important to human life to make its own independent contribution to the existence of a right to education? Or that health is a key good protected by the right to bodily integrity? (Tasioulas 2002, 93)

Similarly, elsewhere, Tasioulas states that human rights to education, work and leisure, while undoubtedly also partly grounded in agency, more directly contribute to the human goods of knowledge, accomplishment and play (Tasioulas 2010, 663). Once we defend agency as a good, there is no logical impediment from also thinking about other rights as grounded in distinctive goods.

Jonathan Quong makes a similar move in his discussion of 'comprehensive anti-perfectionism' (a position similar to my moderate perfectionist liberalism[19]). He asks us to imagine a dialogue between two persons disputing the value of recreational drugs. Mike defends a prohibition of their

---

[19] See note 5 above.

use on perfectionist grounds (they are harmful for the users). Sara defends their free availability on the grounds that if people choose to use these drugs then they must be good for them. Once Sara, pressed by Mike, bases her defence on perfectionist grounds (autonomous choosing is good for people), then the state cannot remain neutral about the good anymore whether it chooses to follow Mike's or Sara's political view. Sara admits this. Her position only 'aims to be neutral with regard to all those conceptions of the good that are compatible with this thesis about the value of living an autonomous life. This is the only kind of neutrality to which liberals can and should aspire' (Quong 2011, 24). To this, Quong objects:

> [L]iberals should be clear that this sort of argument is itself a form of perfectionism: it is only a sound argument if the value of living autonomously (or the importance of promoting autonomy more widely) outweighs the disvalue of whatever activity is under scrutiny. (Quong 2011, 25)

Acknowledgement of autonomy's value brings in a weighing structure. Moreover, Quong is right, I think, in having suspicions about the self-evidence that autonomy will always weigh heavier. Liberal policies depending on that calculation rest on shaky grounds. The passage is followed by the identification of a second problem with Sara's position:

> Suppose that Mike is persuaded by Sara's arguments about the value of autonomy ... Mike can still reject the conclusion that autonomy-based reasons are the *only* valid perfectionist reasons for a liberal state to consider in formulating its policies ... Even if autonomy is of great value, this does not preclude the state from acting for other perfectionist reasons provided it can do so without undermining the autonomy of citizens. (Quong 2011, 25)

Again we see how other values enter the field as competitors once one conceives of autonomy itself as a value (Sher 1997, 56–60). This makes it impossible to sustain this view as a form of moderate perfectionist liberalism: incorporation of other values ('non-liberal goods') makes moderate perfectionist liberalism collapse into one of its right-hand neighbours (see Table 1.1): either strong perfectionist liberalism or even non-liberal perfectionism.

The general strategy I propose to deal with the balancing problem is to deny that autonomous agency is a value on the same plane as other values. The teleological view draws on an analogy between the individual level and the political level that is much too hasty. On the individual level, freedom/autonomy may have the character of a 'value' that can be traded off against other values. At least this is how individuals may sometimes perceive conflicts between freedom/autonomy and other values. But, in the political sphere freedom/autonomy has a special character. It has the status of a *regulative principle*, regulating the behaviours of different citizens wherever they conflict. Or so I will argue over the course of the chapters of Part II. If we can make true on the promise of this strategy then we have good reasons not to balance autonomous agency against other values, but to give it a special status. Such a principle will still require us to balance instantiations of agency against each other when they conflict (either between persons or with respect to different agency-conditions for one person). It does, however, contain this need for balancing within the principle of freedom/autonomy that is used. Some would call such a theory in which autonomous agency is not a value but a principle 'non-perfectionist', a third position between political and perfectionist liberalism, but I will prefer to classify it as minimally perfectionist, in my specific sense, to retain the force of the idea that state policies cannot be completely neutral.[20]

Moderate liberal perfectionism may also be thought vulnerable to a follow-up challenge, which I call the *incorporation problem*. Even if we can bar other values from entering a perfectionist liberal theory as competitors juxtaposed to the ideal of freedom/autonomy, one might still object that a perfectionist liberal view is objectionably perfectionist because specifying the exact conditions of freedom or autonomy will require incorporating other values through the back door. For example, Tasioulas in his critique of Griffin's agency-based human rights theory, has also argued: 'Autonomy and liberty are not "atomistic" values without constitutive relations to other components of a good life; instead their nature and scope is partly determined by their location within a broader web of prudential values' (Tasioulas 2002, 93; see also Tasioulas 2010, 664). If so, then we lose in this second, specification step what we have gained by solving the balancing problem.

A freedom-based capability theory will need to incorporate more substantive views of the good (and will have to, otherwise it remains an empty vessel) at least at three points. First, we have to select a list of basic capabilities that are necessary for every citizen to have free and autonomous agency. However, how can we do this without pronouncing, albeit

---

[20] Although I will not attempt to defend this, I take it that this strategy is basically the one adopted by Immanuel Kant in his *Doctrine of Right* where he defends the view that the state has to regulate interactions between individuals using a principle of equal freedom, the Universal Principle of Right (Kant 1996, 353). For two Kantian assessments of the debate between perfectionist and political liberals, staking out a third position similar to mine here, see Rostbøll (2011) and Pallikkathayil (2016).

implicitly, on the value of the activities that are to form the subject of these basic capabilities? If a capability to marriage, but not a capability to play tennis, is granted a place on the list, don't we implicitly take a stance on the value of marriage versus tennis? Can we separate their importance towards freedom/autonomy from their substantive value? Second, when specifying the details of any basic capability, we would run up to the same problem. If a capability to practice religion is on the list of basic capabilities, can we then have a policy selecting religions which should (not) get state recognition without an implicit understanding of the value of these different religions? Third, we have to balance different instances of freedom/autonomy where they clash. But can we do that without referring to other values? We can measure the length of two persons in terms of the value 'length' in virtue of the undisputed operationalization of this value in terms of a scale of inches or centimetres. Can the same kind of operationalization be done for freedom/autonomy? I defer treatment of this problem to Section 5.1.

The balancing and incorporation problems challenge the view that the moderate liberal-perfectionist commitment to the good of freedom/autonomy (however defined) is on its own *sufficient* for building a political theory. In addition, a commitment to non-liberal goods may be unavoidable. If so, the difference with strong perfectionist liberalism would then be less than originally claimed. The answer I propose to both problems will be different. Against the balancing problem, my moderate perfectionist liberal claim will be to accept the special value of autonomous agency (hence the perfectionist character of liberalism itself), but deny the political relevance of other, competing values. Against the incorporation problem, my response will be to accept that other values may sometimes play a role in specifying the value of autonomous agency, but deny that this renders the theory objectionably perfectionist. All of this requires first laying down the basics of the alternative capability theory of justice suggested at so far.

PART II

The Theory of Navigational Agency

CHAPTER 2

An Agency-Based Capability Theory of Justice

Introduction

The aim of this chapter is to present a dual-level conception of individual agency and to show how this conception can be connected to a capability theory of justice, as the underlying normative ideal to select basic capabilities. If this conceptual connection between agency and capabilities is accepted, then justice becomes a matter of equality of basic capabilities to agency. The main aim of this chapter is to offer a *conceptual analysis* of the notions of agency and capabilities and their connections. This chapter concludes by offering an argument in favour of the agency-based capability theory (see Section 2.4), but this is only a preliminary argument. The full normative *justification* of this view of justice is a separate matter and is the aim of Chapter 3.

Chapter 2 aims to offer two conceptual innovations. Within liberal theory, the innovation is to offer a *dual-level theory of agency*, where a person's agency is immersed in their social practices on one level, but is able to transcend these practices on a higher level. While many liberal theories work with a conception of agency, rarely do they offer such a dual-level theory, at least not explicitly.[1] Section 2.1 presents the two aspects or features of a person's agency which can be described by reference to the individual alone: 'autonomy' and 'freedom'. Section 2.2 adds a social feature to the conception of agency. Here the duality comes in. On the

---

[1] Two exceptions which I encountered are Doyal and Gough's theory of human needs and Carol Gould's theory of agency. The former makes a distinction between a lower and higher level form of agency ('autonomy of agency' and 'critical autonomy')(Gough 2014, 365–6), the latter between basic agency and the exercise of agency in self-development (Gould 2004, 33, 2015, 181). I will have to leave explicit comparisons to these theories for another time. In addition, it may be argued that several theories *implicitly* contain the two levels I have in mind. For example, Christine Korsgaard's moral theory (Korsgaard 1996) distinguishes reflections about how to act on the basis of our personal identity from reflections on our personal identity itself. I will have to leave the search for analogies with other theories which implicitly make a similar distinction in two levels to the reader.

one hand, agency is a form of participation in a social practice – i.e. a cooperative structure characterized by a common set of institutions. This is what I call 'participational agency'. Given the multiplicity of practices, however, we need to acknowledge a second, higher-level form of agency: the ability, not to participate in practices, but to navigate between them: navigational agency (Section 2.3). Hence agency can take two forms: the ability to move autonomously and freely within a social practice and the ability to move autonomously and freely between social practices.

The second aim is to offer an innovation within capability theorizing about justice, by offering an *agency-based capability theory*. This will be achieved by showing how agency itself is a capability-concept and how the conditions for agency must be understood in terms of a set of capabilities. This will lead up to the argument, in Section 2.4, that once we accept this view of agency, justice can be understood as requiring for each citizen a set of basic capabilities for the higher-level form of agency: navigational agency.

2.1   Agency: Freedom and Autonomy

This section discusses the 'individualist' aspects of my conception of agency – i.e. those aspects that can be described without explicit reference to the social context. It defines agency as made up of two individualist components: autonomy and freedom. It then connects both components to the concept of capabilities, and compares the resulting conception of agency to Martha Nussbaum's and Amartya Sen's use of the same term.[2]

Many authors have defined individual agency in purely individualist terms. For example, John Rawls refers to our capacity to construct a rational life plan. His thin theory of the good is centred around this aspect of our deliberative rationality (Rawls 1999a, 358). Joseph Raz offers a conception of personal autonomy consisting of three conditions: appropriate inner abilities, independence and an adequate range of options (Raz 1986, 372). James Griffin, in his theory of human rights, uses a conception of agency consisting of three aspects: freedom, autonomy and minimum provision (Griffin 2008, 149). Alan Gewirth, in his moral theory, offers a conception of agency which consists of two

---

[2] The expression 'free and autonomous agency' which I will regularly use may falsely give the impression that the components 'autonomy' and 'freedom' qualify a third feature, called 'agency'. This is wrong: agency simply exists through its two components. This is more accurately captured by the formula 'agency = freedom + autonomy'.

aspects: voluntariness and purposiveness (Gewirth 1978, 31–42). Despite enormous differences, these and other authors see agency as a feature of individuals. I think these definitions of agency are incomplete, since they do not explicitly incorporate the social aspects of agency which I will add in the next section.[3] However, I first concentrate on the individualist aspects and, here, I have much in common with each of these authors. I offer a characterization which is not meant to be particularly controversial, but which systematizes the concepts of agency of authors like those mentioned.

The most general definition of an agent is that of a person trying to realize an end as the object of their action. Action is intentional or purposive behaviour. The end can be intrinsic to the action (simply to perform the action for its own sake), or instrumental to it (to realize a goal not included in the act-description itself). The end can be simple and short-term or complex and long-term. The concept of an agent's end does not require devising a life plan in which many goals are integrated into a unified whole, or a coherent conception of the good life. Our ends may or may not be hierarchically ranked or commensurated. The only thing that is implied is that the agent *values* his or her ends: they represent whatever he or she considers good to achieve. This implies that his or her goals are not simply cravings, impulses or desires, but purposes that he or she has adopted or endorsed as worthy of pursuit. Agency requires a reflexive stance (i.e. at least the presence of some level/forms of reflection to be specified in more detail).

Purposiveness can be separated into two different stages which are together constitutive of agency. The first stage is when an agent *deliberates* – i.e. forms (or revises) his or her goals and chooses adequate means to realize these goals. The second stage is when an agent tries to *realize* his or her goals in practice. Of course, in the actual experiences of agents these stages are often not neatly separated but intermingled. We re-adjust our goals while acting as much as we re-adjust our actions while deliberating. Nonetheless, it is analytically useful to keep these two stages separate. I will refer to the first stage as the exercise of an agent's 'autonomy' (a capacity also referred to with such terms as self-legislation, self-determination or self-authorship) and the second stage as the exercise of an agent's 'freedom'. Autonomous agents are able to set themselves goals,

---

[3] Note that this does not make their conceptions of agency individualist in the moral sense (as akin to 'egoistic' or betraying an 'individualistic life style'). Nor do I think these conceptions need to deny that agency thus conceived has social preconditions. However, they do not bring the social context into the definition itself. In Section 2.4 I will argue this lack has distinctive disadvantages.

Table 2.1. *Individual agency and its components*

	Autonomy (rational deliberation)	Freedom (free action)
Capacities: internal capabilities	(1a) capacities to set ends and means	(2a) capacities to realize ends
Options: external capabilities	(1b) awareness of options (non-manipulation by others)	(2b) options (non-interference by others)

a free agent is able to act upon them. Full agency requires both freedom and autonomy.

Both freedom and autonomy also have two aspects: they require the presence of *capacities* or 'internal capabilities' on the one hand and *options* or 'external capabilities' on the other hand. This leads to a four-fold scheme (see Table 2.1). With respect to the autonomy part of agency, I need the capacity to set myself goals – i.e. certain mental abilities to deliberate.[4] With respect to the freedom part of agency, I need the capacity to succeed in reaching my goals. There are then two sets of capacities necessary for agency, relating to the two stages of agency: deliberation about, and realization of, my goals. Similarly, there are two sets of conditions with respect to our options. With respect to the autonomy part, others should not interfere with my internal process of setting goals – i.e. that they do not manipulate my deliberations about my options. This safeguard ensures that I am aware of the options that I actually have: others may block my awareness of – i.e. mental access to – these options (Pettit 2003). With respect to the freedom part, it is about the actual access to these options: others should not coerce me into another way of acting than the one I had decided upon myself – i.e. not interfere with my actions.

Summing up, we arrive at the following definition: an agent is an individual who is: (1) able to deliberate autonomously, i.e. (1a) has the capacities necessary to set him/herself goals and decide upon means to reach these goals, (1b) can exercise these capacities without manipulation by others; and is (2) able to act freely, i.e. (2a) has the capacities necessary

---

[4] This definition remains agnostic on the exact nature of the 'capacities' mentioned in the a-clauses (see Table 2.1). Since we require that agents endorse their goals as their own, some minimal level of rational control is implied. We should not assume extensive levels of rationality, however, nor should we assume that we need only cognitive requirements for agency. Emotional and social capacities are all in a complicated way involved in our agency. In the literature on personal autonomy, several competing theories about the exact requirements of autonomy are proposed (J. Anderson and Christman 2005). I will discuss these in Section 5.2.

to act upon his or her choices about goals and means, and (2b) can exercise these capacities without interference by others (see Table 2.1).

What is the relation between this conception of agency and the concept of capabilities? (In the following I relate my framework to Nussbaum's capability theory; I have included Appendix 1 to discuss the relation with Sen's capability theory.)

First, agency itself *is* a capability. A capability is an opportunity or ability to a functioning. A functioning, as Sen has defined it, is any state of 'being' or 'doing', from being healthy to riding a bike. The concept of a functioning is extremely flexible. Being healthy or riding a bike are quite concrete functionings, although they could be specified even more concretely, as being mentally or physically healthy or riding a mountain bike or a city bike. Similarly they could be specified more abstractly, such as when we subsume riding a bike under 'riding a vehicle' or 'moving from place to place'. Because of this flexible structure, it is no stretch of the imagination to see agency itself as consisting of two highly abstract functionings: autonomous deliberation and free action. And if both deliberation and action are functionings, then agency consists of the two 'meta-capabilities' to these functionings. Agency's two central components are not forms of welfare or resources, but capabilities. Agency may require resources, and the exercise of agency may deliver welfare, but agency itself is a capability.

It is rather surprising that the fact that agency is itself a capability has not been noted more often.[5] Nonetheless it is latent in Nussbaum's theory, since Nussbaum presents practical reason as itself a capability. In my terms, however, practical reason covers only the autonomy part of agency, not the freedom part. It is about reasoning about one's ends, not about realizing them in practice. For the latter part, we have to look at all the other central capabilities on Nussbaum's list, which specify privileged action-contexts. Also, Rawls has assimilated Sen's early critique of his theory by noting that he starts from the normative standpoint of capabilities, namely 'the capabilities of citizens as free and equal persons in virtue of their two moral powers' (Rawls 2001a, 169). The primary goods, then, are selected with a view to realizing these two moral powers/capabilities. Finally, in the legal context Simon Deakin has made a strong case for the similarities between the notion of capability and the notion of 'capacity', which refers to the standing before the law one needs to enter into

---

[5] An exception is Hübenthal (2006, 302), who discusses the close relation between Nussbaum's capability theory and Gewirth's theory of agency. See also Claassen and Düwell (2013).

contracts with others (Deakin 2006). The linkages made by these authors are indications of the fruitfulness of a theoretical connection between agency and capabilities that I aim to develop more fully in this chapter.

Second, the different components of agency can be spelled out in terms of a list of capabilities. The conception of agency presented above can be linked to Nussbaum's well-known distinction between three types of capabilities. First, we have 'basic capabilities', the 'innate equipment of individuals' that often 'cannot be directly converted into functioning' (Nussbaum 2000b, 84). I prefer to refer to these as 'innate capabilities' (since I will use the term 'basic capabilities' for what she calls 'central capabilities'). When innate capabilities are sufficiently developed, they become 'internal capabilities' – i.e. 'developed states of the person him/herself that are, so far as the person herself is concerned, sufficient conditions for the exercise of the requisite functions' (Nussbaum 2000b, 84). Finally, when internal capabilities are combined with 'suitable external conditions for the exercise of the function' (Nussbaum 2000b, 85), they become 'combined capabilities'. Only the latter are full capabilities, providing us with effective freedom, with the real opportunities to do or be something. It is, therefore, combined capabilities that are the subject of justice for Nussbaum and Sen.[6]

Internal capabilities correspond to what I have called the 'capacities' necessary for both goal-setting (agency-autonomy) and goal-pursuit (agency-freedom). The options one has access to when non-manipulated and non-interfered with correspond to Nussbaum's suitable external conditions, which I will refer to as 'external capabilities'. Taken together, the two agency capabilities are what Nussbaum calls 'combined capabilities'. In adopting this terminology of 'internal' and 'external' capabilities, a note of caution is in order. The proper development of internal capabilities from our innate capabilities *also* requires suitable external conditions. Both types of capabilities, then, are dependent on suitable social conditions. The words internal and external merely refer to the location of the respective aspect of agency itself (capacities as attributes of the person, options and their manipulation/interference as attributes of the social world external to the person). Moreover, these external conditions for nurturing internal capabilities are not merely negative. For example, it is obvious that from childhood onwards the nurturance of many inner abilities requires a good deal of help from others. In my framework,

---

[6] See also Dowding, who analyses these stages as 'latent ability', 'ability proper' and 'ableness' (Dowding 2006, 325).

however, the more positive conditions are acknowledged by saying that all four aspects of agency require suitable social practices – including legal and social norms – to safeguard both aspects of agency (see next sections). The negative conditions with respect to the agent's options (non-manipulation and non-interference) are part of the definition of agency itself, while the positive conditions are external to the definition of agency. For example, it is part of the description of an agent to say that he is able to display his love for his homosexual partner in public without interference by homophobic others, while this requires the presence of social and legal norms which inhibit these others from interfering.

Note that the fact that the components of agency can be specified in terms of a capability set does not mean that they *must* be specified in this way. Agency is a highly general term, which needs specification. Some may argue that the practical conditions for realizing agency turn out to be best formulated in some other metric than capabilities. This of course is the Rawslian position. As we have seen, he allows the re-description of his two moral powers as capabilities, but continues to think of their conditions in terms of a list of primary goods. Whether one thinks that the conditions for agency can best be spelled out in terms of capabilities or resources depends on arguments in the debate between resourcists and capabilitarians (R. Dworkin 2000; Pogge 2002; Pierik and Robeyns 2007; Sen 2009; E. Anderson 2010a; Brighouse and Robeyns 2010; Kelleher 2015). In this debate the main capabilitarian claim has been that a resourcist metric takes insufficient account of inter-personal variations in agents' abilities to convert resources into functionings. I will not repeat this debate here, but rely on those who have made the capabilitarian case elsewhere.

In conclusion, the concept of agency should not be set apart from the concepts of capabilities and functionings. Agency can be fully captured in the language of capabilities. It is itself a (complex) capability, and can be specified in terms of a set of capabilities that form the components for agency.

2.2 Participational Agency

In this section I will present a conceptualization of the social aspect of agency. This part of the theory does not negate the individualist components of agency, but shows how these have to be embedded in a social context.

The relation between the 'social' and the 'individualist' may lead to endless confusions. First, I restrict myself throughout to agency as the *attribute of individuals*. I will simply stay agnostic about the existence of collective agents. My theory at this point neither presupposes nor denies their existence. Second, I will take it for granted that individual agency has certain *social conditions*. For example, if individual agency requires rational capacities that need to be nurtured from birth, then it requires some social arrangement, like families nurturing babies and teachers educating pupils. In this sense individual agency to a large extent is a social achievement. This kind of 'social thesis' is not where we should look for controversy. It is hardly in dispute, between, say, liberals and communitarians (Taylor 1985, 191; Kymlicka 1989, 75). Indeed, the aim of many liberal theories is precisely to show that individual agency requires certain – liberal – social and political institutions, from the rule of law to the separation of powers, from constitutional rights to a market economy. Note, however, that the fact that agency has social preconditions is compatible with a purely *individualist* notion of action itself (as exemplified by the authors mentioned at the start of Section 2.1).

The definition of agency offered here goes one step beyond this and defines agency itself as *inherently* socially embedded. Action, on my account, will be defined as a *free and autonomous move in or between social practices*. The social aspect is that action is a move in a social practice, while the individualist aspect is that this move has two qualities which make that move an individual's own action: its freedom and autonomy. Hence one cannot really understand actions for what they are without their social context. The description of actions refers to this context for their comprehensibility. As the definition above ('in or between') makes clear, the social aspect refers to two forms of agency: agency within social practices (what I will call 'participational agency') and agency as moves between practices (what I will call 'navigational agency'). These will be the subject of this and the next section, respectively.

Sometimes an even stronger connection is made, that agency is itself a *social status*: to be an agent is to be recognized as such by others (Honneth 1995, 2011; J. Anderson 2008). There are several ways of understanding this recognition claim, some of which come close to the earlier thesis that agency has social preconditions. For example, social recognition can be presented itself as one of the preconditions of agency, next to material and legal requirements (J. Anderson and Honneth 2005). This I will accept. However, at other times the recognition claim goes beyond this, to say that one can only *be* an agent if and to the extent that one is recognized by others. This is often cashed out in terms of roles: 'being an agent' is a role like 'being a mother' or 'being a doctor'; it depends on the right kind of social relationships. The social recognition (either in formal laws or more informally) of one's position as a role-holder constitutes one's agency in that role. I do not rely on this stronger claim. Recognition is best seen, I think, as a response to, not as constitutive of our agency. For recognition is a response to a *capacity* for agency that is itself not dependent for its existence on recognition relations (Laitinen 2007, 248; Baldwin 2009, 325). As a result, agency is not just another role, which only comes into being through social acts of acknowledgment. It is the possibility of being a role-holder in the first place. Arguably, reaching this conclusion will require some work if one has first embedded agency in social practices. To defend this position, we need to separate the ontological from the justificatory relation between agency and recognition. While we may acknowledge that agency and recognition are ontologically co-existent, agency is prior to recognition in the order of justification. This will only become clear as the argument unfolds.

While providing an inherently social definition of action is highly unusual in much moral and political theory, this is more or less customary in much social theory (Winch 1990; Pettit 1993; Giddens 1994; Searle 1995; S. Miller 2001). Such an inherently social definition of agency is also certainly in the spirit of Nussbaum's capability theory. Nussbaum has always stressed that two of her ten capabilities have an architectonic role: practical reason and affiliation. These 'both organize and suffuse all the others, making their pursuit truly human' (Nussbaum 2000b, 82). Affiliation refers to 'being able to live with and toward others, to recognize and show concern for other human beings, to engage in various forms of social interaction' (Nussbaum 2000b, 79). Nussbaum's stress on this capability is meant to provide an antidote to the Kantian tradition in theorizing about justice, which according to her focuses solely on a human being's rationality. This is why she puts the capability of affiliation on the same level as practical reason. Man as rational animal and man as social animal are brought together. My theory has the same reconciliatory ambition, but pursues it through a different route. First, I think it is better to integrate both aspects in *one* conception of agency, thus making clear the connection between rationality and sociality. This connection is lacking in Nussbaum's theory, where the two capabilities remain separate and unconnected items on her list. Second, I do not interpret sociality as necessarily including altruistic motivations ('show concern for other human beings'). I follow those who believe that a justification for political theory should not rely on such motivations, since that presumes what needs to be

proven. Even if we would be entirely egoistic, we are still acting within a
social context. More should not be presupposed.[7]

As a point of entry we can start from the idea that agents have options
that others should not interfere with. If we would not go beyond that,
our theory of agency would presuppose that in the absence of interferences we simply 'have options'. However, most if not all[8] options agents
have are socially constructed, and would not exist without society. The
setting and realizing of ends does not occur in a vacuum, but in social
contexts. For these contexts I will use the generic term 'social practices'.
A social practice is a structure of actions held together by a set of common institutions, in which several agents cooperate to reach their ends.
Structure means that actions obey more- or less-recognizable and stable
patterns, which can be interpreted by the participants to orient themselves in the practice. Structure is brought about by *institutions* – i.e. the
formal and informal rules (norms) that qualify actions within the practice
as legitimate or illegitimate, desirable or undesirable, allowed or prohibited and so forth. Such institutions define *roles* of participants, in terms
of the *rights and duties* they have to follow to be able to participate in
the practice. All of this serves the purpose of allowing the participants to
pursue certain *ends*. These concepts – institutions, roles, rights and duties,
and ends – are the crucial components of a practice. Practices are often
understood through the analogy of a game: they are cooperative structures in which participants pursue their ends, subject to the constraints
presented by the rules of the game.

This definition of a social practice is meant to accommodate a great
variety of practices. Some will be highly stable and exist without much

---

[7] Some authors have explored the social nature of capability theory, proposing collective capabilities
(Gore 1997), 'structures of living together' (Deneulin 2008), or a capabilitarian 'relational ontology' (Smith and Seward 2009). Ingrid Robeyns provides a valuable discussion of the differences
between ethical, ontological and explanatory individualism, see Robeyns (2008, 90–4).

[8] One question that may arise at this stage is whether *all* actions are a matter of moves in (between)
practices. Some will wonder whether at least some actions take place outside of any practice. This
may include both purely individualized interactions with nature outside of any social context
(Robinson Crusoe on his island or I alone in my room brushing my teeth) and social interactions
which do not seem to be embedded in any practical/institutional context (two strangers meeting on
the street). My theory can allow for the existence of such actions. Purely individualized actions (to
the extent that they exist in society – many self-regarding actions can be re-described as part of
larger action types which are a move in a practice) generate no moral consequences and are thus
irrelevant for a theory of justice. Social, but non-practice-bound interactions may still have effects
on the agent's capabilities for participational and navigational agency, by violating its preconditions
(one stranger assaulting the other). As a result, the latter will also be institutionally pre-structured
(e.g. by criminal and tort law and social norms), hence part of a 'quasi-practice' (which isn't positively geared towards the realization of ends but does contain institutions).

change for centuries. Others will be fluid and adopt changing norms rather quickly. Some will be mostly structured by formal rules (such as legal codes), others rather by informal expectations and unwritten social norms (think of the routines of family life). Some practices will be rather self-standing, while others will have porous boundaries and overlap or be nested in other practices – e.g., think of how daily work in a company is structured by its statute and corporate culture, but also by the norms of the market in which it operates. To start with agency as a move in a practice, is not to take a stance on what practices should look like in all these respects. It is merely to give an account of agency's embeddedness in social contexts.

Social practices are essentially normative in two senses.[9] First, they are normative because action is directed to the realization of ends; this is the teleological aspect of practices. Here we need to distinguish individual and collective ends. Every individual always has an individual end in acting: this is what they want to achieve by their own moves. Some practices allow a great variety of individual ends to be pursued: the descriptions of the individual actions, when spelled out, will have little in common. At other times, however, all these individual ends are instantiations, without much variation, of a collectively standardized end for all its participants. The first type of relation we often find in competitive settings (such as adversarial politics or the market), where each individual's end includes the frustration of the ends of others. The collective end here is radically different from the ends individuals strive for; such as to deliver the public benefits from a competitive political process. The second type of relation can be found in cooperative practices, where there is a truly shared end (as when a group builds a house together). But even here, there is a need for agency – i.e. for individualized contributions to the practice, in which a person has her own ends when cooperating towards the collective end. Indeed, freedom and autonomy in a practice are about the individual's decisions how to fulfill his role, how to discharge his duties and make use of his rights, which moves (not) to make, in short, how to play the game (all of this says nothing about who *determines* the ends – more about that later).

Second, practices are normative because the goal-pursuit of agents is structured by institutions, which define roles in terms of rights and duties; this is their deontic aspect (more on this aspect will follow in Chapter 3).

---

[9] Using the term 'normative' does not imply *approval* of the theorist of whatever happens in a practice (MacIntyre 1985; D. Miller 1999, 111–30). Rather it should here be seen as a descriptive term, which allows us to understand the relation between actions and the social structures within which they take place (Rawls 2001b; Young 2011).

This deontic aspect is related to the teleological aspect. Through the adoption of a certain set of norms, a practice gains a specific character, as being a practice of a certain kind. Other norms would have led to another kind of practice, and this will have an impact on the ability of participants to reach their goals. If legal norms prohibit euthanasia, then patients with a wish to end their lives will have difficulty to reach this goal in the medical practice. If legal norms allow euthanasia, then their goals will be more easily facilitated, even though other norms in the same practice (say, a shared medical ethos amongst doctors not to actually perform euthanasia save in highly exceptional circumstances) may still make it difficult, compared to another practice in which these other norms would also be reformed. Norms will often be selected with an eye on the individual ends that ought (not) to be pursued within the practice.

A social practice, then, both enables and constrains individual action. Setting one's own purposes, in a practice, means deciding *how* to fulfill one's duties and make use of one's rights. It is crucial to see that this involves our freedom and autonomy. No deterministic picture of practices is credible. Individuals still (have to) make decisions when they interpret their roles. These role descriptions always leave a certain leeway (Gewirth 1978, 27–28). On the other hand, we should also not be blind to the fact that practices constrain action. First, the capacities to set and execute goals depend on the practice. To be an agent in a football game requires different capacities from being an agent when standing before a legal court, or selling art works, or speaking in parliament. In each of these contexts, different capacities are required. For example, to sell a work of art requires commercial skills in persuasion, affinity with the products traded in that specific market, an ability to attune one's performance to a specific kind of clientele, etc. All of these things are highly specific to the practice. Second, the context of a practice limits our options as well. The reason for this lies in the constraints imposed by institutions. The practice of car traffic needs a rule for driving on the right-side or left-side of the road, to enable participants to engage successfully in movements from one location to another. Norms impose certain patterns of action rather than others, since they are necessary to reconcile the actions of all participants.

The necessarily restricted character of our agency in practices points to a theoretical difficulty in identifying instances of manipulation and interference. It is inevitable that participants constantly influence each other. At which point are we prepared to say that these influences get a manipulative or interfering character, i.e. amount to a form of coercion?

This cannot be discussed in general. If practices make possible our actions (by creating options to act in the first place) and simultaneously restrict it (by creating a limited set of options) then coercion can only be benchmarked against the alternative practices which could also exist, and offer more options than the current practice. In other words, judgments of coercion depend on the overall benefits of having this practice instead of another one (here judgments of proportionality come in as well: could we have this practice but with less restraining rules?). These are essentially normative judgements. Similarly, what counts as objectionable manipulation will also depend on the practice. The same technique of advertizing that is objectionable on TV on Sunday morning in between children's programs will be unobjectionable late at night where it is addressed to adults.

Given the fact that practices offer a restricted context of action, it is natural to wonder about the possibilities for individuals to transcend the specific practices in which they find themselves enmeshed. This will lead us to consider navigational agency (see Section 2.3). Before closing, however, let's discuss the link between participational agency and the concept of a set of capabilities.

On the level of a specific practice participational agency can rather straightforwardly be specified in terms of a set of internal and external capabilities. A practice of teaching is composed of participants with certain internal capabilities, say capabilities to speak and listen, give and understand instructions, etc. It also requires certain external capabilities, say options to access relevant educational resources, the absence of certain inhibiting conditions, etc. Descriptively, it may or may not be difficult to identify the relevant capabilities, depending on the complexity of the practice, the transparency of its institutions, the extent to which the practice is volatile or stable, etc. Normatively, there may be disputes about what these capabilities should be. The only relevant point here is the conceptual one, that in so far as it is possible to identify the demands of successful participation, these can be captured in terms of capabilities, along the lines sketched earlier. The specific set of necessary internal and external capabilities then is *constitutive* of what it is to be an agent-participant in the practice. If being a lawyer requires being able intellectually to handle legal cases plus being able to communicate successfully with clients plus having an entrepreneurial disposition, then these three capabilities together make up the capability of being a lawyer. Agency in a specific practice is simply defined through the capabilities necessary for participation in that practice. If the practice changes then the characterization of agency and the required capabilities change accordingly.

Since agency itself is composed of the four aspects analysed earlier, in studying specific practices we need to trace the linkages between the relevant capabilities and these four aspects. As an example, let's take the freedom of expression, or in capability terms, the capability to express oneself in public. Let's suppose we can identify the set of practices in which this capability is institutionalized (say, television programs, protest marches on the street, internet forums). Links can be drawn between each of these practices and all four parts of the definition of agency. Freedom of expression most obviously contributes directly to a speaker's freedom of action (2b). They can say what they wish to say. It also, however, contributes to a listener's freedom from manipulation (1b), because when listeners have access to a plurality of options they will be less likely to be indoctrinated by a single group able to monopolize public discussion. Moreover, since private deliberation is always influenced by input from others, long-term exposure to such a free public sphere will automatically improve listeners' capacities to deliberate about public issues (1a). Finally, and through a training effect, such a practice will contribute to speakers' capacities to express themselves well (2a). This is, of course, anything but a full analysis of freedom of expression. The point is to illustrate the methodology of identifying agency in a practice: we should look at all participants in a practice (here: speakers and listeners) and all their capabilities.

2.3 Navigational Agency

To bring in navigational agency, we need to enrich the social ontology developed thus far with one additional premise: the existence of a multiplicity of social practices. As we will see, this brings in the possibility of a new type of agency.

Human life consists of participation in several practices, and a society consists of the co-existence of several practices. I take this premise to be uncontroversial. Partly the identification of a practice is an arbitrary matter, which depends as much on the interests of the observer as on the characteristics of social reality. Where one observer sees a boundary between two separate practices, another one sees a practice overlapping with or nested in another – does the enforcement of the criminal code form one practice? Or should we distinguish as many practices as there are crimes defined in the code? Whatever of the exact boundaries, it strains credibility to define society as made up of only one practice. We all participate in different social contexts, with markedly different rules and expectations. This is not just a consequence of the differentiation of spheres in modern society – although there it takes extreme forms – but of living in society in general (one need only think of the conflicts between different normative orders described in ancient Greek tragedies).

As a consequence of the multiplicity of practices, all participational agents will be confronted with two normative problems in addition to the fulfilment of their role within the practices in which they happen to participate. The first problem is: in which practice(s) to participate? This problem is forced upon us by the multiplicity of practices and the practical impossibility of participating in all of them. Different careers, marriage partners, memberships of religious and other communities, etc. are possible; which one(s) to participate in? Second, participational agents need to deal with *conflicts* between the practices in which they participate. The most familiar kind of conflict lies in the necessary scarcity of our time, which forces us to distribute our time between participation in different practices. Beyond that, conflicting norms are also a source of conflicts. For example, holding a certain job may make the observance of a religious custom impossible, so that one will have to choose between one or the other or find another way to solve the conflict.

If and to the extent that participational agents are able to solve these two problems themselves freely and autonomously, they are navigational agents. First, navigational agents are able to choose which practices to participate in – i.e. to make decisions about *entry and exit* in social practices. Second, navigational agents are able to resolve practical conflicts between the practices in which they participate on their own terms. Having these abilities is not self-evident: navigational agency is a mere *possibility*. Not every participational agent necessarily also is a navigational agent. One can be a participant in a multiplicity of social practices *without* having the option of choosing to exit these and enter other ones. Social or political conventions may prohibit these moves and coerce people into participation into certain practices. Similarly, conflicts between practice-based commitments may be resolved by other persons or institutions instead of by our own choices. Navigational agency is a contingent possibility, whereas participational agency is a necessity of human life.[10] Navigational agency requires a specific kind of society, which protects its members' opportunities to navigate the social world as they see fit. The central contention later in this chapter will be that honouring the

---

[10] We could say participational agency is a *descriptive* notion since we are always participating in some practices, while navigational agency is a *normative* notion: this form of agency need not be present, we can strive for it as an ideal/value to be realized for all agents in society.

aspiration to navigational agency defines the struggle for social justice (see Section 2.4).

Navigational agency ensures that one's participation itself in social practices is a free and autonomous choice. However, an objection to the analysis so far may be that it is implicitly biased towards the status quo and may have conservative implications. For each practice constrains the ends that a participant can choose and at any point in time society offers a limited menu of practices and associated possible ends. This menu reduces agency in any society to a choice between pre-set ends. This is particularly painful where a participational agent is not prepared to endorse any of these ends. Here the different levels at which one can identify a practice become relevant. Imagine a labour market consisting of ten companies which all manage to exploit their workers in some ways. If one identifies the relevant practice of participation as that of the single company – given its unique institutional framework of formal and informal rules, compared to its competitors, this identification may be useful for some purposes – one could say workers have a choice to freely exit and try to enter other companies if they disagree with its exploitative features. However, if one identifies the relevant practice as the labour market as a whole, one can say there is no exit option – assuming for the sake of argument there are no other sources of income available – from exploitation.

Navigational agency, as the ability to make free and autonomous choices with respect to one's participation in social life, hence requires more than the ability to exit. The latter sometimes simply is not available, if a set of practices in which one must participate are all similarly structured, as in the labour market example. Therefore, we need to add two forms of navigational agency in addition to exit/entry and conflict resolution. I will call these the *reform* of existing practices and the *creation* of new practices. Opportunities for reform and creation, where they are available, potentially greatly enhance our agency. Reforming practices means being able to *co-govern* these practices. Of course one cannot claim, when dissatisfied with a practice, to have the right to govern the practice on one's own (becoming the new dictator). Reforming (or creating) practices requires the participation of others, so that here one's agency is necessarily limited to the extent that one cannot convince others of the value of supporting the changes one has in mind. Nonetheless it is of great importance in contexts where exit is unavailable. The creation of a completely new practice can be seen as a limit-case of reforming existing practices (when the reforms are drastic enough, what emerges is basically something new), but is seems important to mention separately to stress the creative, spontaneous potential of navigational agency. Practices are not static but evolve, and to the extent that participational agents are also navigational agents, they are not passive subjects but agents of change, innovation and transformation.

In conclusion, where these four abilities of exit and entry, conflict resolution, reform and creation are available, a participational agent is able to freely and autonomously participate in social life and also becomes a navigational agent.[11] Navigational agency is agency at a practice-transcending level, since it is about navigating the social world as a whole: deciding which practices to join and leave, how to resolve conflicts between them, how to create or reform practices. In navigational agency we take up a reflexive stance to social life as we encounter it and as we have participated in it thus far; trying to either change or add to existing social structures or change our own location in the social field. The qualifier 'practice-transcending' should not be misunderstood. Navigational agency is not asocial, since it still concerns choices within or between practices: the agent at all times acts 'on the ground' of social life. It is only about transcending one's *current* participation in *existing* practices, either by moving to other practices or by changing or adding to the menu of existing social practices. In this way, a concept of agency starting from a firmly socially embedded analysis of what it is to act, leads us to acknowledge the possibility of a form of agency that transcends these practices.

This requires that individual agents are able to take their reflection to a higher level, and reach a reflective distance with respect to their current roles. It requires that they may formulate new or different ends in life from the one's assigned to them by the practices they participate in. One may wonder whether individuals are able to do this kind of end-setting, if they are always immersed in social life. Aren't we back to the 'disembedded self'? This ability however, is not more mysterious than the reflective distance needed to fulfil a role – which as we saw also requires one to reflect upon how to use the discretionary space left by the role description, and interpret it in a free and autonomous way. If humans have the reflective abilities to be participational agents, they also have the potential to be

---

[11] Given that I have defined navigational agency through these four abilities, one might wonder whether the 'navigational' label is the best description, since the metaphor of navigation refers primarily to the first task (exit/entry: movement between practices). 'Practice-transcending agency' might be more-encompassing, since all four kinds of agency transcend existing practices (in different ways). This is a somewhat burdensome term. I have decided to stick with navigational agency as a *pars pro toto* given the metaphorical force of the term.

navigational agents. Being neither animals nor automata, human beings should be understood as having these abilities (at least, both fall or stand together. But I will leave out of consideration the possibility that they fall together that some determinists in the free-will debate may want to push).

Let's now turn to the link between navigational agency and capabilities. Navigational agency requires the general ability to choose between practices, as well as the absence of manipulation and interference with respect to these choices. The fact that these requirements are not relative to a specific practice but are general, does not mean that they can somehow (mysteriously) be realized somewhere *outside* social practices. Even these general requirements of agency must be realized within social practices. Navigational agency-capabilities are a subset of participational agency-capabilities. They are those practice-bound capabilities that are causally necessary to realize navigational agency. To illustrate, let's use the example of freedom of expression again. Not all four links between communication practices and participational agency mentioned in Section 2.2 are necessarily also links to navigational agency. It is probably reasonable to say that the direct effects on our agency-freedom (2a and 2b) are mainly important for those who have it as their private ends to be speakers (say, politicians, journalists, activists). They may greatly enjoy doing so and think it important to do so – it makes up their private conceptions of the good life. In this example the value for navigational agency lies mainly or exclusively in the effects on agency-autonomy (1a and 1b) of the listeners: every citizen's capacity to navigate between social practices. Thus some of the value of the freedom of expression is purely practice-bound while another part of it also transcends the practice (concerns navigational agency). Any of these specific claims about freedom of expression might be contested. My point is merely methodological: we can make a full list of all the practice-bound capabilities and then investigate the way they contribute to (or threaten to undo) our navigational agency.

In elaborating this method, it is useful to distinguish between two types of social practices. First, some social practices are positively necessary to develop the required capabilities for navigational agency. Call these *mandatory practices*. Navigational agency will for example require practices of education and health care, to the extent that these are necessary to build up the required mental and physical capacities (internal capabilities) which enable citizens to navigate their societies. It will also require practices which safeguard certain general prohibitions on coercion and manipulation (external capabilities), such as policing and courts to maintain criminal law. This means that certain practices have a special function: they serve to create and sustain our general capabilities for navigational agency. The existence of these practices cannot be left to the spontaneous agency of individuals volunteering to create them, but is a social and political concern if there is to be navigational agency at all.

Second, all other practices, which are not necessary in a positive sense to realize navigational agency, can be conceived of as practices in which agents exercise their agency already developed. Call these *optional practices*. For these practices there is a negative requirement not to violate the navigational agency of their participants. Imagine that someone argues that the practice of marriage (unlike health care or education) is itself not a necessary requirement to become a navigational agent. Rather it is one optional lifestyle choice among others. Whatever of the substantive merits of such an argument, if we grant it, there still is a further point to ask about inequalities within this optional practice. For if the inequality between men and women in marriage arrangements leads to women feeling inferior and unable to act freely and autonomously, this would amount to a violation of their navigational agency. This would be the case where women do not feel free to exit their marriages (so that the practice is a coercive one) or where women would feel unable to act freely and autonomously in other domains of life. The preservation of navigational agency therefore requires monitoring *all* practices to see if insufficient levels of participational agency do not undermine their participants' more general capacity for navigational agency.

Through this method one could use to the concept of navigational agency to generate a list of basic capabilities, understood as capabilities to navigational agency. In Chapters 5, 6 and 7 I will argue for recognition of three sets of basic capabilities, i.e. empowerment, subsistence and political capabilities. I will there also give a rough indication of the capabilities to be included in each of these sets. But whatever list we come up with in the end, it is important to realize that on the method described here it is impossible to make up a completely trans-historical list of basic capabilities. The relation between navigational agency and capabilities is not constitutive but *instrumental*. For depending on the specific sociohistorical character of existing social practices, the task of navigation will require *different* specific capabilities. For example, the skills to navigate between existing practices required in modern societies are different than those in pre-modern societies. The ability to read and write will be necessary for agency in literate societies, whereas this is not the case in societies relying predominantly on oral transmission of information. Similarly, whether one has a realistic possibility of exit from an existing practice (say, a vested religion) depends on the strategies for blocking exit in current practices. As these blocking strategies become more aggressive, more extensive capabilities to exit will be necessary as well. Navigational agency thus serves as a *regulative principle* to select capabilities, which is itself universally valid (this would need further justification), but does not generate a universal list of capabilities. Some items will be pretty durable and constant over time, while others will be less so.

The recognition of the socio-historical specificity of basic capabilities does *not* imply taking a Senian stance on the controversial 'list-issue'. My discussion here about the status of the list (trans-historical versus historically relative) is not to be conflated with the issue of its legitimate authors. On the latter issue, I cannot see what is wrong with granting (political) philosophers (as anyone else) the opportunity to propose capability lists, nor why that would be disrespectful of democracy (Claassen 2011b). That however is a different matter. The point here is that whoever proposes a list, should acknowledge its socio-historical specificity even if the criterion of navigational agency itself can be justified as trans-historically valid (as I think can be argued, see Section 3.3.). With these caveats in mind, in Chapters 5, 6 and 7 I will argue for three sets of basic capabilities as essential in modern developed (if not for many of these capabilities also in other) societies.

2.4   Justice, Agency and Capabilities

So far this chapter has given a rough picture of participational and navigational agency and how these concepts can be specified in terms of a set of capabilities. We can now address the normative question: which capabilities do citizens owe each other in a just society? Justice is normally (and correctly) understood as being about *equality* in some dimension. My theory offers two dimensions as a candidate[12]: those capabilities necessary for agency in all social practices (i.e. participational agency), or those capabilities necessary for navigating social practices (i.e. navigational agency). Is justice about equality of participational or navigational agency?

Let's imagine that justice would require equal rights to participate in all social practices. Inequalities in agency are everywhere in social life.

---

[12] Theoretically, one could imagine two other options: justice as the equal ability to participate in *some* (i.e. any) practice or as the ability to participate equally in *some specific* practice(s). The former seems a redundant ideal; being participational agents, we always already participate in some practices. The latter begs the question: why is equality within these specific practices a requirement? This will have to refer to some external standard (such as the necessity to become a navigational agent).

They may have many origins and reasons. In family life, the inequalities between parents and children find their rationale in the natural inequality of capacities of both these roles. The inequality between husband and wife, in some cultures, finds its origin in beliefs about the aptness of each of these roles for the fulfilment of certain tasks in the household. In business, employee contracts specify rights and duties and most companies differentiate between employees in this respect. It might be dysfunctional for a company to give the same right to make decisions about the long-term strategy of the company to the 25-year-old graduate who just started, and to the 50-year-old senior manager in the strategy department. In such contexts, there may be good reasons for having inequalities of participational agency: it may deliver benefits to all participants (albeit not necessarily equal benefits). The mutuality of these benefits may require and thus legitimize inequality of agency. However, the rationality of having these practices does not preclude their immorality. It may be rational to cooperate within an inegalitarian structure in which one is dominated, because that is still more advantageous than defecting from the practice. The question thus arises when these unequal relations become unjust.

It is here that my theory introduces navigational agency. The powers of a navigational agent, her real opportunities to enter and exit practices, reform existing ones or create new ones, is what ensures that if she participates, she does so (sufficiently) freely and autonomously. This in turn presupposes for each participant that she has basic rights – i.e. rights to the capabilities necessary for navigational agency. These rights guarantee citizens the capacities and options causally necessary to enter and exit social practices. Therefore, at the higher level of navigational agency equality between agents *is* a demand of justice, even if within social practices it is not. For if some citizens would have more or stronger agency rights than others, they would find themselves in (grossly) asymmetrical bargaining positions within practices. This would render them vulnerable to coercion and oppression from other participants. Instances of such coercion are often experienced as unjust. These experiences of injustice are an indicator of what the agency account tries to make explicit. Coercion points to a lack in the voluntariness of one's participation, and that can best be teased out in terms of the absence of sufficient capabilities for navigational agency.

These reflections are only meant to give a first motivation why navigational, but not participational agency should be considered the right *equalisandum*. They merely provide a preliminary justification for navigational over participational agency as the criterion for social justice, by showing that there is no reason to condemn all instances of practice-based inequality as long as individuals have control over their subjection to these instances (either by exit options or by rights to reform). A full justification requires showing how it is rationally inescapable for each person to claim a right to navigational agency. This will be done later (see Chapter 3). They also do not answer the more detailed question: when, at what point, does the lack in navigational capabilities between two partici-pants become so strong that one can no longer speak of voluntary, unco-erced relations in their practice? In other words, we still need an account of the *distributive principles* to apply. Equality of agency does *not* imply that every capability must be distributed in strictly equal portions. It is a separate discussion whether a sufficiency or priority rule may also be legit-imate. At this point, we need not conclude that the distributive principle should be strict equality, or even that we can apply the same rule for each capability in the set of navigational capabilities (see Chapter 4).

Let me now comment on why I think this conception of justice com-pares favourably to Nussbaum's capability theory of justice. The demarca-tion of basic capabilities from non-basic ones is not made on the basis of their importance for a flourishing human life or any other ideal of well-being, as it is for Nussbaum and others in the capability approach. As discussed in Chapter 1, many have (convincingly, in my view) argued that this leads to a strongly perfectionist conception of justice. My alternative capability theory avoids this strong form of perfectionism since naviga-tional agency capabilities fulfil a different and more restricted *function* than capabilities for human flourishing or well-being: navigation in social life. The concept of agency introduced here leads to a capability theory that is focused from the start on the liberal aim of guaranteeing for each agent a measure of practice-transcending freedom and autonomy. The individualistic aspects of agency lead us to single out only those capabili-ties that contribute to such freedom and autonomy.

Now since we need some freedom and autonomy in all social prac-tices, as part of what it is to fulfil social roles, the individualist aspect on its own would still have led us to a conception of justice prescribing capabilities for agency as participation in *all* social practices (analogous to Nussbaum's theory which prescribes capabilities for flourishing in all spheres of life).[13] By embedding this account in a dual-level theory of

---

[13] An example from a different context may help: Liao has argued that Griffin's (single-level) theory of agency does not have the resources to block the implication that a human right to an 'agentic

agency, we can see why that conclusion needs to be resisted. For a just society should restrict itself to those conditions that empower citizens to navigate between social practices. By focusing on citizens' emancipation from social practices, it guarantees that participation is a matter of free choice. Justice then is a matter of using public power to save citizens from private practices of oppression and coercion, so that they can function as autonomous choosers of their own lives. While much more needs to be said, this is hopefully enough to show us how this account can escape the problem associated with Nussbaum's version of the capability approach to justice, of becoming an overly perfectionist theory.

This leaves open the question how the agency-based capability theory offered in this chapter relates to other, non-Nussbaumian versions of the capability approach. Some authors have explored a similar direction, by tying the capability metric to a conception of personal autonomy (Rothstein 1998, 52–54, 157), economic, cultural and political forms of agency (Olson 2006, 94–96, 138–43), a Hegelian concept of social agency (Schuppert 2014), a conception of freedom as 'freedom from duress' (Axelsen and Nielsen 2015) and a conception of 'capabilities to control' (Begon 2017). These theorists all share my basic idea that the metric of capabilities needs to be coupled with an underlying ideal of freedom/agency/autonomy which determines which capabilities are to be selected as basic one, necessary for justice. Obviously, they differ in the conceptions of freedom/agency/autonomy they offer, both among themselves and compared to my theory. This is also true for Philip Pettit's attempts to marry the capability metric to his conception of republican freedom (Pettit 1997, 158, 2001, 2014, 86) and for Elizabeth Anderson's theory, which ties the capability metric to an ideal of democratic equality (E. Anderson 1999, 2010a).[14] (For a discussion of the relation between my capability theory and Pettit's republicanism, see Appendix 2, for Anderson, see Section 4.3). All of these take a distance from the capability approach's orientation to well-being or human flourishing, such as it can be found in Nussbaum's (and also Sen's) work. All of them take the direct route to 'liberalizing' the capability approach by tying it to a concept of freedom/autonomy instead of offering a well-being-based capability list as the object of a political-liberal overlapping consensus.

---

capacity to sail a yacht' may have to granted to all citizens (Liao 2015, 89). This seems to me a problem for Griffin indeed, but my approach solves it by confining basic rights to navigational agency.

[14] For a criticism of Anderson's capability theory, which could be launched mutatis mutandis from an agency-based perspective, see Barclay (2012, 516–17).

Finally, and now abstracting from capability theory, it may be instructive to clarify the kind of intervention I hope the dual-level conception of agency can make in the field of liberal theory more generally. There are two main points I would like to stress at this stage. First, it is a pervasive objection against agency-based liberal theories that they are unable to give a principled reason for why rights to minimal levels of agency (which are clearly compatible with a non-liberal practices such as slavery) would not suffice (Tasioulas 2010, 664; Buchanan 2010, 694–96; Van Duffel 2013, 652–55). Here is Raz's version of the objection, directed at Griffin's and (in an earlier passage) against Alan Gewirth's agency-based theories:

> If human rights are rights of those with the capacity for intentional agency to preserve that capacity, the distinction between capacity and its exercise is relatively clear, and a case for the privileged standing of the capacity can be made, at least so long as it is not claimed that the privilege is absolute. But Griffin quite explicitly extends the grounds of human rights beyond the capacity for intentional action. He includes conditions making its successful exercise likely, conditions such as the availability of education and information, of resources and opportunities. At every point he adds 'minimal' – minimal education and information etc. But if minimal means some information, some resources and opportunities, however little, it is a standard easy to meet, and almost impossible to violate. Just by being alive (and non-comatose) we have some knowledge, resources and opportunities. Slaves have them. Griffin, of course, does not mean his minimal standard to be that skimpy. He suggests a generous standard. But then we lack criteria to determine what it should be. My fear is that this lacuna cannot be filled. There is no principled ground for fixing on one standard rather than another. (Raz 2010, 326)

Thus Griffin's account wavers between a minimal (austere) and a maximal (rich) account of agency. This problem is ultimately related to the incorporation problem (see Section 1.4). For if we want to generate something like the existing lists of human rights, we have to opt for the richer account of agency. This, however, Raz suspects, means 'smuggling a particular ideal of a good life' (Raz 2010, 325) into the agency account. This problem may be unsolvable for a single-level theory of agency.[15]

My account seeks to overcome this problem by searching for a way out of the dichotomy between the merely intentional agency that the slave

---

[15] In response, Gewirth reverts to the idea that the agent has a right to the conditions for successful agency (Gewirth 2007, 224). This however smuggles in rights to a particular agent's conditions for success, thus conditions for fulfilling his particular concept of the good. Perfectionism then is unavoidable. For Griffin's response, which basically denies the problem, see Griffin (2010, 748).

has (a form of participational agency) and the rich value or interest-based conceptions of agency that would go beyond intentional agency. The freedoms and opportunities protected by human rights (which are at the heart of liberal theory) are generated by reflecting on an altogether qualitatively different *kind* of agency, which fulfils a separate function in human life (wherever it is present): being able to navigate social practices, in the sense of exiting and entering them, solving conflicts between multiple practices, reforming existing ones and creating new ones. Fleshing out the conditions for this form of agency may not be easy in practice (as all exercises of application are difficult), but at least at this level of abstraction there is not a direct reliance on a theory of the good life (beyond the good of agency itself) that Raz and others (rightly) claim is necessary for single-level theories like Griffin's to generate a rich concept of agency.

A second point is related. The dual-level account demystifies agency (and its components of freedom and autonomy) by showing how these are embedded in all of human life, in both liberal and non-liberal practices and societies. If liberalism is controversial in a global context, and is accused of falsely making universalist claims, then the dual-level theory suggests that these accusations need to be reinterpreted compared to the way they are usually phrased. The problem, for liberalism, is not to show that freedom and autonomy are important goods to which all citizens should have rights. For all agents, by virtue of existing and participating in social practices, already have certain forms of freedoms and autonomy (which implies having certain rights; as will be discussed in Chapter 3). These forms are restricted to the social context, however. The special claim of liberal theories relates to the possibility of having *practice-transcending forms of agency*. These claims do not seem to be necessary to non-liberals, since one can perfectly imagine living a life without them. Such a life may even be a good life, in some respects, especially if one has internalized the justificatory normative framework (in a myth, religion, or ideology) which restrains one's agency to a specified role in existing practices. It is then up to liberals to show why each agent nonetheless has a right to be more than just a participational agent. The justificatory burden is not less, but located differently: in the possibility of having this qualitatively special form of agency. The split is not between an unencumbered agent and a socially embedded one, but between two types of socially embedded agents, where one has considerably more leeway than the other.

CHAPTER 3

Justifying the Right to Navigational Agency

Introduction

If liberal theorizing's first commandment is to protect and respect everyone's free and autonomous agency, its second commandment is that the political protection of this ideal is realized in the form of a set of basic rights.[1] This 'morality of rights' has been contested as the parochial expression of Western cultural norms, just as much as the ideal of free and autonomous agency itself. In Chapter 2 I have not only presented a conception of capabilities for navigational agency, but also given a preliminary argument that justice should be conceived as a matter of giving citizens an equal set of basic *rights* to such agency. To answer the critics of a morality of rights, we now face the question how such rights can be justified. Chapter 3 argues that a right to navigational agency can be justified.

The problem of justification presents itself in different forms for different theories. I start by explaining the problem as it appears in the theory of navigational agency. I extend the social ontology presented in Chapter 2, making use of John Searle's work. Rights and duties give an institutional description of an agent's role. Agents always already are embedded in such structures of rights and duties. However, there is a gap between agents merely having liberties to do certain actions (mere-participational agents), and agents having certain claim-rights (navigational agents). What needs to be argued for is that agents should have an equal set of claim-rights that gives them navigational agency status. This sets the desideratum for a successful justification. Normative questions about

---

[1] In the legal sphere the idea of human rights is often associated with the international regime of human rights, while in the domestic sphere the term 'constitutional rights' is used. I will speak of *basic rights* to encapsulate both of these, since I want to remain agnostic about the political scale of the polity in which these basic rights are to function. Moreover, my basic rights refer to moral, not legal rights (sometimes the term 'human rights' is also used to refer to moral rights which belong to every human being, akin to 'natural rights') – i.e. to those moral claims about human beings which *should* be politically (hence most often legally) protected.

rights enter the stage as an internal reflection upon existing justifications for the rights and duties always already attributed to oneself and other participants in practices (Section 3.1).

Next, I present the method to be made use of, which is that of a transcendental argument. I explain this method in general, in contrast to its main competitor, the method of reflective equilibrium. Then I present the form the argument will take in my theory: it starts from the phenomenological experience or self-understanding of a mere-participational agent, and then seeks to argue that such an agent – if she or he is rational – is committed to claiming rights to the necessary conditions for navigational agency. This method can be understood as a form of moral constructivism: its conclusion is not that agents 'have' navigational agency rights in a mind-independent sense (as a moral realist would want to have it), but they must claim such rights. If this conclusion is correct for all agents, it establishes the rational necessity of a moral order in which each person claims such rights and accepts duties corresponding to these rights. This is all we need (Section 3.2).

The argument itself proceeds through several steps. The first step shows how rational mere-participational agents are committed, by virtue of fulfilling roles in social practices, to evaluating the social purposes of these practices. The next steps apply basic criteria of rationality to show that such agents must accept that social orders are contingent; and to reject the justification of inegalitarian social orders in terms of an external natural order which claims status differences are mandated by nature. Once this is accepted, the next step is to argue that their own prudential interests commit them to accepting an egalitarian order of navigational agents. A final step is to universalize this result. Since the reasoning holds for all agents, all must accept the rights and duties belonging to themselves and other agents. All of this requires much elaboration, which will be given in due course (Section 3.3).

One terminological question about 'basic rights' needs to be addressed before proceeding. I take seriously the idea put forward by Amartya Sen, Martha Nussbaum and others that a capability theory can be developed as a human rights theory (Nussbaum 1997, 2011a; Sen 2004b, 2005; Vizard 2007; Drydyk 2011; Gilabert 2013).[2] I diverge from much of

---

[2] Henry Richardson has argued that the language of rights cannot easily be accepted by capability theories (Richardson 2007). I would agree with Martin van Hees that the marriage between rights and capabilities is possible: we first need to define a list of capability goals (G), and then a set of rights (R) that are to be seen as the conditions for the realization of these goals (Van Hees 2012, 255). This I take myself to be doing in this book.

the human rights literature in one crucial respect. There is a tendency to speak of human rights claims as *distinct from* (or alternatively: a subset of) claims of justice. The division of labour envisaged between them is one in which human rights claims are supposed to cover urgent, minimal demands of morality, while claims of justice go beyond this. I do not follow this division of the moral field. Rights-claims are the central element in any theory of justice. Justice is about the distribution of rights among the members of a specific political community. The two are conceptually co-extensive in my usage (e.g. Steiner 1994). The reason for others to split the normative field seems to be motivated by practical reasons – e.g. that human rights claims get special judicial protection and serve to correct other public policies when the latter violate these rights, and also that human rights claims are used in international (diplomatic) contexts. In both cases there is enough controversy in bringing forward even minimal moral claims. Courts have a hard time striking down laws, given the democratic legitimacy of governments, and Western governments have a hard time lecturing non-western governments, given some of the latter's resistance to human rights language. These may be good practical reasons to focus on the identification of a minimal morality. However, in theory there is no need to reserve the term 'basic rights' (or human rights) for such a minimum. The rights which express justice ideally provide the program for the whole of political morality, not just a part of it. Whether in a second stage one decides that only a subset of these should be given judicial enforcement mechanisms or elevated to the status of foreign policy goals, is an entirely different matter.

3.1   Agents' Rights: The Deontic Structure of Social Practices

In Chapter 2, we saw that social practices are, among other things, characterized through their institutions: the norms and rules that prescribe what is to count as a correct move within the practice. These institutions specify roles and ascribe them to particular individuals. Each role is characterized by a bundle of rights and duties. The father's role comes with a set of duties to care for his children, as well as rights to make certain choices on behalf of them. I am not concerned, for the moment, with the question of *who* determines these rights and duties. Some may be defined by law, others by custom, or by agreement between the father and mother. The point is that for any practice to get off the ground, the identification of such bundles of rights and duties is necessary. But is it necessarily the case that every practice has such a deontic structure? A positive answer has been given by John Searle, in his social-ontological theory of institutional facts. I will use his theory to explain the tight link between social action and deontic structure.

Searle is concerned with the question how to explain the emergence of institutional facts in a world of brute physical facts. He asks: how do social phenomena such as governments, marriage and money come into existence in a world made up of cells, molecules and atoms? The answer he finds in what he calls 'status functions': 'humans have the capacity to impose functions on objects and people where the objects and the people cannot perform the functions solely in virtue of their physical structure' (Searle 2010, 7). Physical tokens of paper money can only fulfil their social function in the economy through the function we ascribe to them. Status functions, then, require collective acceptance or recognition to be able to function. If they are accepted, then institutional facts come into being. The mechanism through which this happens is what Searle calls a 'constitutive rule', of the form 'X counts as Y in context C', where X is the brute physical fact and Y the institutional fact that is to be explained.

How do we create status functions? Searle stresses the role of language. The vital condition for creating an independent social reality is that humans are language-users. Using his earlier speech-act theory, Searle argues that institutional facts are created through declarations (one of his five speech acts). In declarations we change the world by declaring something to be the case. Examples include the civil servant declaring a couple to be married, or a president declaring war. All institutional facts, Searle claims, are created and maintained through declarations (even if not always in the explicit form of a declarative speech act). I will stay agnostic about this strong claim. The important point, for my purposes, is the more general one: that language fulfils an indispensable role in the creation of institutional reality. Language is the medium which makes it possible to symbolically represent social functions of objects that would otherwise remain physical objects only (Searle 2010, 13).

Searle not only discusses the transformation of physical objects, but also the role of agents in institutional life. He claims that 'without exception, the status functions carry what I call "deontic powers". That is, they carry rights, duties, obligations, requirements, permissions, authorizations, entitlements, and so on' (Searle 2010, 8–9). Their point and purpose is to 'regulate relations between people' (Searle 1995, 100). He distinguishes between positive powers (rights) and negative powers (duties): 'the great divide in the categorization of institutional reality is between what the agent *can* do and what the agent *must* (and must not) do, between what the agent is enabled to do and what he or she is required to do as a result of the assignment of status specified in the Y term' (Searle 1995, 100–1). He also makes it clear (without using the word 'role') that persons have deontic powers by virtue of having been assigned a role: 'we do not just accept that somebody has power, but we accept that they have power in virtue of their institutional status' (Searle 2005, 17). The deontic powers are assigned to persons qua role-bearers; through the creation of institutional life, persons are as much transformed as physical objects are.

Deontic powers, Searle argues, give agents 'desire-independent reasons for action' (Searle 2010, 9, 123). Humans, like animals, can act on the basis of desires in combination with beliefs (instrumental rationality). But since they have consciousness and a sense of free will, humans experience their actions as a matter of choice: they could have acted otherwise. This gives them the potential to act on the basis of reasons, which do not relate to a pre-existing desire. Rather, it is the other way around: these reasons give them a desire to act (Searle 2010, 129). Given this cognitive make-up, Searle then argues, social reality for humans must be structured around deontic powers. Because of the potential gap between what we do and what we could do, social reality must consist of deontic structures that give us reasons for action, that are independent of our immediate desires. This 'must', however, is a conditional one. It depends on Searle's view that to create institutional reality is very advantageous to humans: it creates enormous benefits compared to animal life: 'the deontology makes it possible for rational and conscious agents to use the institutions without destroying them' (Searle 2010, 140). If Searle is right, then deontic powers are a necessary part ('without exception') of any type of social action.[3]

Searle is not the only one offering such a close connection between social practices and roles on the one hand, and rights and duties on the other hand. One particularly interesting contribution is in Leif Wenar's work, where he develops a theory of rights which aspires to provide an alternative to will and interest theories of rights (Wenar 2013). Wenar starts from the position that rights historically derive from socially defined roles. Role-bearers received their rights to be able to fulfil their role-bound duties, as when a policeman has to the right to stop me on the street to be able to fulfil his duty to regulate traffic, or a mother needs certain custody rights over her children to be able to discharge her

---

[3] Similarly, elsewhere Searle states that 'Institutional facts are always matters of deontic powers' (Searle 2004, 93). See also Searle (2010, 24).

parental duties. In broad strokes this leads to a very similar picture as Searle's, with a particular twist of its own: Wenar does not just describe how fulfilling a role is bound up with rights and duties, but, more particularly, emphasizes how duties are primary and rights are derivative as means to fulfil these duties. My position is that this derivative role for rights is problematic as a general claim, as Wenar himself recognizes when he concedes that in modern times pre-given duty descriptions are often absent (see Appendix 3). Therefore, I have stated the connection in Chapter 2 in a more open way: role-bound rights and duties are both meant to help the agent fulfil his role-bound *ends*, whatever they are. Nonetheless, Wenar's claim bears a deep truth in particular contexts, and at two points I will suggest some important basic rights do derive from prior duties (see Sections 6.3 and 7.2).

We need not accept every detail of Searle's or Wenar's theories; and similar insights in the deontic character of practices can be generated also by other theories in social ontology. A theory like's Searle offers what we need here: a clear analytical exposition of the connection between action in social practices and its deontic structure. For the agency-based capability theory this is an important step forward. For now we do not have to worry how to understand the link between certain agential characteristics (capabilities) and claims to rights, i.e. claims to protection of these agential characteristics. Agents always *already have* (some) rights and duties, by virtue of participating in social practices. The establishment of this social-ontological connection bridges the first half of the is-ought-gap: we have shown the existence of a descriptive 'ought' inside the world as it 'is'. Bridging the second half of the gap then means finding a firm answer to the justificatory question so as to reach conclusions about the normative 'ought': within social structures which rights to which capabilities *should* be granted to which agents?[4]

This latter question needs to be refined. I will do so by bringing into play what at first sight may seem to be a problem for the Searlian connection between social life and deontic powers: Joel Feinberg's claim that

---

[4] There may be alternative ways of closing the gap. One particularly important alternative is to show how the concepts of rights/duties are implied in the evaluative structure of all action: the mere fact that an agent considers the purposes of his actions good, implies that he is committed to the claim that others ought to refrain from interfering with them, i.e. that he has a right to non-interference. See Gewirth (1978). Whether this inference from the evaluative to the deontic is valid has been the subject of heated debate. The similarity to my strategy is that both show how rights/duties are part of the concept of acting, the difference is that Gewirth works with a conception of action that makes no immediate/explicit reference to the social context (although one might read him as implicitly doing so).

there is nothing necessary about people having claim-rights. Before going into Feinberg's argument, let's remind ourselves of the meaning of this crucial term, claim-rights.

It comes from Hohfeld's famous analysis of four different types of rights. Following Leif Wenar's recent interpretation of it, we can distinguish first-order from second-order rights. First-order rights relate directly to potential actions. They can be divided into liberties and claim-rights. Liberties (also called 'privileges'), are of the form "A has a right to phi" and imply "A has no duty not to phi". Especially when paired with the contrasting liberty "A has no duty to phi", these liberties give the holder a discretionary power over the object of choice, i.e. whether or not to phi (Wenar 2005, 225–8). Note that liberties do not say anything about other persons than A himself. This is different for claim-rights. Their form is: "A has a right that B phi" which implies "B has a duty to A to phi" (Wenar 2005, 229). Claim-rights go beyond liberties, then, since they introduce duties of others to respect A's liberty to do (or not do) something. Claim-rights secure one's liberties. To have this secured status makes it possible to look others in the eye as equals (at least, presupposing one has a bundle of claim-rights that is not grossly inferior to that of others). Without claim-rights, one's liberties remain at the whim of others. In addition to these first-order rights, there are two second-order rights. These are related to claim-rights: they grant a person the possibility to change his claim-rights (a 'power', which like a liberty provides discretion to the holder to use the power or not) or provide him security against others waiving his claim-rights (an 'immunity') (Wenar 2005, 230–2). We may think of these second-order rights as 'governance rights', since the power to change first-order rights is a power of governing the social practice in which the participants are involved. Persons who have these rights co-determine the institutions which define the roles and bundles of rights and duties involved; they have governing power within the practice.

In a classic thought-experiment Feinberg asks us to imagine a place called Nowheresville. In Nowheresville people have duties but they don't have rights against each other, i.e. there is no correlativity of rights and duties. Inhabitants of Nowheresville are subject to mandatory actions, but they do not know the concept of claiming a right to those mandatory actions as something that is their due. Instead, these duties are owed to 'the Law', to God, or to a sovereign who holds a 'right-monopoly' (Feinberg 1970, 247). This is a third party to whom all duty-holders in the legal system hold their duties. What is absent from such a world, Feinberg claims, is the notion of a claim-right: a right that we can claim against others. When analyzing this, Feinberg argues that the essential point is the absence of the fact that people engage in the activity of claiming: 'they do not claim before they take' (Feinberg 1970, 249). Feinberg insists that such a Nowheresville is a realistic option, one cannot dismiss it as a phantasy. He even tries to make its potential existence more credible by introducing examples such as the obligations of brothers not to hurt each other (which these brothers feel are only really owed to their parents, not to each other) or the marital obligations of spouses (owed not to each other but to God).

At first sight, it may seem that Searle's and Feinberg's insights are incompatible. Didn't Searle argue that rights are a necessary part of social life? And isn't Feinbergs Nowheresville a denial of that argument? However, I think there is a way of making their positions compatible. Let's start by accepting that Feinberg's Nowheresville is a real possibility. There are, have been, or could be, societies in which practice-participants do not have any claim-rights. This does not mean, however, that we have to throw Searle's full deontic structure out of the window. What is left? Up to this point, I have spoken of roles as specified in terms of 'bundles of rights and duties'. In Nowheresville, the inhabitants have duties – so one side of the deontic structure is fully present. On the rights-side, however, something seems to be missing. Nonetheless, the predicament is not well-characterized by saying that the inhabitants 'don't have rights'. They don't have a particular type of rights: claim-rights.[5] A crucial element of the full Hohfeldian deontic structure is missing. They do have something else: liberties.

To fully grasp what such a world could look like, we need an interpretation of what is going on in Nowheresville. Here, I submit, the distinction between participational and navigational agency can shed light. As we have seen, some agents may be 'mere-participational agents', i.e. lack navigational agency (see Section 2.2). Imagine such an agent, enacting her role and fulfilling her duties. She needs to have some freedom, however minimal, in choosing how to discharge her duties. The protection of this freedom, it seems natural to say, is a matter of rights. But this statement requires qualification. The most we can say of a mere-participational agent is that she has several options to choose from. This in turn requires, as a minimum, that she has a liberty with respect to each of these options: she is not under a duty to do the option, nor to refrain from doing it. In this sense of a liberty (absence of a duty) the

---

[5] Since powers and immunities are related to claim-rights, they probably also don't have these.

participational agent has a right. We need not assume, however, that the participational agent also has claim-rights against others.[6] In other words, as soon as she tries out an option, she may discover that another agent will interfere. She is not secure in the options that she has liberties to (let alone that she would have the governance rights to determine what her claim-rights are in the future). Participational agency does not depend for its possibility on the possession of claim-rights.

This kind of situation seems a coherent possibility; it may even have some historical credentials.[7] If so, an argument against such a world needs to be a *normative* one. And indeed Feinberg makes – and thinks we can only make – a normative argument against it:

> Having rights, of course, makes claiming possible; but it is claiming that gives rights their special moral significance. This feature of rights is connected in a way with the customary rhetoric about what it is to be a human being. Having rights enables us to "stand up like men", to look others in the eye, and to feel in some fundamental way the equal of anyone. To think of oneself as the holder of rights is not to be unduly but properly proud, to have that minimal self-respect that is necessary to be worthy of the love and esteem of others. Indeed, respect for others (this is an intriguing idea) may simply be respect for their rights, so that there cannot be the one without the other; and what is called "human dignity" may simply be the recognizable capacity to assert claims. To respect a person then, or to think of him as possessed of human dignity, simply *is* to think of him as a potential maker of claims. (Feinberg 1970, 252)

We cannot presuppose that agents in all possible worlds have (hence: that agency conceptually necessarily implies) the kind of standing that comes with having claim-rights, and that Feinberg associates with respect and dignity. That standing, in my terms, can only be achieved

---

[6] Against this, some readers have objected to me that some (maybe even many) forms of participational agency require claim-rights. People often cannot function (even if their life is solely contained within a practice) without having the guarantees offered by being able to claim non-interference from others. I think this can be admitted, without undercutting the force of the point I want to make here: that one's status as a chooser *between* practices depends on claim-rights (in a strong sense; it cannot exist without), while one's status as a chooser *within* practices need not depend on them (even if in practice it may often come with claim-rights as well); and that this difference sheds a light on Nowheresville's moral unacceptability from a liberal point of view.

[7] In historical studies we find the same ambivalence. On the one, hand the prevalence of rights in social life is not merely a modern invention: Roman and Medieval societies were characterized by extensive legal orders. We can go back even further in time, since anthropologists have shown that so-called primitive societies already had elaborate systems of property rights (see Becker 1980, 199). On the other hand, the idea of people holding *subjective rights* seems to be modern. Although it is a matter of dispute when this idea arose, it seems possible to have a system of objective right (law) without subjective rights (see Tuck 1979; Tierney 1997). How these claims have to be reconciled I have to leave to others.

if participational agents also get navigational agency. By granting agents the rights to exit any practice, we ensure that when they participate in a social practice this is based on a free and autonomous choice. The threat of exit means that all participants have to persuade others to stay and cooperate. They must be treated, then, not as mere role-bearers, but as agents who can decide whether or not to take upon themselves these roles. This is not to say that navigational agents will have exactly equal bundles of claim-rights vis-à-vis other participants (on this, see Chapter 4). But persons who can exit will not normally be content with a completely unsecured bundle of liberties, in which obligations to discharge their role are not matched by any claim-rights which impose duties on others. Some balance may have to be struck, in which some participants may have fewer duties and more rights than others, but the distribution of rights will at least have to be such that all are able to perceive themselves as dignified persons who have equal standing.

We can thus confirm the conclusion that practices (Searle's realm of institutional facts) necessarily have a deontic structure consisting of duties and rights, with the amendment that these rights are sometimes (for some practices, for some participants within them) mere liberties rather than more robust claim-rights. There is a gap between participational and navigational agency, and the job of a successful justification is to close this gap. A justification is needed – i.e. an argument for why it is rationally necessary to create a society of navigational agents who have a set of robust claim-rights. In Appendix 3, I contrast the problem of justification as it has been identified here with the way it presents itself for those following an anthropological method. This prominent alternative type of justification for rights-claims starts from a conception of human nature and then faces the challenge of showing how to justify the elevation of certain elements in human nature to the status of basic rights. If one's descriptive vocabulary is that of human nature then there will inevitably arise a gap between all features which are essential of human nature, and those which deserve moral and political protection through rights-claims. Using the example of Nussbaum's capability theory, I show in Appendix 3 how the anthropological method cannot close this gap without introducing normative elements beyond human nature. As a separate argumentative strategy, therefore, the anthropological method is a dead-end. Once we start from human nature, we cannot leap-frog without external help to the justification of a set of claim-rights. This provides an important motivation for continuing down the road on which I focus in this chapter.

3.2 Method: Exploring the Rational Self-Understanding of Participational Agents

This section will explain the argumentative method that I will use to answer the challenge of justification. I will explain my use of a method of transcendental argumentation, which is itself one way to operationalize a form of moral constructivism. I will argue this method requires us to start from the phenomenology of what I called a 'mere-participational agent' as a starting-point. The argument needs to prove that every rational mere-participational agent is necessarily committed to claiming rights to navigational agency. The next section will then present the argument itself.

Ever since John Rawls started to use the term 'Kantian constructivism' in his 1980 lectures, the term caught on as a label to classify a distinctive approach to moral theorizing (Street 2010; Bagnoli 2013). Following Christine Korsgaard and Onora O'Neill, we can describe constructivism as a position distinct from both moral realism and moral relativism. In contrast to the relativist, constructivists believe it is possible to justify an objective, context-independent morality. However, in contrast to the realist, constructivists reject the idea of a mind-independent moral order as a basis for justification. Moral norms are constructed by and for humans as answers to practical problems. The validity of moral norms is relative to human beings, but objective to the extent that some norms are *necessarily valid* for these human beings. This will involve showing that there are certain necessary implications of the fact that humans have to take up a practical or *first-order standpoint* from which they act (O. O'Neill 1989; Korsgaard 2008).[8] The ambition of this enterprise, in the hands of its proponents, has not just been to justify any type of morality, however, but to justify an 'Enlightenment morality'. For a Kantian constructivist procedure, the challenge is to justify a Kantian morality whose kernel is the idea the persons are, in Rawls's terms, 'free and equal persons'. This is a specifically modern, liberal-egalitarian morality, which often issues in the prescription of a set of basic rights and liberties marking the independent moral and political status of a person who is free to choose his own conception of the good life. If the constructivists are right, of course, this is the only type of morality which can be justified; others are collections of traditional,

---

[8] This description of constructivism focuses on Kantian constructivism. For other variations, such as Humean constructivism, see Street (2010).

parochial, inegalitarian norms which haven't undergone the test of reason. Hence the stakes are high.

A choice for moral constructivism (against relativist or realist alternatives) does not yet dictate what one can call a specific 'method of operationalization'. The most dominant method by far for constructivists has been reflective equilibrium.

In reflective equilibrium, reasoners are supposed to shift backwards and forwards from their considered convictions about concrete cases and possible moral principles, adjusting, refining and changing both until a mutually satisfactory equilibrium is found. This method has been attacked on multiple fronts. First, the method ultimately delivers only an internally coherent set of moral statements and has often been attacked for its relativist implications (for a discussion of this claim see Scanlon 2003a, 151–3). Second, depending on who is reflecting, the moral conclusions reached may be immoral. The reflective equilibrium of a racist will yield racist moral principles (this point raises a worry, but cannot be decisive for it assumes a standpoint from which this judgement can be made). Third, nothing prevents multiple equilibria from arising for different persons. The method doesn't have any resources for adjudicating between these. Indeed, tellingly, much work in applied ethics is claimed to be generated by this method, but with very different positions as outcomes: from cosmopolitanism to nationalism, from luck egalitarianism to prioritarianism, philosophers from all persuasions assemble under reflective equilibrium's flag (De Maagt 2017).

Defenders of reflective equilibrium have tried to strengthen the method as a response to these criticisms, but by and large, I agree with those who argue these problems cannot be remedied within the framework of reflective equilibrium itself. If so, then it is problematic that defenders of reflective equilibrium continue to treat the conclusions reached in reflective equilibrium as morally objective results. Instead, they should acknowledge they have reached a position which makes moral validity *relative* to the individual or group reaching the equilibrium (Kelly and McGrath 2010; De Maagt 2017). This raises the big question: is there are an alternative? Some claim a stronger basis to derive the unconstructed materials which are the input in any constructivist procedure is indeed possible. For them, the core of constructivism would be to come up with starting points that do not merely match our considered convictions, but are necessarily characteristic of all rational agents (Street 2010; Bagnoli 2014). The point of constructivism is to reconstruct the first-person practical point of view, and derive the demands of morality from the necessary presuppositions of this reconstructed point of view.[9] This method is also referred to as 'consti-tutivism' (Enoch 2006; Ferrero 2009; Bertea 2013), or, in earlier literature, as transcendental argumentation.

A transcendental argument rests on two premises. The first premise posits a starting point within our experience (X), which is deemed ines-capable. The second premise states that there is a necessary condition for the possibility of X, namely Y. The conclusion is that this condition (Y) is validated as rationally inescapable. These arguments have been used in theoretical as well as in practical philosophy. In theoretical philoso-phy René Descartes' 'cogito ergo sum' is an example, which attempts to show that the first-person experience of thinking has a necessary pre-supposition, being in existence, so that the 'I' has to conclude that he/she exists. Several general points about transcendental arguments are noteworthy. First, the starting point usually is a very broad feature of our self-understanding, such as action, speech, experience or thought. Its inescapability is a *phenomenological* claim. Second, the derivation of the conclusion from this starting point is a matter of *rational argumenta-tion*. Typically, it is claimed that an agent who accepts the starting point but denies the conclusion commits a performative self-contradiction: he denies something he cannot deny on pains of denying that he is the act-ing, speaking, thinking, etc. being that he is. Any rational agent must necessarily, by virtue of his rationality, accept the conclusion Y (an irra-tional agent can deny everything and therefore is not an interesting test case). Finally, the validity of the conclusions of transcendental arguments, i.e. the 'objectivity' that is claimed, remains dependent on the first-personal perspective. Strictly, on the basis of Descartes' argument we can thus never claim the conclusion 'I exist', but only 'I must necessarily hold (as a thinking being) that I exist.' Whether one considers this a 'proof' of the conclusions depends on the expectations one has from philosophical argument in a certain context.[10]

When employed in ethics, the starting point of a transcendental argument is a reconstruction of our practical self-understanding. For example, Alan Gewirth has presented an argument which focuses on

[9] Some propose theories which work from a 'second-person', not 'first-person' standpoint. Habermas can arguably be classified under this label. The most recent leading example is (Darwall (2006).) The question is whether second-person theorizing can avoid being reduced to first-person theoriz-ing. For a critique along these lines, see (Korsgaard (2007).)

[10] The inability to prove the transcendental conclusion as a realist conclusion (showing not merely that I must not only hold that I exist, but that I really do exist) is taken to point to a deficiency in transcendental arguments (Stroud 1968). However, arguably this objection, while having some force in the context of theoretical philosophy, doesn't affect the strength of such arguments in eth-ics for those who want to establish constructivist conclusions (De Maagt 2016).

our self-understanding as purposive agents, who act voluntarily and purposefully in the world (Gewirth 1978). Another good example is Jürgen Habermas, who offered a discourse ethics based on a reconstruction in terms of communicative agency (Habermas 1990). The implications of the transcendental starting point (X) can be spelled out over several steps, but their end point is the proof of a categorical and universal moral principle. For Gewirth this is his Principle of Generic Consistency (PGC), for Habermas his Universalization Principle (U). Further down the line, such principles can then be applied to generate valid moral norms in concrete cases. I find these and other examples of transcendental reasoning in ethics promising – more promising anyhow than relying on the method of reflective equilibrium or accepting a moral realist or relativist position; but I cannot argue this here. I also think existing arguments, like Gewirth's or Habermas's, may contain problematic assumptions; but I also cannot argue this here.[11] Instead, the remainder of the chapter gives my own attempt at providing a transcendental argument for the justification of rights to navigational agency.

The first question for the theory of participational and navigational agency is: what is the inescapable transcendental starting point (X)? The sought-for argument could in fact start from one of three conceptions of agency. We should remember that the relation between participational and navigational agency is one of a subset. All agents are participational agents, given the practice-bound nature of all human action. There are two types of participational agents in this broad sense: mere-participational agents and those who are also navigational agents. Participational agents are characterized by the fact that they live their life by participating in social practices. Mere-participational agents participate while being confined to their specific social roles, while navigational agents are not so confined. So, we have three options to start a transcendental argument from: (i) participational agency (the general concept), or one of its subtypes; (ii) mere-participational agency; or (iii) navigational agency.

Starting from the general concept of participational agency would seem to be a good starting point, since this type of agency is what is truly inescapable, being shared by both navigational and mere-participational agents. A transcendental argument would then ask what the conditions of possibility of participational agency are. However, participational agency in general would be overinclusive as a starting-point. We don't need rights to move between social practices – i.e. navigational agency

---

[11] I am working on an attempt at this in a manuscript provisionally entitled *Constructivism's Challenge: Justifying a Modern Self-Understanding* (Claassen 2018b).

rights – as a condition to live our lives within specific social practices – mere-participational agency. Hence, an argument starting from the experience of participational agency in general would only be able to generate rights to the conditions for its least-demanding subpart, mere-participational agency. As an argument for navigational agency it can never work. On the other hand, starting from navigational agency would be like pulling the rabbit out of the hat. We cannot presume that navigational agency is an inescapable starting point, since some agents do not have an understanding of themselves as navigational agents – i.e. as agents who should have the right to the full spectrum of navigational agency rights (note how the claim is not about the rights they have, as a matter of legal protection, but about the rights they hold they *ought* to have a right to). Mere-participational agents conceive of themselves as of lower worth or standing than others, and as rightfully holding a place in the social order with more restricted possibilities for free action and autonomous deliberation than others. They display a lack of self-respect in the specific sense of respecting oneself as *equal* in social standing to others. Cases standardly referred to in debates about self-respect includes examples of deferential housewives, or slaves like Uncle Tom (Hill, Jr. 1991; Stark 1997; Westlund 2003). A transcendental argument will have to start from the phenomenological standpoint of such mere-participational agents and then show how they – when rational – are implicitly committed to claim rights to navigational agency.

An objection against this would be that mere-participational agency is an unsuitable starting-point for a transcendental argument since it is not inescapable in a phenomenological sense. That would seem to disqualify it as a type of transcendental argument. This objection seems correct, given the definition of transcendental arguments above. A reply will help to explain the special form my transcendental argument has. The argumentative strategy can be summarized as follows:

(i) navigational and mere-participational agency together logically exhaust all possibilities: every agent either is one or the other;

(ii) all rational navigational agents necessarily claim rights to navigational agency;

(iii) all rational mere-participational agents must upon reflection necessarily understand themselves as navigational agents instead – hence, claim rights to navigational agency as well, see option (ii); and

(iv) hence, all rational agents necessarily claim rights to navigational agency

The first proposition is a matter of definition, and has been explained above. The second proposition is tautological once the deontic order sketched in Section 3.1 is accepted. To be an agent is to have the rights (and duties) belonging to your social position; to be a rational agent is to claim those rights which are justifiably owed to you; for a navigational agent these are her navigational agency rights, since these are the conditions of possibility of her being a navigational agent. The navigational agent has a 'sense of entitlement' in an egalitarian sense: she or he claims to be recognized on an equal basis with all others, and this claim is cashed out in terms of a bundle of agency-rights. The hard case is proposition (iii) and the transcendental argument in the next section aims to establish it. If that succeeds, the conclusion (iv) follows automatically. By parallel testing for both subtypes of agency whether claims to navigational agency can be reached from the phenomenological experience of each subtype, we find a combined argument which is inescapable for *every* agent, *disregarding* the subtype she or he originally belongs to.

In light of this, it is paradoxical that mere-participational agents may themselves consider their type of agency to be inescapable (it is only the theorist, who already has decided there is such a thing as navigational agency as well, who can present mere-participational agency as only an optional form of agency). But of course we do not have to take mere-participational agents at their first word. They may be wrong about their self-understanding. As much as I have emphasized that we should start from phenomenological descriptions of the self-understanding of actually existing agents, this cannot mean that these descriptions are subject to no demands of rationality at all. Obviously, if a person would be drunk or mentally severely disabled, it is at least possible that her self-reports do not qualify as an accurate description of her self-understanding. So, we need to think about what qualifies as an accurate form of self-understanding, and this in turn depends on the requirements of rationality that one imposes. The transcendental argument aims to convince the mere-participational agent that her first word shouldn't be her last one; that she is wrong, on second consideration. It is a condition of the possibility of her understanding herself as a mere-participational agent that she considers herself to be aspiring to be a navigational agent instead.

These considerations open up a route for a transcendental argument that would lead to the conclusion that all agents must accept rights to navigational agency. If we can show that mere-participational agents are irrational in adopting a self-understanding of themselves as mere-participational agents, then we can argue that they must accept, on pain

of contradicting themselves, adopting a self-understanding as navigational agents. This includes claiming rights to the preconditions of their
navigational agency. Can we make such a rational assessment of their self-
understanding? And what conclusions would it lead to?

3.3 An Argument for the Inescapability of Claiming Rights to Navigational Agency

In this section I propose a rational assessment of the mere-participational
agent's self-understanding in five steps. First, we must show how such
an agent is necessitated to reason about his or her own social status in
practice. Second, we must show how the inegalitarian social relations in
which he or she is held captive cannot be justified by a mere appeal to
logical consistency, nor, third, by an appeal to an external natural order.
This third step creates a transition to navigational agency as a potential
confronting the agent. The fourth step is to show how this potential must
be capitalized upon by showing how it is prudentially beneficial for the
mere-participational agent to make the transition. The fifth step univer-
salizes this result.

Step 1: The Necessity of Reasoning about One's Agency Status. The first
step is to show that mere-participational agents cannot escape reasoning
about the correctness of their mere-participational status. This requires a
demanding conception of rationality that goes beyond the requirement
that when a person reasons, she or he does not violate the 'canons of
inductive and deductive logic' (Gewirth 1978, 22). Agents are required
to actually *use* their capacities to reason, to *exercise* their capacities to
reason by testing the prevailing ideologies to see if there are good reasons
for upholding them. One is not only irrational, on such a conception,
when one makes a failure of reason; one is also irrational when one fails
to reason. This conception of rationality is not self-evident. Persons
with low self-respect, who do not see themselves as ends-in-themselves
(think again of the archetypical examples of the Deferential Housewife
and Uncle Tom), do not make failures of reason; but they do fail to reason. Often, they are excused for doing so because they cannot be held
responsible for this given their circumstances. However, the point is not
to assign moral blame. We can avoid blaming the victim and accept that
such individuals are not making an error of logical consistency (their
self-understanding matches with the claims they think they can make
on others, both are just very restricted). Still, we can try to argue that a

minimally reflective mere-participational agent can be shown to make a failure of rational inquiry when such an inquiry is an indispensable part of his role-fulfilment, inextricably bound up with what it is to be fulfilling a role. The following is an attempt at this argument.

A participational agent has been defined as someone fulfilling a socially defined role. Fulfilling a role contains two exercises, which are closely connected. On the one hand, the agent needs to *interpret* the normative structure of the practice. This normative structure contains two elements: social purposes and social norms. The description of the agent's role (their rights and duties) is inscribed in the social norms (which can be formal or informal). These norms are means to the social purposes of the practice. If a group of people sets themselves the end of playing tennis together, they will then use, as functionally necessary to that end, norms to give practical shape to this end. They will, for example, write up a constitution which specifies the rights and duties of membership of the club, rules for how to become member and terminate membership, the fees that are due, etc. The agent who must interpret his role must be aware of these social purposes and social norms. The norms more directly define his rights and duties, but often, he will only be able to understand the norms in light of their animating purpose(s). Interpretation serves the primary function, for the agent, to see what his leeway is: what space of discretion is open for him in fulfilling his role. Rights will enable certain moves, while duties will constrain his actions in certain ways. Once he understands these, he knows what his space for free and creative action is.

On the other hand, then, he must decide how to *give shape to his role*, i.e. how to fill this leeway. This requires that the agent think of himself as an individual purpose-setter, as a source of individual ends in so far as this is possible within his role. He is someone thinking and deciding autonomously and freely about how he will make use of his rights and fulfil his duties. He constitutes himself and his personal identity by the way he operates within the given normative structure of the practice. In seeing himself as a source of individual ends, the agent's rationality stretches beyond mere instrumental rationality. The agent can rationally select the means to his ends but also deliberate about his ends. We do not need to take a stance on the long philosophical discussion about what this implies. It is sufficient that agents somehow can reflect on their first-order preferences and rationally endorse some of them while rejecting others (Frankfurt 1988), test maxims for actions for consistency with his practical identity (Korsgaard 2009) or deliberate about his final ends (Richardson 1997). For the agent to set his ends requires her or him to bridge the gap between the abstract demands of his role and his personal situation; display a personal understanding of what the role requires which relies on his personal insights and capacities. He must invent his own way of being a football player, father or architect: say, a creative football player, a demanding father, a modernist architect. This requires creativity and expresses the spontaneity inherent in all forms of agency.

Now let's focus on the first element: the interpretation of the normative structure. The interpretative task that the agent needs to engage in relates in the first instance to the content of the norms that define the role: what do these norms actually require of him? When interpreting these norms, he can bring in all kinds of materials (own ideas, previous experiences, etc.). However, to the extent that such norm-interpretation is to be rational, it will also need to bring in the second element of the normative structure: the purposes of the practice. The interpretative activity can therefore be expected to shift upwards, to these purposes (these can be found in numerous places depending on the practice. Sometimes they will merely reside in informal understandings between participants. In other times they may be codified. An example would be the legal study of parliamentary proceedings to understand why a certain legal text was approved as it is, i.e. to reconstruct the legislative intent of the law-maker). Where this will not result in an unequivocal result, because the purposes themselves are not clearly stated, the agent may need to shift his reasoning even further upwards (or outwards), and draw on other resources, for example those in other, parallel practices in other societies, to give a determinate shape to his interpretations of his role. We see here a gradual expansion of the practice of interpretation, which happens because the meaning of one term in the normative network (the role) depends on others (the norms) which yet depends on others (the purposes). An adequate grasp of one part of this living social network requires an adequate grasp of the totality of the lifeform that the practice is. Interpretation is a holistic activity.

In this process the agent cannot neatly separate interpretation of these normative elements from *evaluation*. We imagine him not to start out as a critic of the practice, since he is a faithful mere-participational agent. However, the activity of interpretation forces upon him evaluative questions, since interpreting means choosing between competing interpretations, endorsing one above the other as the better one. In the first instance he can question what the best interpretation of his social role may be given the stated norms. For example, he may question whether the norm to be a fair player in tennis requires of him to protest an arbiter's decision or not. Such a process of rational inquiry is further expanded when the agent starts to question whether the norms are justified, in terms of their suitability as means to reach the purposes of the practice. If the goal of the group is to organize tennis-playing, how prudent is a rule which prohibits the club from becoming member of the National Tennis Federation (imagine this federation could help the club with resources to be more effective)? Further expansion of rational inquiry happens where the agent comes to question the social purposes themselves: are they justified?[12] Should we spend our time playing tennis, rather than something else? (The fact that it is unclear in light of what that question should be answered, doesn't mean it does not arise for the rational agent). The inescapability of evaluation should be no surprise: the agent's individual end-setting is a matter of evaluation (the ends that he deems best for him) and to be able to set his ends the agent needs to follow the chain of interpretation upwards. Each time it is the same rational capacities that the agent takes resort to. It is only their object that becomes ever wider in this sequence.

So far, we have seen how the exercise of rational capacities for interpretation is part of what it is to act. Moreover, given its practice-bound nature, this necessity is bound up with evaluative questions about the goodness and badness of what is interpreted: the agent's own role-description and the purposes of the social practices themselves. Minimally rational participational agents *cannot avoid reflecting on the justifiability of the social practices in which they participate.* But what must such a reflection lead a

---

[12] Some readers have been critical of assuming the rational (not factual – i.e. always calibrated to what can be required of a sufficiently rational agent) inescapability of agents evaluating their practices as a whole. Alasdair MacIntyre has provided what I think is a very clear and convincing reply to this worry: 'There are some roles that may seem purely mechanical, since the individual who plays the role can always be replaced by a machine: where there was once a ticket seller, there is now a ticket-machine. But the ticket seller always faced choices that machines never confront: *how* to play her or his role, cheerfully or sullenly, carelessly or conscientiously, efficiently or inefficiently. And for all roles, the way in which the role is enacted presupposes not only an answer to a question posed to and by the role-player: "How is it best for me to play this role?," but also to such further questions: "By what standards am I to judge what is best?" and "Should I continue to play this role in this way?" *"It is the inescapability on occasion of such questions that suggests that practical reasoning that is adequate for doing what a particular role requires will itself generate reasons for acting beyond those requirements and even sometimes against those requirements. To resist asking such questions, to insist upon terminating one's practical reasoning whenever it directs one beyond one's role requires a peculiar kind of self-discipline."* To be able to restrict one's practical reasoning to what will enable one to discharge the responsibilities of one's socially approved roles is to have imposed on one's thinking a set of artificial restrictions. It is to have arbitrarily closed one's mind to certain possibilities of action. And, although others may provide one with motives for effecting such a closure, it is only with one's own active co-operation that the habits of mind can be developed which make such closure possible' (MacIntyre 1999, 326) [emphasis mine, R.C.].

mere-participational agent to believe? Use of his reflective capacities forces upon him the conclusion that social practices – and the ideologies justifying them – stand in need of justification. What can provide this justification?

Step 2: Consistency with the Present Order. The second step is to show that it is irrational for a mere-participational agent to accept her current self-understanding as the type of agent she is, just because it is logically consistent with her current social position and the ideology legitimizing that position. Such a recourse to logical consistency provides a form of reasoning which does appeal to reason, but nonetheless contains a rationality deficit.

Before proceeding to make these points, I will now slightly change the set-up and terminology within which the argument works. The reason for this is that we need to focus, even more than before, on the issue of hierarchical versus egalitarian social relations. Therefore, it is necessary to decide how the agency concepts used so far relate to social ranks. In a hierarchical society, we face a spectrum consisting of distinct positions of social status (think of a social ladder or pyramid). Let's for simplicity work with a two-class society, in which some agents have a superior social rank, others have an inferior social rank. In an egalitarian society, the spectrum consists of only one class position (intermediate between superior and inferior), which we can call an equal rank. In terms of agency, persons with an equal rank are navigational agents. They can all, to the extent compatible with the agency of others, move freely in society. In the present context, call them 'equivalent agents'. Inferior persons are mere-participational agents, but in the present context I will call them 'inferior agents'. Agents in superior positions have all the rights of navigational agents and more: they can command the inferiors and get them to do things which egalitarian navigational agents cannot demand from each other. Call them 'superior agents'. To these three positions correspond bundles of rights and duties, as is familiar from the social ontology developed earlier. Hence, we have three positions that each reflect (i) a social status or rank, as expressed in practice by (ii) a corresponding bundle of rights and duties, which (iii) realize a corresponding level of agency. Figure 3.1 graphically illustrates this, with the vertical arrows representing the rank, rights and agency spectrums and horizontal arrows representing corresponding points on these spectrums which together form a social position.

Now one could try to justify the self-understanding of inferior agents as rational by arguing that (i) the self-understanding of such agents is

Superior social rank	Large bundle of rights	High level of agency
Equal social rank	Equal bundle of rights	Equal level of agency
Inferior social rank	Small bundle of rights	Low level of agency

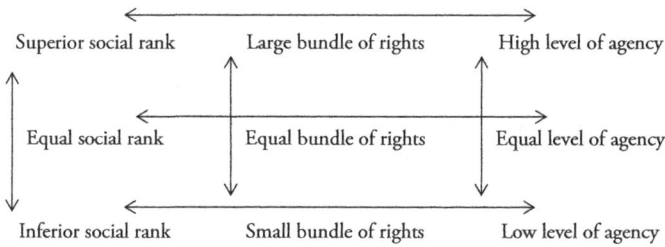

Figure 3.1. Relations between social rank, rights and agency

consistent with their social positions in the practice(s) in which they participate and (ii) a social order containing these inegalitarian positions is not logically inconsistent. Both points of consistency together would provide a justification of the present, hierarchical order for the inferior agent.

The claim made by the first point should be accepted. An inferior agent considers that her practical identity is given by her social role, and to the extent that the role-description portrays her as inferior to others, she has accepted this portrayal and interiorized a lower sense of self-worth. This description implies that each inferior agent accepts a view of the world that fixes her place in the social order. Such an ideology is what she believes in. It would seem no counter to this argument that it is irrational per se to believe in an ideology. After all, there is no theory-neutral access to reality. We all use systems-of-reasons to orient ourselves in the world, both practically and theoretically. Rationality as the mere standards of logic does not preclude such an adherence to an ideology, and participation in social life seems to even practically require adherence to ideology, or at least to some beliefs which help to orient ourselves in the world. All of this can be accepted, but still we cannot infer from this that consistency between one's self-understanding and the present social order makes the latter rationally justified. One may be mistaken about the rational justification of this social order through some ideology, and then being consistent with this mistaken ideology doesn't save the agent from the charge of irrationality. Rationality might require a change in the social order, and then an inconsistency with the present order would be what is required, not a consistency.

Similarly, the consistency claim made by the second point is correct, but it doesn't provide a justification either. We should grant that logical consistency is not a completely powerless criterion of justification. It does rule out two types of society: (i) those where all agents are superior agents; and (ii) those where all are inferior agents. Social standing is a zero-sum concept. The concept of a society in which all are superior agents is as non-sensical as the concept of a football match which is won or lost by both teams. The idea of superiority presupposes the idea of inferiority, and the existence of superior positions presumes the existence of inferior positions. So what consistency cannot rule out is (iii), the idea of a society where some are superiors and others inferiors. This is familiar from daily practice in modern societies, which contain many social practices marked by inequality, which (seemingly) rational agents accept as legitimate. We accept the authority of parents over children (even if this is considered illegitimate by the child liberation movement), the authority of managers in the workplace (even if this is contested by those calling for workplace democracy), and the authority of governments over citizens (even if some think civil disobedience is rationally warranted and anarchists think all government is illegitimate). There seems to be nothing inherently contradictory about such inegalitarian social practices in a modern society. The same seems to be true for societies as a whole, which function on an inegalitarian basis. Hence an inferior agent might seem not to be *prima facie* irrational (i.e. on the basis of consistency alone) if she considers an inegalitarian social order to be justified.

However, the problem with this is that it seems that the standard of logical consistency puts the bar too low. What hasn't happened is that the inferior agent has examined whether the inegalitarian ideology is warranted, justified in a sense which is stronger than mere consistency. This is necessary because there are at least two consistent social schemes: an inegalitarian and an egalitarian one. Like a society where some are superior and others inferior, (iv) a society where all are equals is also logically consistent. So, a choice needs to be made between option (iii) and (iv). Logical consistency cannot determine which of these two remaining social options is to be preferred. In the context of this final choice, the appeal to the present order is question-begging, unless it is argued why continuation of the present order above all others is to rationally preferred. Note, for example, that even the preference for the status quo and against social change which is found in many conservative texts is always backed up by further substantive reasons, such as the value of whatever order has grown gradually and spontaneously, or the disvalue of disruption.

The criterion of rationality introduced at this step is still not very substantive, I would argue. Rationality, at least in its practical form, requires that one can make (i) an assessment of options to act (ii) in terms of the substantive value of each of the alternatives. The first point presumes that there is a plurality of options which can be imagined, and that it makes sense to speak of the possibility of a choice between these options. The second point presumes that logical consistency is not enough and that there need to be independent reasons for valuing each of these options. Both points together refute an unquestioned adherence to the status quo and show the *contingency* of the present social order. It could be otherwise, and whether it should depends on a more substantive rational engagement with the reasons for and against the present order and alternative orders. Note however, that this contingency is at this point only a hypothesis. One might still try to show that while such contingency is in principle bound up with the structure of practical reason, in actual fact there is only one type of social order fit for us humans, namely an inegalitarian one.

Step 3: Consistency of the Present Order with a Natural Order. The third step is to show that it is irrational for the inferior agent – our mere-participational agent in the context of a hierarchical society – to claim that appeal to a natural order can justify her present self-understanding. In this step the agent goes beyond logical consistency and presents reasons; and these reasons show her that the present hierarchical order is just because it is natural: an unavoidable consequence of the essential truth about (human) nature. This too must be shown to contain a rationality deficit.

This step is especially important because throughout history a rational reflection on the justifiability of social practices has most often brought exactly the opposite result of the conclusion that only an egalitarian society can be rationally justified. Instead of a criticism in the name of liberal-egalitarian norms, it has brought an affirmation of existing inegalitarian social orders. As Larry Siedentop writes about the ancient Greek city states:

> [T]he assumption that reason 'governed' shaped the understanding of both the social and the physical world. In the physical world, the assumption emerged as a belief that purposes or ends (what Aristotle called 'final causes') governed all processes and entities. In that way relationships within the non-human world were assimilated to reasons for acting in human life. It followed that reason could identify that towards which each thing 'naturally' tends, finding its proper place in a 'great chain of being'. In the social world, the assumption emerged as belief that there was a natural hierarchy, a superior class entitled by 'nature' to rule, constrain and, if need be, coerce. Thus, in a society where some were born to command

and others born to obey, the motivational power of reason seemed self-
evident. (Siedentop 2014, 35)

As this reminds us, rational reflection for the Greeks (and many other
societies) meant insight into a naturally determined social order which
is hierarchical in nature. Each has its place, as fixed by nature, and
these places are unequal. Can we show that this very common form of
rational (!) self-understanding of non-modern, hierarchical societies is, at
second thoughts, not rational at all, and should be replaced by the self-
understanding of modern, egalitarian society?

Ideologies arguing in favour of inegalitarianism on the basis of a putative natural order rest on an unsubstantiated link between the natural
characteristics of agents on the one hand and the type of agency and
social rank that should be socially ascribed to them on the other hand.
For example, some ideologies argue that women are bound to be housewives because the natural characteristics of women make them good only
for cleaning, cooking and childrearing. The implicit claim is that women
cannot do other things: they cannot work outside the home, engage in
politics, or whatever else. Similarly, slaves would be good for working
hard and obeying their masters and not for being masters themselves.
These naturalistic impossibility claims of the form 'X cannot do Y' can
in principle be empirically tested. One can try to bring inferior agents
in different social roles from the ones naturally ascribed to them (including roles attached to superior positions) and see what happens. I'll take it
as uncontroversial that the empirical evidence has falsified such claims.
Emancipated slaves, working women, and many others have shown that
the naturalistic claims of racism and sexism are mere pretence.[13] Stated
philosophically, the type of agency one can realize depends neither on
one's starting position nor on the alleged claims of natural abilities made
by naturalistic ideologies, but on the capabilities for agency one can
acquire by socially being granted rights to these capabilities. If you give
inferior agents access to education, more money and political power, they
can change status and become superior agents themselves. The rationality claim made here is not, I take it, very substantive. The only thing we
need to accept is that naturalistic ideologies contain a rather basic error
in social ontology: they misconceive the dependence relation between a

---

[13] A potential problem for my argument at this stage is that this does not disprove naturalistic claims
at a lower level of abstraction – i.e. as applied not the group as a whole (e.g. black persons,
women), but to single individuals. Individuals do differ in their potentialities for fulfilling certain
roles. Here more fine-tuned claims are needed to show that even less-talented individuals can still
fulfil such a diversity of social roles that they still have the same potential for navigational agency.

person's agency and capabilities on the one hand and the rights ascribed to a person on the other hand (as depicted in Figure 3.1). The error in the end goes back on ignoring the empirical evidence. The agency one can realize can be shown to empirically vary with (hence depend on) one's rights, so one cannot justify the latter by looking at the former.

The *contingency* of the social order – which in the previous step was a hypothesis – is now substantiated. The social order can be different because the social rank of agents can be changed, by changing the laws and norms determining the rights to their capabilities. The realization of this contingency is important, for it implies the idea that all mere-participational agents share something, namely a potentiality for fulfilling several social roles, which includes a potential for switching between such roles and choosing themselves which ones to fulfil. This is nothing more or less than the realization that all mere-participational agents are on a par in terms of their *potential for navigational agency*. This is not a trivial point, for the same cannot be said of those who are not participational agents. In contrast to non-rational, so-called 'marginal' agents (such as animals and mentally severely disabled persons, see the Conclusion) as well as non-agents (such as roads, tables and lamps), all participational agents share this potential. The basis for this claim is their capacity for participational agency (based on the kinds of rational capacities which makes one fulfil social roles within social practices) in combination with acceptance of the rational arguments provided in the previous three steps of the argument.

However, while these considerations show the irrationality of claims to a fixed natural order, they still do not show individuals have a *right* to the potential which has just been discovered, thereby justifying an egalitarian society in which all participational agents are equivalent agents. They merely show that we cannot base a justification for a hierarchical society on naturalistic claims. The possibility is still open to argue that such a society can be rationally justified for some other reason.

Step 4: A Rational Assessment of Inegalitarian Social Practices. The fourth step of the argument aims to show that an inferior agent would be irrational if he would not claim a right to the potentiality he has discovered in himself – i.e. to be a navigational agent. The argument will try to establish this by showing that he prudentially must claim this right.

From the perspective of the inferior agent, if naturalistic reasons for his inferiority are not good reasons, what could be good reasons that he should rationally accept? At this point I think the rationality concept can only refer to what I will call 'prudential reasons', reasons that refer to the interest of the agent, as these are conceived by himself in his own set of preferences, given his own beliefs. The concept of interests used here is purely formal: it may relate to monetary gain, spiritual experiences, fulfilling social relations, or whatever else an agent may think worthwhile. Once the grip of external reasons originating in a natural world order is lost on the agent, this is the only basis for further rational argumentation. At the limit, agents may continue to believe in the validity of an external moral order which dictates a specific social ordering, but they now must recognize this cannot be something which can provide a valid reason to others in a process of rational argumentation. Hence if they continue to have a belief in such an order and a preference to have this realized in society, this counts as a reason in the sense of being their *subjective reason* for such a putatively objective natural order. As we will see below, such a subjective reason as such will not be the basis of this step in the argument.

We are familiar with the idea of prudential reasons for inegalitarian relations within social practices. Based on claims of superior expertise or other capabilities, many social practices are hierarchically organized. The argument for such an organization is that this delivers superior benefits over an egalitarian organization of the same practices, benefits which can be distributed such that all participants gain. One can therefore accept an inferior role within a social practice for prudential reasons: to gain benefits that otherwise would not be available. The internal organization of one specific practice can therefore be seen as dependent on a sort of 'social contract' in which hierarchical relations are justifiable to all involved to the extent that they all benefit. This is a good reason within social practices, but can a similar case be made for prudential reasons to accept remaining with an inferior state in society as a whole? Can there be a good reason for voluntary submission at this higher level?

The inegalitarianism at the social level as a whole is expressed in the fact of having one's option set restricted from two options (x = continuing one's current role, y = taking up other roles) to one option (x only). There cannot, as far as I am able to see, be a good reason for the inferior agent to restrict himself into such a position of inferiority when there is an option of not being so restricted. For any prudential reason to this effect that we could try to come up with, we can claim that it will not necessarily apply to all participational agents. Take one of the more plausible reasons for some inferior agents to prudentially claim such a confinement to their inferior status: that it is beneficial to them because being a navigational agent is much more existentially frightening. Navigational agents will seriously have to confront that there are important choices in one's life which one can only make oneself. This is not an easy thing to do, and one could prefer the option of not having that choice because it avoids the stress of making these choices. It is more comforting (and comfortable) to lack personal responsibility for the good and bad things that happen to oneself. But this kind of reason will not appeal to all participational agents; it depends on a contingent psychological fact about certain inferior agents. Hence an inferior agent, generically understood, cannot invoke it. Of course, the same reasoning shows that inferior agents without anxiety to become navigational agents can also not claim that it is rationally justified to have that option because they psychologically *like* to have that option (because they value and enjoy their social freedom). Either way, contingent-prudential reasons are not good reasons in the context of a transcendental argument.

The argument must be based on a necessary-prudential reason. If we remove the *content* of their subjective reasons – given their variability between specific individuals – the only thing we are left with is a *formal* reason: *to have their subjective reasons realized, whatever their content is.* From this perspective, accepting an inferior position is irrational. For an inferior agent it is prudentially rational to have a choice between continuing to function in one's present social roles or not. Having such a larger choice set (x, y) delivers objective benefits to the inferior agent. Having more choices ensures that there are greater chances of living a life that fit his personal preferences and abilities, hence greater chances for a life with more objective benefits for him. This is a valid prudential reason (whatever his specific subjective reasons are) which provides the justification for him to claim that he should be able to become a navigational agent. The reasoning is analogous to the objective benefits delivered to agents within inegalitarian social practices, which may provide a basis for mutually accepting them. The argument does not assume any content to these benefits, it only assumes a probabilistic point: the chances of getting more benefits for oneself are higher when one has a more diverse set of social possibilities at one's disposal. The disanalogy with the same question about a specific social practice should be noted. In a specific practice the objective benefits may legitimize an inegalitarian scheme of social relations, because the inegalitarian logic at this 'local' level is based on capacity differentials which are given and to a certain extent necessary to get the job done: we can only get the benefits of a nice sailing trip together on the lake if I submit to your authority and follow your orders, given your knowledge of how to sail and my lack thereof. This kind of reason fails to generalize to the social level as a whole. At that level, capacity differentials cannot be treated as starting points which can be taken for granted, but they need to be justified themselves (see step 3). Moreover, I have a greater chance of realizing more benefits if I have the choice to change roles – again, the benefit does not relate to my *liking* to have this kind of choice or not. The failure to see that good local inegalitarian reasons do not generalize may have led many to accept some forms of inegalitarianism, but the analogy is unwarranted.

It may be objected that an inferior agent who continues to hold a subjective belief in the justification of a hierarchical order will experience a conflict between the reasons emanating from the content of his personal beliefs and this formal reason. On the one hand, he wants to abdicate control over his social position to those he beliefs to be his superiors, while on the other hand, he wants to retain such control. How can we argue the formal reason should be trumping *for him*? But this disregards that this agent, as much as others, also needs control to be able to realize his specific subjective beliefs. Imagine a society with two competing religions which each want to establish a hierarchical social order, but on a different basis. Agents adhering to religion A will want to retain control over the political community and have the possibility to exit the social practices of religion B, when they are threatened to be coerced into them. Even those among religion A's believers who see themselves as natural inferiors in its internal value-system, must wish for this control, so as to be able to have the power to create – together with the other believers in A – the social practices congenial to A, in which they can then live a life in this submissive role (see Section 5.2 for more on this paradox).

This may trigger another objection, in the opposite direction: that the argument proofs too much. It may now seem to proof that every agent must, from the formal reason which I have taken as driving the argument, not just claim rights to be able to choose for himself which practices to exit or enter, on a par with others, i.e. equal control to make personal choices. Rather, he must claim maximum control over the direction of society as a whole, i.e. a dictatorial, superior role. For such a maximum control is a better – indeed the best – guarantee that his subjective interests are fulfilled, whatever their content is, than a merely equal control. The choice set (x, y) from the perspective of this objection was artificially restricted, and should be extended with option (z = determining the roles of all others). Every rational agent would prefer to have (x, y, z). In reply, I would claim that while this may be more effective for the agent, such a claim would not pass the universalization step of the argument which follows (given the earlier point, argued for in step 3, that not all can be superiors in a social order, by definition). The objection forgets that the argumentation is supposed to be rational, which means consistent. Consistency in the universalization step hereafter requires restricting oneself to make claims which are acceptable to other agents, given that they are symmetrically situated. Once one cannot convince others to take on an inferior position by pointing to the rationality of the status quo and/or the authority of an external natural order, one is in no position to make that claim merely on account of one's personal beliefs.

Step 5: Universalization. The argument offered here shows why agents need to claim rights to navigational agency. It is only through a reflection upon their social standing, in turn triggered by a reflection upon their participation in social practices, that they come (indeed must come) to the realization that each of them deserves rights to navigational agency. The mere-participational agent should renounce her self-understanding as a mere-participational agent and accept a self-understanding of herself as a navigational agent for if she wouldn't, she would deny that she has the potential for being a navigational agent (step 3) and/or that she has a good prudential reason to realize this potential (step 4). Both of these denials have been shown to be irrational. The final step of the argument proceeds through universalizing this result.

A navigational agent who claims a right to navigational agency, must on the same basis also grant the same rights to other navigational agents (originally inferior or not), since she claims this right on the basis of her navigational agency (not some other, person-specific characteristic). This granting of a right implies an accepting a duty to respect that right of others. The implication is of course also true for other agents, hence a reciprocal system of rights-and-duties for everyone is justified. The argument for an egalitarian distribution of rights to navigational agency is established. It is proven that every agent *has* a right to navigational agency. This 'has' remains confined to the first-person perspective all agents share: it means 'must necessarily claim'. An external, realist argument for 'having' these rights is not what the constructivist has been after; it is not clear to me (but those with realist intuitions will surely disagree) that such an argument is possible nor that it is needed. I take it that this universalization step is itself not particularly controversial, and will therefore not elaborate upon it here.

Some final remarks are in order. One important qualification about the argument so far is that it can best be read as a moral argument, but only when this is understood as arguing for a moral claim about one specific subset of all moral duties: moral-political duties. The right to navigational agency is a moral claim to have a politically protected (i.e. legal) set of rights, protected by one's political community. Honouring this claim is what social justice within such a community requires. Strictly speaking, this requires an additional (anti-anarchist) step in the argument: that navigational agency rights can only effectively be secured through a political authority – i.e. that the creation of such a political authority is causally necessary to have the moral claim-rights to navigational agency honoured. The argument for this is presented in Section 7.2. For now, the reader is asked to proceed on the assumption such an argument can be successfully made.

Another point is about the status of the 'proof' the argument aims to provide. It is quite natural to read the steps taken above as steps in a psychological developmental process, a gradual liberation from the grip of purportedly self-evident justifications of a social order one has accepted *ab initio*, which one scrutinizes and then rejects one-by-one. Similarly, on a macro-level, they could be read as an abstract representation of an historical developmental process of societies as a whole (Habermas makes such claims about the rationalization trajectory of modern societies). We could point to literature which attempts to show that individuals in highly vulnerable positions, such as the slaves in the nineteenth-century United States, or women in traditional patriarchal cultures around the world, have always retained a sense of self-worth, a self-understanding which – however socialized to accept inferiority – gives at least some starting points for the kinds of reflections offered here. While this offers some sort of valuable side-support, the argument here is not (indeed could not) be meant as representing a series of empirical claims. Instead, it holds (and must hold) that a *rational* agent must make these steps. Here the only thing one can do is make the criteria of rationality sufficiently weak, so as to make the steps of the argument acceptable to all kinds of sceptics. Once these criteria become too strong, the argument becomes question-begging. The argument however cannot answer the ultimate question: why accept what rationality is (if correct) dictating us to accept? Rationality cannot give an argument in favour of being rational. Nor is it clear that we should need such an argument. The practice of philosophy is, if anything, self-validating.

Finally, the argument in this chapter is embedded in larger debates between moral constructivists and moral realists, and between proponents and critics of a diversity of transcendental arguments. I am unable to address these debates here. Nonetheless, I hope at least that the considerations in this chapter serve the purpose of providing a proposal for justification that is interestingly different from the often-found references in political philosophy that a method of reflective equilibrium has been used to generate whatever the text is arguing for. My proposal tries to assume as little as possible at the outset (in the guise of the self-understanding of a merely-participational agent), and by reflecting on the necessary implications of this starting point, to make the steps transparent which are needed to get from there to a conclusion which establishes equal rights to navigational agency. One may doubt whether every step is as rationally warranted as I presented it to be, or more radically, whether such a rational justification can ever be had. Such doubts I have had as well, both about every specific step and in some moments of despair about the project of rational justification as a whole. While it would be naïve to think that this chapter will be the last word on these matters, the abdication of the justificatory project as such would issue in the acceptance of a relativist position, which I take it does not match the self-understanding agents betray when they issue and argue about moral claims in daily practice.

CHAPTER 4

The Distribution of Capabilities

Introduction

Once we have identified a certain capability as basic, the distributive question is: *how much* of this capability is each person entitled to? This question is at least analytically distinct from the preceding questions about the metric (whether or not to adopt a capability metric instead of a welfarist or resourcist metric) and the normative criterion for selecting basic capabilities. Now that I have defended the view that capabilities are basic if they are a necessary condition of what I called navigational agency, we can address the distributive question. As I will show, even if they are analytically distinct, my answer to the first two questions does have implications for answering the distributive question.

In the literature on the capability approach, much less attention has been spent on the question: which distributive principle is the right one? Amartya Sen has explicitly endorsed an agnostic stance about this question, calling for flexibility in the use of different principles for capability distributions (Sen 2010, 248–9).[1] Nonetheless, there is a somewhat received view, which is that the capability approach is sufficientarian. I will start with an overview of Martha Nussbaum's position on this issue, since her theory arguably has been most influential in framing the capability approach as a sufficientarian theory (Section 4.1). The remainder of the chapter will be structured around three objections to sufficientarianism.

The first objection, coming from *prioritarians*, is that sufficientarianism suffers from 'threshold fetishism': it is implausible in giving priority to bringing people across the threshold compared to reducing their distance to the threshold, and even worse, in prioritizing small sub-threshold gains over large supra-threshold gains (Section 4.2). The second

---

[1] He has also been sceptical about general discussions of distributive principles (Sen 2009, 10–15).

objection, coming from *egalitarians*, is that sufficientarianism ignores above-threshold inequalities as irrelevant to justice. Once the threshold is realized for all individuals, any further inequalities are deemed morally unproblematic. Egalitarians argue that justice considerations do have a role to play above the threshold (Section 4.3). The third objection, coming from *luck egalitarians*, is that sufficientarianism fails to take into account personal responsibility. People who due to their own choices fall below the threshold should be allowed to do so, instead of being saved by new rounds of redistribution (Section 4.4). This chapter assesses these objections in more detail. It will first give a defence of a modified form of sufficientarianism to take account of some prioritarian concerns, then take egalitarian principles on board for one class of cases, so-called positional capabilities and, finally, reject the luck egalitarian charge.

Three preliminary remarks are in order. First, the metric of capabilities refers to capacities (internal capabilities) and options (external capabilities) (see Section 2.1). Both of these cannot be (re-)distributed directly by some central agency such as government. Governments can only create rights to resources – material goods as well as access to services – and use other measures to try to create or change cultural or social norms. These resources and norms subsequently lead to a certain capability distribution in a population. Linkages between resources/norms on the one hand and the realization of capabilities on the other hand can be incredibly complex and uncertain. This chapter abstracts from this complexity in talking about abstract distributional schemes, and assumes we can identify the package of resources and tweak the social norms so as to attain the favoured scheme. This is a heroic assumption, but it is necessary to make if we want to have any abstract discussion of distributive principles.

Second, this chapter only provides a framework for capability justice. In reality, different capabilities – from education to health, from security to mobility – will need separate discussions. In the literature, arguments often proceed by creating numerical examples in which anonymous parties have different levels of some metric – welfare, resources or capabilities – and some central planner distributes additional units of this metric. These examples are meant to play on our intuitions by revealing counter-intuitive implications of competing principles. We need to be careful in generalizing from such examples, since when the details are filled in and abstract numbers stand for specific goods, our intuitions may lead to different conclusions. This chapter follows this literature discussing abstract distributive principles and is, thus, useful only in a limited sense. The considerations at best provide a framework to guide work on specific capabilities.

Third, this chapter assumes that distributive principles will be applied at the level of a single capability. The reader is asked to keep in mind one separate capability and think about distributive conflicts between a group of individuals as they attempt to distribute (the resources necessary for) this capability among themselves. I leave out of consideration distributive trade-offs between different capabilities. It makes sense first to work out an ideal distribution of separate capabilities. To the extent that scarcity of resources makes it necessary to find an index of (dis-)advantage overall, this will need to happen in a second stage, which I do not address here (see the remarks about conflicts between capabilities in the Conclusion).

4.1 Capability Sufficientarianism

Throughout her work, Nussbaum refers to the need for specifying a minimum threshold for each capability. This central place of the idea of a threshold is what has given the impression that she is an unqualified sufficientarian. However, I want to argue that this is misleading in two ways.[2]

First, Nussbaum actually adheres to at least *three* distributive principles, but she subsumes all of these under the notion of an adequate threshold. She says that 'we must indicate where, and to what extent, equality itself is part of the very idea of the threshold itself' (Nussbaum 2006, 292). Her first commitment is to a principle of strict equality: 'It appears that all the political, religious, and civil liberties can be *adequately* secured only if they are *equally* secured' (Nussbaum 2006, 292–3). Under this principle each citizen gets exactly the same amount. I will not follow Nussbaum's terminological subsumption of strict equality under adequacy (threshold) but reserve the term 'threshold' for a properly sufficientarian principle. Next, Nussbaum endorses the idea that for some 'instrumental goods' we need such a sufficientarian principle: here 'what seems appropriate is *enough*' (Nussbaum 2006, 293). She argues that inequalities in house size, above a certain threshold, should not matter:

> Insofar as envy and competition make people feel that an unequal house is a sign of unequal dignity, we might wonder whether these judgments are not based on an excessive valuation of material goods, which a just society might decide not to honor... At least sometimes we may find that excessive valuation of competitive goods lies behind a social norm; a just society could decide not to honor that valuation. (Nussbaum 2006, 293)

[2] I focus on Nussbaum (2006). A similar statement can be found in Nussbaum (2011b, 40–2).

Finally, she argues that 'grossly unequal shares' may not be adequate for some material goods. She mentions basic education and basic health care as examples. What is warranted here is 'something close to equality, or at least a very high minimum' (Nussbaum 2006, 294). This is not strict equality, but a more or less-equal distribution – i.e. justice as requiring keeping shares within a *range*. I will refer to this as a 'range equality' principle. In conclusion, Nussbaum's theory is only sufficientarian for some, not all capabilities.

The second qualification is that Nussbaum repeatedly emphasizes that she offers a partial or minimal theory of justice (Nussbaum 2006, 71, 274, 290). Her theory remains agnostic about distribution above the threshold: 'The approach does not yet take a stand on how far it would be imperative to pursue equality of wealth and income above the threshold' (Nussbaum 2006, 381). Nussbaum's theory would be compatible with using several other distributive principles above the threshold – this is simply left open. This stance is *not* distinctively sufficientarian, at least according to a widespread definition of sufficientarianism as characterized by two theses. The first one, the so-called 'positive thesis', states that absolute priority should be given to bringing those below the threshold beyond it. The 'negative thesis' is that *no* moral consideration should be given to further benefits above the threshold (Casal 2007, 298–300). Sufficientarianism is not agnostic but *rejects* justice-relevant considerations above the threshold. This is important, for it determines sufficientarian's stance in cases of conflict between below and above-threshold benefits.

The question is, however, whether Nussbaum's position is really as minimal as she claims. We saw that she recognizes principles of strict equality and range equality that say something about above-threshold situations; these are not minimal because they completely determine the distributive pattern for the relevant capability. Also, we have seen in the quoted passage that when Nussbaum discusses capabilities properly governed by a sufficientarian principle she argues that a just society 'might' or 'could' not honour pleas for a more egalitarian distribution. Here she seems to be not agnostic but (cautiously) negative about doing anything beyond securing a threshold. While this is no explicit acknowledgment that above-threshold interests should not count, it comes as close as possible. When following these passages, Nussbaum could be interpreted as a full sufficientarian after all, who endorses both the positive and the negative thesis.

This brief overview shows that matters are bound to be more complex: a mix of distributive principles is as much a possibility as a simple-minded adherence to sufficiency for every capability. Besides Nussbaum other authors have also offered sufficientarian capability theories (E. Anderson 1999; Schuppert 2014; Axelsen and Nielsen 2015, 2017) while others combine a capability metric with prioritarianism (Wolff and De-Shalit 2007). This chapter will systematically research the case for capability sufficientarianism by confronting it with its three most important competitors, and the objections they raise against sufficientarianism.

(1) The *threshold fetishism objection* protests against the importance of setting a threshold in the name of a less dichotomous and more continuous picture of people's interests. Any threshold is arbitrary given the continuous nature of the moral spectrum. For example, Paula Casal argues that 'it is strange to think that individuals can suddenly plummet from having absolute priority to no priority whatsoever' (Casal 2007, 317). Similarly, Richard Arneson explicitly attacks the capability approach for its sufficientarianism in the name of continuity: 'A small shift in the values of the factors that morally matter should not generate a large shift in what we morally ought to do' (Arneson 2006, 30). This fundamental point about arbitrariness can be worked out in terms of two concrete problems. One is that sufficientarian is committed to giving priority to raising people beyond the threshold even over larger gains to those further below the threshold.[3] The other is that sufficientarians must give priority to small, even tiny sub-threshold gains over large beyond-threshold gains.

(2) The *inequality objection* also objects to thresholds, but for different reasons. Egalitarians object that comparative considerations should count in our moral assessments. Sufficientarianism, structured as it is by an asymmetry between parties on either side of some absolute threshold, rejects such considerations about being relatively well-off. But egalitarians argue that it is unjust when two persons are more unequal in their holdings than they could be. For example, Larry Temkin has objected to Roger Crisp's sufficientarian argument that we should set the threshold at the level where an impartial spectator would no longer feel any compassion (Crisp 2003). Temkin states: 'considerations of fairness are distinct from those of compassion, and they do not

---

[3] Stein extensively discusses Nussbaum's stance on below-threshold conflicts, concluding that she remains silent about it for reasons of incommensurability. He argues in favour of a utilitarian benefit-maximizing rule to resolve this silence (Stein 2009, 504–14).

give out once people are "sufficiently" well off' (Temkin 2003a, 772).[4] Similarly, Richard Arneson has argued against Anderson's sufficientarianism that issues of tax policy in a polity of citizens who are all well-off still raise issues of fairness between those well-off and those even better-off (Arneson 2000a, 347).[5]

(3) The *responsibility objection* cuts across the previous two objections, which objected to sufficientarians' adherence to thresholds. Whether one ultimately comes down on the egalitarian, prioritarian or sufficientarian side of these debates, there is a further question about factoring in responsibility. Thus, Temkin argues for a responsibility-sensitive egalitarianism by defining egalitarians as those who believe that 'it is bad for some to be worse off than others through no fault or choice of their own' (Temkin 2003b, 62). Arneson argues for 'responsibility-catering prioritarianism' in which 'the moral value of altering a state of affairs in a way that makes someone better-off or worse-off depends, other things being equal, on the degree of responsibility the person bears for her present condition' (Arneson 2000a, 344). Responsibility for one's own choices is an issue which arises after one has decided on an initial distribution along the lines of egalitarianism, prioritarianism or sufficientarianism: Should one allow that pattern to be altered due to individuals' own choices?

Let's now discuss these three objections in more depth in order to see how my agency-based capability theory would respond to each.

4.2 The Prioritarian Challenge: Threshold Fetishism

I will start with the two more practical problems that prioritarians have brought to the debate; about sub-threshold and cross-threshold conflicts. Only through arguing about them we will reach the fundamental point about the moral arbitrariness of thresholds.

Prioritarians object to sufficientarians for committing themselves to giving priority to moving people beyond the threshold. In the case depicted in Table 4.1, where the threshold is set at 25 and with a choice of moving

---

[4] The same objection to sufficientarianism's indifference for inequalities above some threshold can be made from a prioritarian standpoint, even though prioritarianism strictly speaking is not intrinsically concerned about inequality in the relations between people's levels of welfare (Holtug 2007, 150).

[5] The problem is not just that sufficientarians ignore relative considerations above the threshold, however: they also ignore them below the threshold and this is equally problematic (Casal 2007, 307).

Table 4.1. *Sufficientarianism: A sub-threshold conflict*

	Individual A	Individual B
Status quo	24	15
Situation X	26	15
Situation Y	24	24

from the Status quo either to X or Y, sufficientarians would be committed to choosing X which brings A across the threshold, instead of Y, which brings a larger but sub-threshold capability-increase to B. Wolff and De-Shalit, calling this the 'strong threshold view', argue convincingly, that this seems both absurd and inefficient (Wolff and De-Shalit 2007, 92–3).[6] It is absurd since a far larger gain (in terms of justice!) can be made with the same resources by choosing the improvement of B's position, and it is inefficient since resources are thus not spent most efficiently.

Most sufficientarians in response to such criticisms revert to a 'weak threshold view which, in cases of sub-threshold conflict, gives priority to those who are worse off: they introduce a prioritarian principle below the threshold. The resulting view is prioritarian up to the threshold but sufficientarian overall in that the moral field is still divided by the threshold with those above it having their benefits not being given any consideration (Crisp 2003, 757–9; Benbaji 2005, 311; Casal 2007, 317–18; Holtug 2007, 149–51; Huseby 2010, 184–5). The prioritarian structure below the threshold seems clearly more satisfactory and the resulting *weak sufficientarianism* an important improvement over strong sufficientarianism.[7] It rightly mandates choosing Y over X and this not just because Y makes a larger gain, but primarily because B should receive priority because he or she is the worst-off person (imagine B getting to just 16 or 17 in Y; it is still better to choose Y over X).

However, there are two variants of prioritarianism,: absolute and weighted prioritarianism (Crisp 2003, 752; Holtug 2007, 133–4). Which one should a weak sufficientarian adopt? In the situation depicted in Table 4.2, absolute prioritarians choose F over G, H and I. The gain in one

---

[6] Arneson calls this the 'strict sufficiency doctrine' and distinguishes it from the moderate one, which roughly coincides with the weak threshold view in Wolff and De-Shalit (Arneson 2006, 27). For a discussion, see Shields (2012, 103).

[7] Sometimes threshold-crossings may have a special moral significance, e.g. when they are a matter of life-and-death (Frankfurt 1987, 30; Casal 2007, 307).

Table 4.2. *Absolute versus weighted prioritarianism*

	Individual A	Individual B
Status quo	20	15
Situation F	20	16
Situation G	21	15
Situation H	22	15
Situation I	24	15

increment for the worst-off (B from 15 to 16) outweighs whatever gains can be made to A. This requires potentially very large foregone benefits of A to realize a small benefit to B. Weighted forms of prioritarianism introduce weights, such that benefits of the worst-off count as heavier than benefits to those closer to the threshold, but not as absolutely heavier. Thus, a weighted form of prioritarianism could choose I (but not G and H) over F, judging that in this situation the four increments gain for A are large enough to weigh heavier than the one increment gain to worst-off B.[8] In fact, however, weighted prioritarianism is a family of principles, depending on how much weight it attaches to the worse off. For example, an even more strongly weighted view will already give priority to A in situation H, requiring a mere two-increment increase for A to off-sets B's one-increment gain. We are now on our way to a simple maximizing principle where an increment for everyone counts equally (in the utility metric, this would be simple aggregative utilitarianism). Prioritarians (and weak sufficientarians) will stop short of that point, but it is difficult in general to say where.

Weak sufficientarianism's accommodation to prioritarianism seems a reasonable end-point, and I will defend it in what follows. However, prioritarians – not content with a partial victory – will want to convince us to go further. They can do so by introducing cross-threshold conflicts.

Prioritarians argue that prioritarian considerations should be allowed above the threshold as well. This comes down to abolishing the threshold altogether.[9] The argument can be illustrated using Table 4.3 (adapted from Crisp 2003, 758). Individual A still has to cross the threshold of 25,

---

[8] I leave aside conflicts between groups with different numbers. Here too prioritarianism introduces weights.

[9] An exception is sufficiency-constrained prioritarianism (Casal 2007, 320). Note the difference between this view and weak (prioritarian-introducing) sufficientarian (Huseby 2010, 184).

Table 4.3. *Prioritarianism versus sufficientarianism*

	Individual A	Individual B
Status quo	22	26
Situation K	24	26
Situation L	22	100

so it seems that his or her increase from 22 to 24 should count heavier than any increase for B who already is above the threshold. This suggests that we should prefer K over L, as both weak sufficientarians and absolute prioritarians would do. However, the increase for B in situation L is impressive, so shouldn't it get priority on grounds of efficiency? (One sees the analogy with the efficiency reason for moving from strong to weak sufficientarianism.) Most weighted prioritarians as well as straightforward maximizers would defend that move.[10] Mark Stein makes a big deal out of this in his critique of Nussbaum. He argues extensively that her theory falls prey to the 'insatiable entitlements' (or 'bottomless-pit') problem. It is always possible to spend more and more to those below the threshold, to get them slightly higher up towards it, without reaching that point. This is especially true for those with expensive natural handicaps. Should the capability approach be spending these enormous efforts on such small gains? (Pogge 2002, 212; Stein 2009, 499–504).[11]

Cross-threshold conflicts bring out prioritarians' fundamental charge of arbitrariness: why should we follow sufficientarians in treating two parts of the moral spectrum so differently (Casal 2007, 312–14)? In Arneson's words: 'What we have is a smooth continuum of possible levels of overall capability for flourishing. Higher capability is always better than lower capability. But I do not see how any unique level (not even a broad thick line) can be picked out such that if a person has that level she has "enough"' (Arneson 2000b, 56). This is the main challenge for (weak) sufficientarianism.

---

[10] This is why it doesn't help much to counter, as sufficientarian Huseby does, that prioritarians face the same problem. For this is only true for absolute prioritarians. Huseby recognizes this in what follows (Huseby 2010, 186–7).

[11] The costs of prioritizing capability increases for below-threshold individuals can be either spelled out in terms of the sacrifices of those paying for this (as Pogge and Stein do), or in terms of the foregone capability gains of spending the same resources rather on those above the threshold (as prioritarians would do).

Apart from conversion to prioritarianism, sufficientarians have three options. One is to adopt a threshold 'that is so high that virtually all of humanity lives below it and therefore within prioritarian territory' (Casal 2007, 318; see also Holtug 2007, 154). There may be cases where setting a high – but still interesting – threshold can reasonably be seen as the right thing to do. For example, one can imagine public benefit schedules for sharing in the costs of health care, child care or other expenses, which make the amount of income support available dependent on household income, and phase out such support to finally reach zero at some fairly high threshold level of income; say 100.000 euros. The question is whether this solution is sufficientarian in an interesting sense or rather prioritarian dressed up in sufficientarian clothes.

A second option is to redefine sufficientarianism by rejecting the negative thesis. Sufficientarianism then amounts to the positive thesis combined with 'the shift thesis' (Shields 2012, 108): beyond the threshold there is not a zero value attached to individual benefits, but rather a shift towards another distributive principle. For example, above the threshold we simply apply straightforward maximizing principles (Crisp 2003, 755, 758; Benbaji 2005, 312) or a Rawlsian difference principle (Casal 2007, 318–26). If we adopt one of these schemes, a threshold is important not to mark where our moral consideration for individual benefits ends, but where a different kind of moral terrain begins. Nussbaum may be interpreted as adopting this solution, while leaving it open what the best principle above the threshold would be. I will argue against this solution by maintaining and defending the negative thesis, as the third option does.

The third option is to bite the bullet. Robert Huseby does so when he states that aggregative theories also have their deficiencies (such as allowing large pain for one person to be offset by small gains to many people), and that on balance he prefers to accept the counterintuitive implications of sufficientarianism over those of aggregative theories (Huseby 2010, 187). Similarly, Crisp accepts the implication, arguing from his compassion-based theory that this is 'not as implausible as it seems once we give proper recognition to the fact that the threshold is the point at which compassion no longer applies. There really is something special to be said for benefitting the worst-off individual which cannot be said for benefiting those above the threshold' (Crisp 2003, 758). Crisps's argument hinges on his justification in terms of a compassionate impartial spectator. In the welfarist part of the literature the special importance of the threshold is explained in terms of the notion of a point of *satiation*. One's welfare (in a certain dimension) can be satiated at a certain point so that the notion of increasing welfare any further in that dimension carries no weight (Shields 2012, 113; see also Frankfurt 1987, 37–41).[12] In terms of my theory of justice, however, this satiation point must be explained differently.

The agency-based capability theory of justice is concerned to justify political action. Political action is by its nature coercive. Even where it does not directly use violent means, its effects cannot be escaped by those who are subject to it, as citizens of the relevant political community. Therefore it needs special justification (Blake 2002; Ripstein 2004). This special justification is in terms of justice. Political action serves to create the conditions for just living together of citizens. Justice is the only norm for political action; other, possibly conflicting norms (freedom, equality, efficiency, etc.) are to be understood as parts of the concept of justice (see Introduction). Given these assumptions, there is an *endpoint* to political action: to establish conditions of just living together between citizens. Political action should stop where this endpoint is reached.

If justice is concerned with creating navigational agency, then a further investigation of this property will help us to understand the need for thresholds of capabilities. It is customary to think of the property of being a person as, in Rawls's terms, a range property (i.e. a binary property) which itself is based on a scalar property (Rawls 1999a, 444; Benbaji 2005, 324; Carter 2011, 548). The set of person-making capacities is scalar (gradual) in nature. However, the property of being-a-person is itself not scalar. At some level of this set, personhood sets in. The same thought can be applied to agency. While the capabilities for agency and thus agency itself can be thought of as scalar, we also need to consider agency – for political purposes – as a range property. Since social practices can be understood on the analogy with games in which we participate, we need to make a distinction between *developing* and *exercising* agency: the distinction between preparing for a game, and playing that game. Preparations, however long and torturous they might be, make no sense except by reference to that for which they are preparations. At some point, the games must begin. The distinction between agency development and exercise points to a discontinuous feature at the heart of political action in the name of justice: between the time for and after the start of the game.[13]

---

[12] Benbaji has another proposal: to distinguish good and bad lives on the analogy with the asymmetry between pleasure and pain (Benbaji 2005, 316–17).

[13] The temporal expressions are deceptive: when a series of matches is played, players' preparations will always continue alongside their matches. Even then the time and energy spent on the preparations is restricted and set off from the time spent in the game.

On this model, political action is meant to create conditions for the sufficient preparation of citizens for the game of social life. It requires deciding on a cut-off point where citizens are presumed to have the prerequisites to qualify for the game of social life that is to be played. This is a pragmatic demand: in many cases the law needs to define cut-off points to be applicable to social life (Feinberg 1986). However, the case for thresholds goes beyond this. Given the nature of any game, we can make an estimate of what would be necessary to play this game with reasonable success. Compare this to a trainer in basketball, gymnastics or rowing, who, one day, after a long training session with one of his pupils says to her: 'Now you are ready for it!' Somehow a line has been crossed at that day. Where possible, such a professional judgement could be backed up with formalized test results, such that when a pupil is able to score above a certain level on a training test, then one can predict with reasonable certainty that she will be able to sufficiently maintain herself in a real competition (operationalization of 'being ready for it' requires: a test score threshold, a real competition score threshold and setting a percentage of the pupils who made the test score threshold also making the game score threshold).

Let's illustrate this by reconsidering the example introduced by Casal (see Table 4.3). This example misrepresents what is at stake in typical justice-related policy issues, in two ways. First, the numbers are misleading. The example sets a threshold at 25 and then uses a four-fold increase to 100 to get prioritarian intuitions going. Let's take a more realistic example in terms of public policy, illustrated by Table 4.4. Suppose that a bliss level of health can be represented by 100. Suppose that a government guarantees financial support to 70 per cent of that level. This level of healthcare is judged to represent what individuals need to get 'in the game' of social life. Anything between 70 and 100 is – in the face of scarce resources and because of diminishing returns of treatments to overall population health – 'luxury health' which is not funded publicly.

Table 4.4. *Thresholds in public policy*

	Individual A	Individual B
Status quo	65	71
Situation P	70	71
Situation Q	65	100

Now suppose a middle-income country struggles to improve healthcare. It can spend additional resources on getting A finally across the threshold health level (situation P) or use the same resources for an increase which is almost six-times as large, and move B from the threshold to the bliss point (situation Q). I take it that here it seems much more plausible to give weight to the threshold. This seems partly because the threshold is set much higher compared to the bliss point than in the earlier example and partly because we have filled in the abstract details behind the numbers (we are talking about medical treatments) so that the pull of getting from a lower to higher level at an absolutely lower level can be more clearly felt.

A second way in which Casal's example is misleading is that the capability numbers in the table do not convey the fact that weak sufficientarianism has a *gradualist* structure in weighing capability increases at different parts of the spectrum. The moral value of benefits to individuals is already diminishing as they approach the threshold (this can be seen by representing sufficientarianism as a concave curve up to the threshold, see Holtug 2007, 150; Meyer and Roser 2009, 223). Individual A's capability level in Table 4.4 already has a value which has been sharply diminishing compared to individuals further below the threshold. The step to the zero value of individual B is not so big. Indeed, one could turn the charge around, and ask prioritarians why, if they recognize the (starkly) diminished value of individual benefits higher up some scale, it would be so implausible that at some point it approaches zero. If moral value diminishes gradually, why not assume a soft landing at ground zero?

Setting thresholds itself is a normative decision with various components – there is no threshold for agency to be found in (human) nature. Threshold-setting can always be attacked as relying on disputable elements; why use this test level, that percentage? However, vagueness is no objection against my argument based on the dichotomy of agency development and agency exercise: that the political decision necessarily has the structure of setting a threshold-level of capabilities necessary for agency, after which no further concerns of justice are to be allowed. This is necessary for defining a sufficient level of agency, and agency needs to be defined because otherwise agency exercise can never be marked off from agency development, so that no agents can actually use their developed capacities to act. Moreover, competing distributive theories also need to be operationalized. Sufficientarianism is in the same boat as these other theories in having to specify the principle for concrete capabilities in concrete practices.

All in all, a sufficientarian threshold principle for distributing capabilities arises as a defensible position that need not give in to the challenges of prioritarianism except for accepting a prioritarian structure below the threshold. In Section 6.1 I will come back to threshold-setting, and add one important specification to what has been argued here: that the sufficientarian threshold for subsistence capabilities must be seen as socially relative. But let's now continue our debate with competing distributive principles, and venture into the possible attractions of egalitarian principles.

4.3 The Egalitarian Challenge: Levelling Down

Egalitarianism as a distributive view can be distinguished from prioritarianism and sufficientarianism in two ways. First, egalitarianism permits levelling down and, second, egalitarianism gives an *intrinsic* justification for reducing inequalities. In this section, I will defend that we sometimes have good reasons to level down, but not for intrinsic egalitarian reasons. Instead, I will appeal to one type of instrumental reason: the positional nature of some capabilities. This reason can be embedded in the sufficientarian account developed thus far.

We need to distinguish egalitarian principles from principles with egalitarian effects. A principle is *egalitarian* if it levels down, i.e. when it makes some worse off while no one is made better off (Parfit 2000, 98). A principle has *egalitarian effects* if it narrows the range between the best-off and the worst-off. The latter, but not the former, is acceptable to sufficientarians and prioritarians. In Table 4.5, situations D, E, F, G and H all reduce the

Table 4.5. *Bringing in egalitarianism*

	Individual A	Individual B
Status quo	40	80
Situation D	45	80
Situation E	45	76
Situation F	45	73
Situation G	40	75
Situation H	38	70

range between individuals A and B; all have egalitarian effects. Prioritarians and sufficientarians will mandate moving from the status quo to situation D, albeit for different reasons (bringing A closer to the threshold, set at 45, or making A better-off). This egalitarian effect is reached because – as is customary in the literature – additional resources (which have fallen like manna from heaven) are made available to serve A's interests. Often in political practice, however, there are no painless ways to raise the well-being of the worst-off and/or those below the threshold. In order to pay for public services, taxes need to be levied and the tax-and-benefit scheme will involve redistribution. This is exemplified by situations E and F, where B's welfare diminishes, so that these moves both violate the Pareto-principle. Sufficientarians and prioritarians can still endorse these moves.[14]

Situations G and H also narrow the gap between A and B, but here lowering B's welfare is not accompanied by an offsetting gain in A's welfare. A remains at the same level (situation G, call this *moderate egalitarianism*) or even sees his or her welfare diminished (situation H, *strong egalitarianism*). This is levelling down, which sufficientarians and prioritarians cannot accept, for it is a properly egalitarian principle (in contrast with non-egalitarian principles with egalitarian effects). The question is: can anything justify levelling down? Non-egalitarians often assume that levelling down must be based on envy and so is illegitimate. Is that true? One might either try to find a justification on egalitarian grounds – i.e. by showing that narrowing the gap has itself an intrinsic moral significance – or by showing that narrowing the gap is justified on instrumental grounds (Scanlon 2003b, 207; M. O'Neill 2008, 123). I will here remain agnostic about intrinsic defences and argue for an important instrumental justification: the positionality of some goods. I believe that most egalitarian intuitions can be explained through reference to these goods (Axelsen and Nielsen 2015, 14).[15]

Positional goods are goods whose absolute value for us depends on our relative position with respect to their distribution. As Harry Brighouse and Adam Swift state: 'The very fact that one is worse off than others with respect to a positional good means that one is worse off, in some respect, than one would be if that good were distributed equally.'

---

[14] E represents a Kaldor-Hicks improvement (total welfare increases), in F we face a net-loss. It is a matter of some dispute whether prioritarianism can accept these consequences. One can define prioritarianism so that it only mandates Pareto-improvements (as in D), but this seems to me an unnecessary restriction of its scope (Holtug 2007, 132, 134). See the example mentioned in Benbaji (2005, 314).

[15] Positional goods justify but do not *require* levelling-down – they require narrowing the range of inequality. If this can be done by making everyone absolutely better-off as well, all the better.

(Brighouse and Swift 2006, 472). Because of the relativity of their value, competition for positional goods has a zero-sum structure: one person's gain is another person's loss. The reason that all scramble for a fixed amount of value is that these goods are inelastic in their supply. This inelasticity can go back to either physical causes (such as their being only one exemplar of a particular Rembrandt painting) or social causes. The latter, in turn, can be divided into two categories. Goods can be socially scarce because they are valued for their scarcity – i.e. the social status derived from possessing something that is scarce; these are sometimes called 'snob goods' – or because of the competitive structure of the good itself, like attractive jobs or educational positions, which form a hierarchy by definition (Hirsch 1999, 30).

Positional goods relate the possession of a good to 'something else'. Let's call this the *Ultimate Good*. Person A prefers positional-good B for its value in terms of C. While positional goods are always resources, the *Ultimate Good* can be expressed in different metrics. We need to be careful in how we specify the links (Brighouse and Swift 2006, 478). In the utilitarian tradition it is customary to express the *Ultimate Good* in terms of subjective well-being levels. Our utility level with respect to a sports car depends on the distribution of sports cars amongst our friends. Sometimes however a relation between two goods is at stake – i.e. the *Ultimate Good* is itself a resource. For example, our relative place in the distribution of education co-determines our absolute chances on the labour market.[16] Finally, we can apply the capabilities metric. The value of a positional good, like educational services, can be considered in terms of our capabilities like literacy and other abilities. Unsurprisingly, I will adopt a capability metric as the *Ultimate Good*.

Now what does distributive justice require with respect to positional goods? The standard economic response, embedded in the welfarist tradition, is that positional competition is inefficient. In a zero-sum game, the fact that everyone is putting in extra effort (time and resources) to the fight doesn't change anyone's relative position. In an arms race, bringing extra ammunition doesn't help anyone but does exhaust all the competitor's resources which could have been put to productive use elsewhere.

---

[16] This structure shows why we cannot see the positional rationale of levelling down from a Table like 4.5. The units in these tables cannot represent quantities of resources but must represent some conception of well-being/advantage (Parfit 2000, 83). Situations G and H in the table show diminishing values. However, in the case of positional goods we would need to see rising values for individual A (the levelling-down happens in the dimension of resources, which is behind these welfare numbers).

The proposed solution is akin to an arms control agreement: to prohibit or discourage all participants from spending additional resources on the competition – e.g. through a consumption tax on positional goods (Frank 1985, 1999; Hirsch 1999; Heath 2005, 2006).

The line Brighouse and Swift take is not to maximize overall welfare but to apply prioritarian principles. They propose to level-down for positional goods because this benefits those who are worse-off in the competition. They recognize that an analogous argument could be made by sufficientarians: to level down because of concern for some falling below a threshold with respect to positional goods. Hence prioritarians and sufficientarians can both accept levelling-down for positional goods – albeit for different reasons. One does *not* need to resort to intrinsic egalitarian reasons to level down. Critics cannot point to envy to refute levelling-down since people's concern for relative equality does not stem from envious motivations but from the positional character of these goods (Brighouse and Swift 2006, 475). Given the arguably large range of positional goods in the economy (indeed one's income and consumption level as a whole may be qualified as such) this would have major repercussions.[17]

However, these conclusions by Brighouse and Swift are too quick. I want to show that critics can reassert the envy-objection to levelling-down, even with respect to positional goods. The renewed objection cannot be answered in a welfarist framework such as Brighouse and Swift use. We need an agency-based capability framework to secure the case for levelling-down with respect to positional goods.

The value of the *Ultimate Good* can itself be either absolute or positional. As an example of the former, imagine a positional competition for scarce places in a lifeboat. The positional good 'places in the lifeboat' is valuable towards the capability of 'life' as an *Ultimate Good*. Those who plea for levelling-down – say, by increasing the allowed number in the boat, so that more people will have a chance of survival; albeit everyone a smaller chance because of the increased weight – do not do so because they are envious of those who happen to get hold of the best places, but because of a sincere concern for the absolute value of the lives of those who may not happen to make it. As an example of the latter, consider that education has value for job opportunities, which are themselves also positional. This shifts the question to the *Ultimate Good* itself – we now

---

[17] While the economist's arms control agreement may or may not be egalitarian, the link with prioritarianism/sufficientarianism is that status anxiety may raise the price for all in an unequal distribution so that levelling-down may be the most effective way to decrease the intensity (waste) of the competition (Wilkinson and Pickett 2010).

need to ask whether the value of these job opportunities is absolute or positional; and if positional, towards which other (even more Ultimate) goods, and so on *ad inifinitum*. A chain of goods/capabilities can be formed at the end of which stands a final good/capability which is itself either absolute or positional.

This quest brings us to ever higher levels of abstraction. In the end, the most *Ultimate Good* is variously expressed as social standing, social status, rank or power. Here we have arrived at the kinds of goods that make up the *instrumental* reasons that relational egalitarians often put forward in favour of egalitarian principles. Equality of standing as the most abstract ideal for society is the ultimate reason to level-down (E. Anderson 1999; Scanlon 2003b; M. O'Neill 2008; Schemmel 2011). However, the non-egalitarian critic can argue that at this point the distinction between instrumental and intrinsic reasons for egalitarian principles breaks down. The critic can argue that these relational egalitarians should not ally with people's wish for high social status but instead preach that one should be content with one's own life. Relational egalitarians' ultimate reference to 'equality of standing' to defend egalitarian distributions of positional goods itself betrays an envious concern.

In response, those who take positional goods seriously tend to argue that preferences for social status are legitimate because they are *inescapable*. Thus, Joseph Heath argues: 'All of the major components of the good life have a deeply competitive structure. The person with the above-average income can buy the house of his choosing, can walk into any restaurant without checking the prices, has access to exclusive clubs, has access to a wider range of sexual and marriage partners, and so on' (Heath 2006, 18). Similarly, Robert Frank argues that negative positional externalities should only be corrected by the government if people cannot psychologically adjust to the costs imposed upon them. Explaining this through an example of people being dissatisfied because of having relatively smaller houses than others, he claims: 'positional externalities in the housing market also entail far more tangible costs, most notably that failure to keep up with community spending patterns means having to send one's children to schools of below-average quality' (Frank 2008, 1783). Critics however may still object to these kinds of explanations that egalitarians should stop defining 'the good life' in such materialist terms (see the passage quoted from Nussbaum in Section 4.1) and adopt the long-standing view of the ethical codebooks of many of the great world religions, that happiness (or salvation) lies in focusing on the quality of the life of our inner self (and/ or the relation to transcendent powers). Preferences are malleable and while we may not all be capable of becoming a Mother Theresa, most of us can still progress a long way in that direction.[18]

Whatever the truth of these claims on either side, the *psychological* route of defending the legitimacy of the ideal of equality of standing/ status seems to me a dead end. Whether the fact that some competition is psychologically (in)escapable is a good reason to level-down ultimately depends on which expectations we can legitimately impose on people. It is better to turn to that moral debate directly. A better approach to positional competition, I will now argue, should consist of two desiderata. We need a *moral* defence of the absolute (i.e. non-positional) value of equality of standing, and a *practical* assessment of the legitimacy of positional competition in light of this moral value.

An agency-based capability theory is well-positioned to provide the first desideratum. The capabilities necessary for navigational agency will sometimes be non-positional, in which case the sufficientarian principle defended in the previous section applies. When they are positional in nature, the value of a capability in enhancing individual agency is decided in a zero-sum competitive social practice. Relative inequalities in capabilities then affect the level of agency we can achieve. Agency itself, however, remains an absolute value, which brings the chain to an end. We may sometimes legitimately compete for positional capabilities, but these remain instrumental, in the final analysis, to an individual's ability to act – which is to devise and execute one's purposes and lead a good life. Equality in terms of a sufficiency threshold of agency (a sufficiently free and sufficiently autonomous life) is a legitimate demand that each individual can make, at least if the ultimate justification for this ability (see Chapter 3) is convincing; that it lies in its being something whose value agents cannot seriously deny to themselves.

This agency-based justification can be taken as a basis for the relational egalitarian's claim about equality of standing. 'Status' and 'standing' are closely related terms referring to an individual's social position. Nonetheless, 'standing' strongly suggests a legitimate demand to be taken seriously as an equal (and is therefore used by relational egalitarians), while 'status' often suggests a reproachable obsession with one's social position based on envy (as critics of egalitarianism argue). Both can only be clearly differentiated if we bring in an argument for the legitimacy of the concrete demands related to equality of standing. My theory suggests that for such an argument, the necessary conditions of free and autonomous

---

[18] For an earlier critique of Frank's externalities-based approach, see Claassen (2007, 1040).

agency need to brought in – this can be seen as an alternative to the relational egalitarian appeal to the conditions of democratic citizenship.

Let's turn to the second desideratum. On this moral basis, an individual's concern with possession of specific positional capabilities may be legitimized, but only to the extent that the competitive structure of the social practices in which these capabilities are realized is itself legitimized as the *best possible form* of that practice. Practices are structures of social cooperation which produce a surplus (over non-cooperating autarkic individuals). To create that surplus one option is to set participants up in a competition, as many important practices do: politics, the market, law courts, sports, science, etc. This explains the positional character of capabilities in these practices. If one parliamentarian has less intellectual skills, financial resources, well-trained staff, etc. than the others, she or he will obviously be less able to function effectively as a parliamentarian: be less able to draw attention for her positions from the media, be less able to make a convincing case to a minister, etc. The capabilities are positional because the social practice is competitively structured. The crucial point is that having a competitive set-up is not inevitable. We could have political decision-making based on a lottery, dictatorship or a plan economy. These are institutional design choices, for which there may or may not be *good reasons*. Sometimes we value the competitive element intrinsically (think of sports practices, constituted by rivalry). Sometimes competitive set-ups create incentives for productive agency that would otherwise be absent, and are thus justified in the end by welfare gains. Whatever the reason, positional goods cannot be eliminated unless we eliminate all adversarily structured practices. Should we? To decide this question, practical reasoning is necessary. Here an agency-based capability theory suggests a two-step process.

First, the theory only cares about positional capabilities to the extent that they are necessary for the *development* of navigational agency. It will not authorize the use of coercive political power to end the positional competition between John Lennon and Paul McCartney for being the best songwriter, not because of the off-setting welfare gains (non-positional aspect) of their competition to music lovers, but because artistic rivalry is an *exercise* of agency, not (also) a necessary condition for the development of navigational agency. Hence the sufficiency threshold marks off a field of practices which – even if they are fiercely competitive – should be left untouched by political action as justice-irrelevant. On this point, the theory clearly differs from welfarist approaches to positional competition that make political action dependent on calculations ranging over all instances of positional competition that arise, even those unrelated to agency-concerns.

Second, if a practice is necessary for agency development, the benefits and costs of structuring the practice competitively need to be weighed. On the benefit side, there may be good reasons for a competitive set-up. One reason is that positional goods may also have non-positional aspects. Strictly speaking we should not speak about positional goods but about *positional aspects* of goods, because goods can have both positional and non-positional aspects (hence, value) at the same time. To the extent that a good is non-positional, its value for the consumer is not dependent on relative distributions. For example, education has positional value in delivering competitive advantages on the labour market, but it has direct value in making people more knowledgeable (Brighouse and Swift 2006, 482). There may also be wider benefits to others beyond direct consumers. The waste between the competitors needs to be balanced against gains due to the incentive effects of competition: third parties may profit from the superior products made by fiercely competing parties (Hirsch 1999, 52). Positional competition is only a zero-sum game for the participants but may be a positive-sum for the wider society.

On the cost side, there will be reasons to level-down to the point necessary to ensure the exercise of sufficient capabilities to agency of all. Where that point is, will depend on the capability in question and its relation to agency. In the abstract, this could range all the way from some range (ratio) between the worst-off and the best-off (say, 1:10 or 1:100) to strict equality (1:1) – as much as is necessary to avoid instances of domination, marginalization or oppression that mark the absence of navigational agency. The allowed capability range serves as a tipping point or threshold beyond which efforts to equalize are not a matter of justice. So, strict equality as well as an egalitarian range (i.e. a threshold *and* a ceiling) are possible distributive principles *embedded in a sufficientarian view*.[19]

The argument in this section, thus, shows how the three different distributive principles Nussbaum mentions (strict equality, sufficiency threshold and a range) all are grounded in one and the same view. We need sufficiency thresholds where the demands of agency require sufficiency in an absolute sense, but we need strict or range equality where having less than others would discount some as agent-participants in the relevant practice. It will remain controversial which principle to apply

---

[19] For non-positional-good related cases for establishing limits/ceilings in the capability approach, see Holland (2008) and Robeyns (2017a).

in which context. The main theoretical point has been to show how an agency-based argument is particularly suitable to an absolute grounding for the relative concerns behind positional goods arguments, a grounding that is necessary if we are simultaneously to escape falling prey to envy-based objections and do justice to relative concerns where they seem appropriate.

4.4 The Luck-Egalitarian Challenge: Personal Responsibility

The luck-egalitarian challenge is that sufficientarianism does not properly take personal responsibility for one's own choices into account. The issue of responsibility is orthogonal to the discussion between sufficientarianism, prioritarianism and egalitarianism (see Section 4.1). Whatever pattern of distribution one ends up supporting, whether that pattern should be altered by taking responsibility for one's own choices into account is a separate question.

The difference between capability sufficientarians and luck-egalitarians is not that the latter but not the former takes responsibility into account. Capability sufficientarians take responsibility into account by dividing the moral domain into two parts, one where responsibility is deliberately ignored (below the threshold) and another where responsibility is fully factored in (above the threshold). In luck-egalitarian terminology, bad option luck and bad brute luck are compensated below the threshold, whereas neither is compensated above the threshold. Luck-egalitarians by contrast defend a unitary moral domain without a threshold, in which outcomes due to bad brute luck are always compensated and outcomes due to bad option luck always go uncompensated.[20] Similarly, the difference is not that luck-egalitarians but not capability sufficientarians compensate for the arbitrariness of the natural lottery (E. Anderson 2010b). The whole point of a capability theory is to give more resources to those who – either because of natural or social causes – have a lower conversion rate than others (i.e. they need more resources to reach the same level of functionings). The point is that a capability theory compensates for natural shortfalls only up to a threshold and not across the whole moral domain, and that it does so not *because* of the arbitrariness of nature in itself but because of a separate ideal that inspires the threshold

---

[20] Luck-egalitarianism comes in several varieties, depending on where one places the 'cut' between choice and circumstances: at the level of a person's preferences (R. Dworkin 2000), or at the level of whatever is under a person's control (Arneson 1989; G. A. Cohen 1989). I will disregard these differences here.

(whatever that ideal is: human dignity, democratic equality or individual agency).

There are, then, two main differences. First, sufficientarians but not luck-egalitarians compensate bad option luck in below-threshold cases. Sufficientarians have always considered this a main weakness of luck-egalitarianism. For example, Anderson has objected that luck-egalitarians do not do enough for uninsured victims of car accidents and other victims of bad option luck (E. Anderson 1999, 295). Luck-egalitarians would be harsh and unforgiving in their tendency to leave dire consequences of individual choices uncompensated. However, luck-egalitarians can also launch the opposite objection, i.e. that sufficientarians sometimes do too much for those who continuously mess up and waste public resources spent on them. Second, luck-egalitarians but not sufficientarians compensate for bad brute luck in above-threshold cases. Above the threshold, the objections are reversed. Sufficientarians now claim luck egalitarians do too much and should stop worrying about differences once certain basic concerns have been met (this parallels sufficientarian arguments against prioritarians about moral concern for above-threshold cases). Luck-egalitarians will now claim that sufficientarians are not doing enough: above-threshold differences due to bad brute luck deserve compensation just as much as below-threshold differences.

Here I will assume that sufficientarian unconcern in cases above the threshold is justified. Political action to correct for undeservingness between individuals who are already well-enough off in agency-terms is unjustified. The argument for this has been given in Section 4.2 in the discussion against prioritarians, and will not be rehearsed here. My focus will be on below-threshold cases. If sufficientarians need to acknowledge considerations of responsibility, it will be in this realm.

Some luck-egalitarians have accommodated the criticism about the harshness of their theories by proposing a hybrid theory, which Casal calls 'sufficiency-constrained luck egalitarianism' (Casal 2007, 322). The idea is to build in a floor to cover cases of dire need, but then apply the luck-egalitarian scheme above that threshold. For example, Kok-Chor Tan argues that basic subsistence needs should be fulfilled first. Luck-egalitarianism only applies to cases arising beyond these needs. In his view such a division is neither problematic nor new. In the international context we make such divisions all the time, by thinking of foreign cases as needing humanitarian assistance, and domestic cases as requiring more stringent duties of justice (Tan 2008, 670). Ronald Dworkin's proposal to add to his original theory a mandatory insurance scheme for cases of destitution has the same effect (R. Dworkin 2002, 114), as does Shlomi Segall's invocation of a principle of solidarity in addition to the luck-egalitarian principle (Segall 2007, 195). In all these cases the main principle remains luck-egalitarian, but an important exception is built in. Isn't such a hybrid luck-egalitarian theory better, all things considered, than pure sufficientarianism?

Luck-egalitarianism's creation of a threshold is a welcome concession. The new hybrid recognizes, like sufficientarianism, the legitimacy of unconditionally supporting those in need (call this a domain in which a policy of *unconditional support* applies). However, the hybrid view is still objectionable, for two reasons. One is the point about luck egalitarianism's problematic treatment of above-threshold cases which sufficientarians can still press (call this a domain in which a policy of *no support* should apply). Second, while nothing prohibits luck-egalitarians from making all kinds of ad hoc concessions to a pure-luck-egalitarian scheme, this requires some kind of unified explanation why one (responsibility disregarding) principle is suitable below a threshold and another (responsibility sensitive) principle should be applied above a threshold. So far, no such unified explanation has been proposed. One could therefore argue that pure sufficientarianism is preferable because it already recognizes the attractions of unconditional support in below-threshold cases, but is theoretically unified and has a better answer in above-threshold cases.

However, it is too early for a total victory for sufficientarianism. For the point that has not yet been addressed is the luck-egalitarian's counter-attack: that in some below-threshold cases we actually should take responsibility into account. To see the force of this point, consider Arneson who brings this out in reflecting on a similar car accident example (which he associates with a fictitious person called Bert):

> The Bert example decisively undercuts a strict or absolutist luck egalitarianism... The example combines several features. If we vary these features in thought, our reactions shift. In the example, helping Bert will benefit him enormously at moderate cost. If you vary the case by degrees so that he benefits less and less at increasing cost, my confidence that justice demands provision of aid weakens and then turns around, into confidence that justice no longer demands provision. In the example as described, Bert will be extremely badly off in lifetime well-being if he does not get help; varying that feature gradually dampens one's sense that we *must* help him. Finally, as described, Bert is at fault, but only slightly at fault; he has very bad option luck. Varying that feature, one finds again that the claim that scarce resources should go to Bert rather than someone else who could benefit from them gradually weakens. (Arneson 2010a, 30–1)

Here Arneson goes on the offense, arguing that depending on factors like the size of the cost, the size of the benefit and the size of the fault, our intuitions are not clear about whether we actually should help victims of bad option luck. Such an offensive point can stand besides a defensive concession by the hybrid luck egalitarian who builds in unconditional support for *other* below-threshold cases.[21]

My response to Arneson-type objections will come in two parts – one developed in the remainder of this section, and one developed in the context of my discussion of subsistence capabilities (see the end of Section 6.2). Each of these replies draws attention to a different reason to factor in personal responsibility below the threshold, albeit in each case for agency-based, not luck-egalitarian, reasons. I submit that both replies taken together go a long way to diffuse the intuitive strength of the objection.

To explain the first reason for an agency-based capability theory to make room for considerations of personal responsibility below the threshold, we need to start by dividing up the moral domain into three instead of two parts. In the upper part, above the threshold, all choices still go uncompensated.[22] The bottom part, below the threshold, consists as before of those cases where unconditional support is the appropriate response. In this domain sufficientarians (like sufficiency-constrained luck-egalitarians) will provide capabilities disregarding an individual's choices. Those who fall below the threshold on a certain capability due to their own choices will still receive new resources to reach the threshold capability level. A third and new domain, however, consists of below-threshold cases where sufficientarians can provide resources so that individuals can improve their capabilities, but on condition that these individuals cooperate in converting these capabilities into functionings. Here individuals who choose to squander resources are punished in the sense that their shortfall with respect to the second threshold will go uncompensated. Call this the domain of *conditional support*.

The reason for introducing such a differentiation (giving it theoretical unity) is provided by the fact that there is good reason to reconsider the

---

[21] Note that by putting the threshold sufficiently low, such sufficiency-constrained luck-egalitarians may be able to escape falling prey to their own criticisms about cases where individuals squander public resources. For these cases will typically fall above *their* (but not the sufficientarian's) minimal threshold. In this way the sufficiency-constrained luck-egalitarian accommodates both the sufficientarian and the luck-egalitarian intuitions about below-threshold cases.

[22] Keeping this upper domain as it is differentiates my responsibility-constrained sufficientarianism from the sufficiency-constrained luck-egalitarianism mentioned earlier, to the strength of the former.

dichotomy between agency development and agency exercise which up to this point has marked off below- and above-threshold cases. On the analogy with games, I have proposed that political action should cease where agency is sufficiently developed to start 'playing the game' and participate in social practices (see Section 4.2). This continues to be true, and marks the second, higher threshold. However, we should also within the theory give expression to the practical phenomenon that individuals already start to *exercise* (some) agency during their own agency development. Healthcare may again provide an example. Publicly supported healthcare must be given up to the second, higher threshold to restore health (as far as possible) so that individuals are able to function as agents. Above that level, we assume a capability to health to be attained, with further healthcare treatments making no essential impact on people's agency. Below that level, however, while entitlements to certain treatments may be given unconditionally, other treatments are only effective if people cooperate. It does not make much sense to give expensive pills to patients who have repeatedly refused to take them. Neither does it make sense to spend teachers' time on students who repeatedly refuse to do their homework. Developing agency does often not require a mere producer–consumer relation, but rather a relation of co-production in which the prospective agent needs to do her or his part of the job.

Such exercises of agency below the threshold are ubiquitous. In many cases others can only promote a person's capability, but it requires a choice for the person to actually function in that way. Jonathan Wolff and Avner De-Shalit rightly remark: 'In general, it is impossible for a government to guarantee the functioning level of its citizens without extreme coercion. The old adage "you can take a horse to water but you can't make it drink" applies. Short of force-feeding you cannot guarantee nutrition levels, and short of incarceration you cannot guarantee shelter' (Wolff and De-Shalit 2007, 75).[23] So, in most cases the development of agency requires choices – i.e. exercises of agency. If an agent uses his agency to deliberately refuse a treatment (say he does not want further healthcare treatments because he wants to die), then this exercise of agency might in certain cases have to be respected. What concerns us here, however, are cases where an agent wants to benefit from treatment

[23] Wolff and de-Shalit are a little one-sided here. In some cases, coercion may be legitimate, most notably where there is a complete absence of individual's agency. These are cases of promoting actual functionings instead of mere capabilities (Claassen 2014a). We do sometimes force-feed. And while compulsory education cannot guarantee learning in the mind, it is coercive in restricting a pupil's freedom of movement.

(as a meta-preference) and in principle has a right to do so under the sufficientarian scheme, but exercises his agency in such a problematic way
that the capability cannot be realized, and spending resources on him
turns out to be wasteful.

These are the types of cases where individuals may be held responsible
for their failure to cooperate. Where it is costly to spend resources to realize capabilities for people who have no intention of functioning, then
spending may be made conditional on cooperative behaviour. A society
in which everyone has the capability to vote may continue to give opportunities to vote to those who did not vote in the last election(s): the right
remains unconditional despite non-cooperation in previous rounds.
However, this example of forgiveness is almost costless. Giving expensive
medical treatment to un-cooperative patients is a wholly different matter.
Here, at least, the moral value of alternative ways of spending the same
funds (in terms of agency development of others) needs to be balanced
against the right of the non-cooperating patient. The theoretical space
for drawing upon efficiency considerations below the threshold is something that we have already accepted by accepting the weighed prioritarian
structure of dealing with below-threshold cases (see Section 4.2). Here
we see a further application. Efficiency considerations can be invoked
in choices about spending benefits either on one (cooperating) below-
threshold person or another (non-cooperating) one.

In this way we should give personal responsibility a place in a sufficientarian theory. Note however that the reason for doing so is different than
the luck-egalitarian's reason. My theory does not condition support on
willingness to cooperate because the individual is assumed to be able to
control his or her behaviour (that may or may not be the case). Rather,
the conditionality is justified because of competing moral considerations
of others. Thus the sufficientarian theory *assumes* that people are responsible for their non-cooperation without enquiring into the causes.[24]
Holding people responsible for non-cooperation does not require delving
into the 'metaphysical swamp' (Wolff and De-Shalit 2007, 77) or 'metaphysical dead end' (Fleurbaey 2008, 247) of checking whether people
'really were responsible' for their behaviour in some deep sense connected
to debates about the freedom of the will.

---

[24] Segall rightly draws attention to the fact that the discussion of the abandonment objection against
luck-egalitarians has almost always been conducted in terms of interpreting option luck as a matter
of 'reckless risk-taking', while in other cases individuals may rather be in the business of 'deliberate
waste and self-harm' (Segall 2007, 186).

This section has defended the sufficientarian's commitment of holding individuals responsible for their choices above the threshold, but it has added a requirement to hold individuals responsible for their non-cooperation below the threshold where (a) such cooperation is necessary to develop agency and (b) more agency development can be realized by spending resources on others who do cooperate. In these cases, they may lose their right to the resources needed for developing the capability. This leaves open all kinds of further questions (What counts as non-cooperation? How stringently do we apply this? Can the right be permanently withdrawn or only temporarily?) which would need to be discussed with respect to particular capabilities.

Overall, the picture that emerges from this chapter is that an agency-based capability theory – like other capability theories – will predominantly use sufficientarian principles. The key argument is the one given in Section 4.2: that political action to realize individual agency has a dichotomous structure (agency development versus agency exercise) that requires threshold-setting. This chapter has, in addition, argued in favour of three complications. First, conflicts between below-threshold cases should be handled through a weighed prioritarian scheme (see Section 4.2). Second, for some capabilities, namely those with a positional character, an egalitarian range principle (settings ceilings as well as thresholds) or even strict equality is justified (see Section 4.3). Third, for some capabilities, where their realization requires agency exercise, rights should be conditional on cooperation for which individuals are held responsible (see Section 4.4). These complications are not arbitrary concessions to the sufficientarian's opponents, but they have all been shown to arise out of a sustained reflection about the nature of my metric (agency-enhancing capabilities) itself. Where the thresholds should be set and when each of these complications invoked, depends on concrete cases. This chapter has merely offered a general toolkit or framework to facilitate such discussions of concrete capabilities.

PART III

Three Sets of Basic Capabilities

CHAPTER 5

Empowerment Capabilities and Civil Freedom

Introduction

Freedom of expression, religion, association and other civil liberties belong to the core of the idea of what it is to be free. They set out the shape and boundaries of what it is to be able to navigate freely and autonomously in society. I will refer to protecting these civil rights (and some other rights) as protecting our 'empowerment capabilities' – real opportunities for being empowered as a navigational agent.

Inclusion of these capabilities on a list of basic capabilities is relatively uncontroversial, at least compared to the socio-economic and political capabilities that are central to Chapters 6 and 7. Thus, whereas much of the coming two chapters is spent on justifying the inclusion of these socio-economic and political capabilities, here my focus is different. Making the case for the functionally indispensable contribution each of these empowerment capabilities to navigational agency would amount to repeating much of the autonomy-based defences of each of these liberties already available in the literature.[1] Instead, I will use this chapter to give an answer to the incorporation problem as an important challenge for moderate perfectionist forms of liberalism (see Section 1.4). As a reminder, any theory of autonomous agency risks being as objectionably perfectionist as the theories that are more directly perfectionist, because when specifying what autonomous agency requires in practice, one needs to appeal to *other values*, which are themselves not justified by arguments justifying the focus on autonomous agency itself.[2] These other values

---

[1] By way of example: for an autonomy-based defence of freedom of association, see L. Green (1998), for freedom of expression Scanlon (1972), for privacy Rössler (2004).

[2] More accurately, the incorporation problem arises as a challenge for three parts of the theory: (1) the selection of basic capabilities itself; (2) their specification; and (3) cases of conflict between them. On capability conflicts, I will say something in the conclusion. The selection of navigational agency capabilities has been extensively discussed earlier (second half of Section 2.3). Hence here I focus on specification.

express views of the good life that may not be shared by all citizens, hence cannot form a basis for state action in the name of justice.[3] The aim of this chapter is to solve this problem, and show how one can specify empowerment capabilities, without taking recourse to perfectionist values.

After a general definition of the category of empowerment capabilities, I argue that the agency-based capability theory can deal with the incorporation problem by either reducing other values to agency or by remaining indifferent between them (Section 5.1). After this general strategy is set, the remainder of the chapter will then study the incorporation problem in two contexts.

The first context is a general problem, which arises when dealing with many capabilities in practice, the problem of adaptive preferences. Adaptive preferences are important because they are often taken as cases where individuals themselves apparently consent to their own deprivation or oppression – i.e. their own sub-threshold functioning on one or more capabilities. In these cases it is hard to justify public interference because liberalism requires abstinence when individuals consent to their own harm. To judge otherwise requires arguing that there is something deficient about these preferences. Martha Nussbaum and others have argued that adaptive preferences can only be dealt with by relying on a theory of the good. I will distinguish adaptive preferences from closely related agency-failures on the basis of a procedural theory of autonomy in combination with the agency-based list of basic capabilities itself, thus avoiding recourse to a set of perfectionist values (Section 5.2). Moreover, I show how and when these agency failures are a reason for paternalist intervention (Section 5.3).

The second context is one specific empowerment capability, on which I zoom in, by way of a case study, the freedom of association. Freedom of association is a coin with two sides: exit and entry. I first discuss the problem of specifying the right of individuals to exit social practices to which they belong as a member. I argue that the list of basic capabilities

---

[3] This debate is as old as Hegel's charge of 'empty formalism' against Kant's ethics. Four contemporary debates in which this problem has been debated are worth mentioning. First, Arthur Ripstein's neo-Kantian theory claims that an equal right to freedom-as-independence can ground political theory, without relying on further claims about the values or interests represented by particular instances of freedom/independence (Ripstein 2009). This formalist strategy has been attacked with substantive counterexamples by, among others (Ebels-Duggan 2011; Sangiovanni 2012; Valentini 2012). Second, Carter (1999) criticizes value-based theories of freedom, but as Sugden (2003) shows, similar problems arise for the quantitatively oriented theories of freedom of Steiner (1994) and Carter himself. This debate is assessed in Garnett (2016). Third, there is the context of theories of personal autonomy, see Christman (2004), Mackenzie (2008), Richardson (2001) and J. Anderson (2014). This debate is further assessed in Section 5.2. For the fourth debate, see note 7 hereafter.

can be invoked to specify the costs of exit, so that we do not require going beyond agency to include perfectionist values (Section 5.4). Second, there is also a question whether individuals have a right to associate – i.e. to enter social practices. I endorse a conditional version of the right to inclusion, based on whether a practice is indispensable to the realization of the basic capabilities on the list (Section 5.5).

5.1 Empowerment Capabilities

A main aim of the theory of navigational agency is to argue for empowering individuals. I first discuss how to define empowerment capabilities. Subsequently I argue that a further specification of each of these capabilities need not run into the 'incorporation problem' raised earlier as a potential problem for liberal-perfectionist theories.

Navigational agents were defined as those capable of: (1) entering and exiting social practices; (2) resolving conflicts between practices; (3) reforming existing practices; and (4) creating new practices (see Section 2.3). An agent who is able to do this is empowered. This four-fold typology of elements of agency can be reduced to two basic categories, on a rough analogy with Albert Hirschman's distinction between exit and voice (Hirschman 1970). The capabilities to exit and enter social practices and to resolve conflicting demands are capabilities for an individual to choose her or his own *location* amid existing practices, characterized by existing institutions. The individual's freedom is a freedom not to participate, or to participate on her or his own terms, to certain parts of social life. Individual empowerment doesn't require social practices to change to accommodate everyone's wishes, but it requires leaving individuals a choice whether or not to take part in them. By contrast, the capability to reform practices – with creating new practices as a limit case of reform – does change the existing *institutions* which characterize social practices. Empowerment in this mode means giving individuals the ability to participate in the governance of social practices, giving them voice. It requires second-order, governance rights (see Section 3.1). Hence empowerment has two modes: it refers to the ability to change one's location in an existing structure or to change the institutions of the social practices in which one participates.[4]

---

[4] The terminology of empowerment fits well within a capability approach, for it is not far-fetched to claim that capabilities are powers. For a discussion of the concept of empowerment in the context of development ethics and the capability approach, see Drydyk (2008, 2013) and Khader (2011). See also Peter Morriss who has rightly claimed that Sen's notion of a capability is just another term

Empowerment capabilities have a central place since they are those capabilities that distinguish navigational from participational agents. The distinction between both types of agents maps onto the distinction between subsistence capabilities (the topic of the next chapter) and empowerment capabilities. To participate in social practices one needs to subsist, and for that one needs to have access to nourishment, food, shelter, etc. These subsistence capabilities, however, do not make one into an agent who has the two modes of control over her or his location and participation in social practices described above. For that one needs specific empowerment capabilities. The subsistence/empowerment dichotomy is based on this distinction between two modes of social existence, that of a participational and a navigational agent. However, it should not be understood normatively, as referring to the *rights* of both types of agent. A mere-participational agent doesn't necessarily have claim-rights to subsistence (or to anything else, see Section 3.1). Only a society in which individuals have the standing of navigational agents grants rights to both subsistence and empowerment to all citizens. Finally, rights to political capabilities (to be dealt with in Chapter 7) are instrumental to both subsistence and empowerment rights. They give citizens the opportunity to specify and enforce claims to these rights. While having one's political capabilities guaranteed is a form of empowerment itself, I will – to avoid confusion – only use the term empowerment for the direct empowerment of agents in civil (as distinct from political) life.

What belongs into the category of empowerment capabilities? Following the distinction between the freedom-side and the autonomy-side of agency (see Section 2.1), two subsets of empowerment capabilities can be usefully distinguished. One subset is the traditional civil rights found in human rights documents, at least the freedom of assembly and association, freedom of movement, freedom of conscience, thought and religion, freedom of expression, privacy and the right to property.[5] These can be understood as giving people freedom to action-possibilities, in space (freedom of movement for public space, privacy for private space), encounters with others (freedom of association), communication with others (freedom of expression) and control of objects (property), etc. On the other hand, there are those capabilities necessary to develop

---

for a 'power-to' (Morriss 2002, xxii–xxv), i.e. an ability to do something. Despite this association, I have chosen to use the term empowerment for a subset of all capabilities.

[5] I will here stay agnostic on some other capabilities, which are often included in human rights treaties: rights to non-discrimination, a right to (meaningful) work and/or leisure, and a right to marry (and to reproduce and have a family life). Whether, and in which sense, these are strictly necessary for navigational agency and/or not already (implicitly) captured by other basic capabilities, requires further study.

the capacities for autonomous deliberation as well as the knowledge of society necessary to orient oneself in the existing social world. In this subset belongs a capability for being educated, where I take education to encompass both formal education as well as (more controversially) being brought up by parents in a way that stimulates a child's autonomy. We should not make too much of the distinction between the freedom-based and the autonomy-based subsets, however, since the civil liberties also contribute indirectly to autonomy (and some of them are also highly important in effective exercises of the political capabilities, or should themselves also belong on the list of political capabilities).

This rough indication of the content of the set of empowerment capabilities obviously leaves open many questions of specification. Let's assume that a specific capability is selected as necessary for navigational agency, and then ask whether we can give concrete content to this capability without referring to other values. Take the capability of free movement and imagine the following situation. A new city is built and the city council needs to decide whether to build infrastructure for cars or for public transport (imagine there is no space for both). Car transport appears to be on average more costly for citizens, less environmentally friendly for future generations, offering less opportunities for spontaneous social interactions between strangers, but quicker in terms of reaching one's destination. What should the council choose? The example shows how making a decision about how to specify citizens' rights to freedom of movement requires an institutional choice between options which differ in terms of four other values: (1) environmental sustainability; (2) monetary cost; (3) community formation; and (4) speed of transportation. Now the strategy for responding to the incorporation problem is to distinguish between two different relations between navigational agency and other values. Some values may be reducible to agency while others are irreducible. The theory incorporates both sets of values, but in a very different way.

Reducible values are values that represent an interest which, on further analysis, is an interest in navigational agency. Values give us reasons for action, and the reason adduced by reducible values is an agency-interest after all. Arguably, sustainability is such a reducible value. It normally refers to considerations about protecting the ecological environment which go back to the necessary role of the environment in sustaining the life of human agents (and, if one includes animals in the category of agents as well, animals). Hence, conflicts between freedom/autonomy and sustainability are better modelled as conflicts between the agency of different (groups of) agents. One prominent conflict, in the context of sustainability, is the conflict between preserving the conditions of agency for current generations and for future generations. But there may be other conflicts as well (e.g., internationally, between Northern and Southern states, or inter-species conflicts between human and animal agents). In all these cases, however, there isn't really an 'other values problem' for liberal theorizing in general and my theory in particular. Arguably, the value of monetary cost in this case is also a reducible value. Politics requires making decisions about conflicting demands, and fights over budgets are one particularly prominent form that these conflicts take. The city council doesn't balance the agency-interest of freedom of movement against monetary cost, but against the set of other agency-interests that also press on the city budget.[6]

Irreducible values are other values which are non-reducible to agency. Here we are only considering those irreducible values that *need* to be taken into account when making a specific decision about how to realize an agency-interest, i.e. those values which are practically unavoidable when trying to protect conditions for navigational agency. Arguably community formation and speed of transportation are in this category. Within a normal range, having more or less speedy transport will not make a difference for the threshold-level of agency-capabilities of those who are transported, and similarly having more community interactions will not have an effect upon agency. Note that not making a decision about these irreducible values is not an option, if one wants to decide on a transportation system. Any transportation system by its nature has its own characteristics pertaining to speed and community formation; and hence one needs to consciously deliberate how to weigh them in the decision (this is different from, say, values which are arguably unaffected by transportation system choices, such as, let's assume, the level of artistic production or the sense of humour available in the community).

I propose the agency-theory's stance is to be *indifferent* with respect to competing choices about how to deal with practically necessary irreducible values.[7] As long as some transportation system is chosen which

---

[6] None of this implies that reducible values are wholly reducible. Some may be only partially reducible. When they contain aspects that are irreducible to agency (e.g. beauty considerations in the case of environmental sustainability), these should be treated under the second category.

[7] Philip Pettit comes to a similar conclusion, distinguishing the value of republican freedom from whatever value decisions are necessary in making systems of rules necessary to realise basic liberties (Pettit 2008). The difference is that he has a very different conceptualization of the relation between republic freedom and basic liberties than I have between navigational agency and basic capabilities. He thinks that republican freedom requires that the basic liberties should be 'as numerous as

realizes the agency-related capability at stake up to the required threshold level, the theory is indifferent about the choices concerning the non-agency aspects of transportation. From the point of view of justice, all of them are equally good. The condition for the justice of such decisions about irreducible non-agency values here is the more general one that the decision is made in a democratically legitimated procedure (that this is a condition of agency is the subject of Chapter 7). There is no reason to think that this is a weakness; that a moderate perfectionist liberal theory would have to abstain from making judgements which include a stance on non-liberal values. There is a real difference between a theory which focuses the state's efforts on free and autonomous agency and allows for other values to influence choices between equally just, but different, ways of realizing agency and a theory which focuses on the realization of non-agency values as a legitimizing ground of state action directly and separately.

A related critique on liberal theories has been that they – just as much as other theories – require *judgement* in the application of principles to concrete circumstances. Such judgements would bring all kinds of new considerations into the picture, which were not contained in the principles themselves. But it is no fault of the theory that deciding which values are reducible to agency and which ones aren't requires judgement (e.g., some may try to argue that a more speedy transportation system brings in options for accepting jobs farther away from home, hence has a liberating, navigational effect on agents; others may dispute this claim). Judgement is also needed to select capabilities themselves, deal with conflicts between them, and also to assess the importance of the many empirical uncertainties that surround public-policy problems. But this ubiquitous need for judgement doesn't remove the guiding force of normative principles (such as navigational agency or its competitors) in making those judgements. Hence it doesn't remove the usefulness of a philosophical discussion about which of these principles to adopt. Obviously, this requires showing how principles guide and constrain – without deductively determining – judgements in concrete application, something I cannot go into here (Nussbaum 2000a; O. O'Neill 2001, 2007; Ronzoni 2010).

---

possible', while I would state that they are selected for their functional role in making people into navigational agents. Pettit follows up on a debate about the formulation of the basic liberties principle in John Rawls. Here the question is how to define the 'most extensive' system of liberties without recourse to other values than liberty itself. See Hart (1983), O. O'Neill (1979) and Rawls (2005).

With this general position in mind, let's now dive more deeply into the two hard cases of adaptive preferences and the freedom of association, where the challenge of the incorporation problem will return as well.

5.2 Autonomy and Adaptive Preferences

Sometimes people, especially in the face of oppression or deprivation, adapt their preferences to their circumstances. This phenomenon has been a reason for Sen (1985a, 1992) and Nussbaum (2000b, 2001) to criticize utilitarianism's potential for correctly identifying injustices.[8] When subjective reports of well-being are unreliable to identify morally just states of affairs, a move to more objective indicators is needed; this insight was an important inspiration behind the development of the capability approach. However, this does not yet help us how to deal with adaptive preferences in a constructive way. Some, like Nussbaum, understand the move to objective indicators as calling for a separate theory of the good. This would lead to a directly perfectionist theory. I will argue that my theory of autonomous agency can provide a credible alternative. It does not fall prey to the incorporation problem: we can specify a theory of autonomy without bringing in other (objectionably perfectionist) values through the back door.

Adaptive preferences were introduced by Jon Elster to describe cases in which people adjust their preferences to their circumstances. His main example was that of a fox, who, having noticed that he cannot get the grapes that he would like to eat, deceives himself into believing that they are sour, and changes his preferences accordingly (Elster 1982). In contrast to this thought example, the literature on autonomy takes as central cases of adaptive preferences real-life cases in which people suffering from various forms of oppression come to accept their social circumstances and abandon any wishes for improving their lot. Women in traditional patriarchal cultures being oppressed by their husbands and leading a confined life within the household are a paradigmatic example. Nussbaum discusses the case of a woman named Vasanti who was abused by her husband and who cannot come to conceive of the situation as one

---

[8] For other treatments from a capability perspective, see Teschl and Comim (2005), Khader (2011, 2012), Conradie and Robeyns (2013) and Begon (2015). For philosophical treatments of adaptive preferences outside of the capability approach, which mainly respond to Elster, see for example Baber (2007), Bruckner (2009) and Colburn (2011). The issue is also widely discussed in the literature on autonomy, in relation to the question of oppression of vulnerable groups. See Christman (2014) and Stoljar (2014) and further references therein.

in which her rights are violated and decides to stay with her husband and put up with the abuse. Another example she gives is of Jamayamma who does not protest against the discrimination she experiences in getting paid less for her work than men and in doing more of the household work than her husband (Nussbaum 2001, 68–9). These and other cases suggest something is wrong when people adapt their preferences to their circumstances. But when, exactly, and why should we speak of adaptive preferences? The practical importance of this question is that if a person's preference is an expression of problematic adaptation to her or his deprivation, this may provide a ground for paternalist interventions by public authorities, while if the preference is a genuinely voluntarily formed preference, such intervention would be disrespectful and unwarranted. The diagnosis of what is going on in cases of adaptive preference thus has real-life consequences for determining the legitimacy of public actions.

Nussbaum has rightly argued that the mere causal phenomenon of adaptation to circumstance cannot be problematic in itself. We all adjust our childhood wishes to become famous opera singers or basketball players as our lives unfold and we realize our shortcomings, Nussbaum notes, and this kind of realism is normally a good thing. The concept of adaptive preferences is introduced with a specific normative aim: to identify *bad* cases of adaptation and the mere idea of adaptation is not going to do the work. Elster introduces the idea of a lack of a 'freedom to do otherwise' (Elster 1982, 228). An autonomous want for X is formed under the condition that one has the freedom to do both X or not. Since the fox is not free to get to the grapes, his decision is non-autonomous. For him adaptive preferences are a sign of non-autonomous decision-making. Nussbaum claims that this focus on autonomy misidentifies the real problem. The adult adapting her or his career plans when seeing she or he doesn't have a real talent for opera singing doesn't have the freedom to become an opera-singer. But the cases which interest us are ones in which we have a right to the alternative, and we are deprived of that right. We need to evaluate the different cases according to whether the individuals expressing the preference were in a situation of oppression, understood as the violation of their rights. Here Nussbaum claims that we need 'a substantive theory of justice and central goods' to identify these rights (Nussbaum 2001, 79). Her list of central capabilities she proposes to do this work. Similarly, Serene Khader has criticized autonomy-based theories of adaptive preferences and proposes a perfectionist theory in which a preference is adaptive when it is 'incompatible with an agent's basic welfare and is causally related to the conditions of oppression under which it formed' (Khader 2012, 310, see also 2011, 42).

I will not argue directly against perfectionist theories here, since I have done this elaborately in Chapter 1. The same criticisms made there also apply to perfectionism in identifying adaptive preferences, as argued convincingly by Terlazzo (2014).[9] Instead I will show how my theory of navigational agency, suitably applied, can take a convincing view with respect to the problem of adaptive preferences.

The challenge confronting the construction of such an autonomy-based alternative is that it will be indirectly perfectionist, and in that sense no better than more straightforwardly perfectionist views. Let's explain this by reference to the two main types of theories of personal autonomy. So-called procedural (or content-neutral) theories of autonomy require certain competences for reflective deliberation but do not engage with the content of the preferences once these competences are available (Frankfurt 1971; G. Dworkin 1988; Christman 2009). Substantive theories in addition to these competences put certain content-requirements on the preferences of autonomous decision-makers. One prominent example would be a substantive theory requiring that persons must value their own capacities for autonomous decision-making; hence a person 'choosing' an action which undermines her or his own status as an autonomous person would be classified as making that choice non-autonomously. Under these theories, it is ruled out as unthinkable that we bring ourselves in certain oppressive, humiliating or depraved conditions; hence an ideal of the autonomous person as a substantively independent person emerges (Oshana 1998; Stoljar 2000). Using this distinction Rosa Terlazzo has argued that we can reconstruct a dilemma. If we accept a procedural theory, we are bound to have too little critical purchase on adaptive preferences. Since many of them are made in conformity with the competencies of critical reflection central to procedural theories, they cannot be classified as non-autonomous, hence state interference with them is unjustified. But if we accept a substantive theory we are bound to classify too many preferences as adaptive, condemning as non-autonomous some preferences which may be made by persons in full awareness of what they are doing (Terlazzo 2016, 213–14). In terms of the standard example of the deferential housewife,

---

[9] Terlazzo (2014) only responds to Nussbaum. Khader's deliberative approach to the formulation of human flourishing makes her less vulnerable to Terlazzo's critique. For criticisms of Khader from the perspective of autonomy-based theories, see Stoljar (2014) and Terlazzo (2016).

who voluntarily chooses a lifestyle marked by a traditional gender-based division of labour and submission to the judgements of her husband, a procedural theory would classify her always as autonomous (if minimal critical reflection was present) while a substantial theory would always classify her as non-autonomous (if the submission was bad enough).[10]

Substantive theories of autonomy, it is often argued, risk bringing in perfectionism within one's theory of autonomy. John Christman is representative of this complaint where he addresses it against a species of substantive views, i.e. relational theories of autonomy:

> Relational theorists who decry procedural views on the grounds that they would allow voluntary slavery to masquerade as autonomy are in fact supporting a conception of autonomy which is an *ideal* of individualized self-government, an ideal that those who choose strict obedience or hierarchical power structures have decided to reject. Those whose value conceptions manifest relatively blurred lines between self and other, who downplay the value of individualized judgments and embrace devotion to an externally defined normative structure (which may include obedience to particular human authorities) stand in defiance of the normative ideals that relational views of autonomy put forward. (Christman 2004, 151)

To avoid perfectionism, it is better to defend a procedural theory of autonomy. And indeed, as I show in a moment, the theory of autonomous agency presented in Chapter 2 can best be seen as such a theory.

---

[10] To keep my discussion tractable, I ignore the subtilities of the debate between these positions and especially the emergence of a weakly substantive position which in addition to procedural conditions also requires that autonomous agents possess some sense of self-worth (Benson 1994), responsiveness to others (Westlund 2003) or active self-governance (Kristinsson 2000). Each of these additional requirements would be incompatible with certain values, in the sense that it would condemn particular types of self-deprecating and deferential attitudes (characteristic of persons with adaptive preferences) as non-autonomous. Hence it would not be neutral to these attitudes. Strinkingly, some proceduralists (Christman 2014, 216) and strong substantivists (Stoljar 2014, 240, n. 61) now converge on this compromise position. In the main text I have chosen to proceed on the assumption that a procedural theory is *sufficient*, and such a weakly substantive position is thus *unnecessary* for diagnosing why persons who wish for their own submission are to be judged non-autonomous: i.e. they can be understood as failing the authenticity conditions (for a defence along this line see Christman 2009, 156–63). However, there is something attractive about the weak-substantive position as well (especially in light of the egalitarian self-respect our rational mere-participational agent in Chapter 3 has been shown to be committed to). I think the weak-substantive position would also be compatible with my conclusions in this section. Accepting it would mean introducing in my analysis – in the terminology of the incorporation problem – certain *irreducible* values (self-respect, etc.) and defend them as a *necessary* by-product of the specification of agency (see Section 5.1). It should be noted that the only difference between the procedural and the weak-substantive positions in practical terms is in the status of the phenomenon of voluntary submission (row 4 in Table 5.1) and one's political attitude towards this phenomenon (as discussed in Section 5.3). It is questionable whether this is pragmatically and politically a very significant category anyhow, compared to the other categories in Table 5.1.

This means that (in terms of Terlazzo's dilemma) the risk for me is to err on the side of not taking cases of adaptive preferences seriously enough, sanctioning them too quickly as autonomous; and while staving off this risk at the same time remaining on the procedural, non-perfectionist side of autonomy theories. Can this be done?

Earlier I presented agency as consisting of an autonomy-part and a freedom-part. A free and autonomous agent (1a) has capacities for autonomous deliberation, (1b) is non-manipulated when exercising these capacities, (2a) has capacities to act freely and (2b) has options for free action without coercion by others. The a-clauses are internal to the person, the b-clauses external to the person (see Section 2.1, especially Table 2.1). Here I will use the two conditions for autonomy (1a, b) and the options requirement (2b) to diagnose adaptive preferences. Moreover, I propose to understand my non-manipulation clause (1b) in terms of what John Christman has called the 'authenticity requirement'. According to him, and many others, autonomy consists of two sets of conditions. On the one hand, one must have competences for practical reasoning, critical reflection, or as I have called it autonomous deliberation (1a). On the other hand, autonomous agents have to be authentic. The values, plans and desires which they hold must somehow be endorsed by them, truly as their own. This requirement can be spelled out in various ways. Christman argues there is authenticity when a hypothetical reflection in the absence of 'reflection-distorting factors' leads to 'non-alienation'. Many desires, traits and choices in daily life are not consciously reflected upon; this is in itself not problematic. However, for the autonomous person it must be true that were she to critically reflect on them, she would continue to feel satisfied with having these desires, etc. Was she to feel repelled or alienated by them ('Is this me? This is not who I want to be'), then she is non-autonomous. Such a reflection cannot take place under conditions which distort one's reasoning, for otherwise one's reasoning process would not count as one's own, but as manipulated by others (Christman 2009, 149–56).

With this definition of procedural autonomy in hand, we can now diagnose the problem of adaptive preferences. I will distinguish several types of agency-deficits, which, although they may superficially resemble adaptive preferences, need to be understood as really different types of problems (see Table 5.1).

First, there are cases where people suffer from a lack of critical-reflection skills. Call these cases of *incompetent reasoning* (row 1 in Table 5.1). Typical examples in this category include young children or

Table 5.1. *Typology of submissive preferences*

Diagnosis: does the agent display...	Capacities for deliberation	Authenticity (non-manipulation)	Options to act (non-coercion)	Political response
1. Incompetent reasoning	No	No	Yes or no	Paternalist action
2. Adaptive preference	Yes	No	Yes or no	Critical deliberation
3. Adaptive choice	Yes	Yes	No	Improve options
4. Voluntary submission	Yes	Yes	Yes	Abstention or prohibition

severely mentally disabled persons, or those with more local autonomy deficits in particular situations. I would disagree with those who conflate adaptive preferences with lack of critical reflection skills. The reasons for this are well explained by Serene Khader who stresses that when procedural theories of autonomy are put to work on the problem of adaptive preferences, they serve to classify many preferences as non-autonomous. However, she argues, many oppressed women in third-world countries show ample capacities of critical reflection, even when they decide to submit to their circumstances (Khader 2011, 80–3). For example, they may be submissive to their husbands, but then show highly critical levels of reflectiveness when dealing with other family members. In doing so, they may be strategically negotiating their limited options in a way which defies the judgement that they lack critical capacities for reflection in general. Khader is right to assume that in cases we are intuitively classifying as adaptive preferences there still is a capacity for reflection available, which deserves respect. Hence, we need to locate the problem of adaptive preferences in situations where capacities for critical thinking and reflective endorsement are present, but they are exercised in such a way as to endorse states of voluntary submission.

The second type of situation is one of what I will call *adaptive choices* (row 3 in Table 5.1). While this is in my view an important class of cases of adaptation, I would also argue that these are not cases of adaptive preference. In these situations, the problem is not internal to the agent (as with a lack of critical reflection skills), but a person adapts to the fact that external options for action are restricted. This requires identifying those options to which adaptation is problematic, which – according to Nussbaum and Khader – requires a perfectionist theory of human flourishing. In response, I would first of all diagnose these cases not in terms of a theory of the good but in terms of a theory of agency requirements. Reading the options-requirement in terms of basic capabilities to navigational agency gives us a non-perfectionist way of singling out the problematic cases of adaptation. Where persons do not have access to speaking or moving freely in public spaces, sufficient nourishment or shelter, or any of the other basic capabilities, they may adapt to these deprivations. This allows us to refrain from adopting a non-perfectionist framework while nonetheless recognizing and respecting the capacities for autonomous deliberation of the oppressed.[11] If so, Elster was right, after all, to focus on the importance of the 'freedom to do otherwise', albeit that he should have understood this as applying to specific freedoms (capabilities) in order to single out the problematic cases of adaptation.

What makes this category different from adaptive preferences is that these agents are not manipulated into making certain choices they themselves see as worthwhile. Rather, they have authentically chosen for the best choice given the (poor) circumstances. The causes of the latter may vary: a government may have failed to make certain capabilities available to all, or private third-parties (husbands) may be coercing others (housewives) so that they do not really have access to these capabilities. Admittedly, it can be tricky in practice to distinguish such cases of coercion from manipulation. When a husband regularly beats his wife when she leaves the house without his permission this counts as coercion, but when such a pattern of violence in the end socializes her into believing that a restricted pattern of movement is the best for her, then it becomes a case of adaptive preference. However difficult to observe in practice, adaptive choice (non-coercion) and adaptive preference (non-manipulation) should be seen as distinct phenomena. The widespread reported strategic behaviour under conditions of oppression testifies to the conclusion that many oppressed persons remain (in thought) at a real distance from consenting to their oppression. They make the best of a difficult situation (Baber 2007). They might be repelled and feel alienated

---

[11] Terlazzo builds an options-requirement into the concept of autonomy. The main difference is that she does not specify these 'valuable alternative options' by reference to a theory of free and autonomous agency itself (Terlazzo 2016, 215). She remains agnostic on how to specify them, but hints at an 'informed desire approach'. Here perfectionism may creep in through the backdoor.

from their situation as a whole, but not from the particular strategy which they have chosen to deal with the situation, given the constraints of the circumstances.

Third, then, we have *adaptive preferences* which occur where manipulation works so as to distort a process of (hypothetical) critical reflection (row 2 in Table 5.1). Persons with adaptive preferences have a genuine preference for their submission, oppression or deprivation, but this preference is formed under suspect conditions (Colburn 2011; Stoljar 2014, 236–8). These persons do not believe their constraints cannot be changed, but rather that these constraints should not be changed; that they are justified constraints on their freedom of action. Manipulation can take two forms. The most direct form is where a person withholds information or exerts pressure on another person so as to make that person believe something she or he wouldn't otherwise believe (the belief can relate to empirical information about the availability of outside options, but also to the assessment of value-patterns). Less directly, however, are cases where social norms exert a manipulating influence, for example where a group maintains a system of social norms that manipulates the preferences of its members, by making them believe that certain society-widely available options for action are to be condemned as immoral. Whatever the form of manipulation, the test case for identifying an adaptive preference is: would the person endorse the preference if she or he reflected on it under conditions of non-manipulation? Hence the framework of a procedural theory of autonomy, it seems to me, is sufficient to identify adaptive preferences.[12]

This test of manipulation should be understood as applicable to the same range of options as the ones which are problematic for adaptive choices: the option being blocked by manipulation needs to be one from the set of basic capabilities. Both adaptive choices and adaptive preferences are only problematic in a political sense if they pertain to this set (remembering Nussbaum's earlier point: we still need to distinguish healthy from problematic cases of adaption). Note that in the category of adaptive preferences we sometimes may find situations where the outside

---

[12] Some may object that – since there is always a system of social norms in place – it is impossible to identify manipulation. How to distinguish manipulation from innocent forms of social influences on individual preferences? While this may be difficult in practice, theoretically it seems to me there is no need for perfectionism here. One first needs to identify the class of *suspect* preferences, which is those for a sub-threshold level of functioning on one or more of the basic capabilities. Second, one needs to test whether the suspicion is correct, by analyzing the *causal mechanism* leading to the acceptance of the social norm: was it the direct influence of the social norm itself or (also) the (hypothetical) endorsement of the agent? (see also Section 5.3).

options (basic capabilities) will actually be available, in the sense that the person, if not manipulated, would have been able to choose them. In other cases of adaptive preferences, however, these options may not be available. In the latter cases, society as a whole converges with the directly manipulating individual or group in putting an option beyond the reach of the person; for example, society prohibits women from divorcing without the consent of their husbands, and the group in which a woman is embedded makes her believe such a rule is justified. Here the manipulation is doing the real (causal) work, we assume (otherwise it is a case of adaptive choices), but the option would not have been available anyhow. Then two battles are necessary, instead of one.

Finally, adaptive preferences can also subtly resemble, yet diverge from, yet another category, where preferences for submission or oppression are formed without any form of manipulation or coercion: cases of *voluntary submission* (row 4 in Table 5.1). These preferences we must respect as in line with both the freedom-conditions and the autonomy-conditions of agency. Purely substantive theories of autonomy would deny that such a category of cases exists, the denial being based upon a reformulation of autonomy that makes submission definitionally incompatible with autonomy. On a procedural theory of autonomy, however, we do recognize the existence of such cases. How to deal with them in terms of political response is another matter, which I will discuss in the next section.

While in this section I have engaged in the definitional battles over what 'really' is a case of adaptive preferences, the upshot should be that reality offers different types of problems which all superficially have some affinity with the diagnosis of 'someone consenting to her own oppression'. Which of these phenomena in the end we lend the name 'adaptive preference' is not so important. What is important is to have a clear diagnostic tool to distinguish different types of cases, in order to be able to also differentiate our reactions to them in an appropriate way. The typology offered here hopefully helps for such clear-headed diagnoses. The next section discusses appropriate responses.

5.3   The Legitimation of Paternalist Interferences

In the capability literature the question of paternalism is generally discussed in terms of promoting functionings instead of capabilities (Nussbaum 2000b; Carter 2014; Claassen 2014a, 2019a). One might think that capability theories can only mandate states to intervene in citizen's lives in order to promote their capabilities (here: capabilities for agency) – i.e. there never is a justice-based justification for governments to act on the paternalist ground that citizens' wellbeing should be promoted directly, by promoting their functionings instead of capabilities. However, this would be a mistake. While focusing on capabilities is the rule, the idea is that there may be exceptional cases when people are justifiably forced into functioning in specific ways. But when, how many and for what reasons? In this section I will show how the political response needs to differ depending on the situations we encountered in the previous section.

An argument for paternalist interferences in the case of autonomy-deficits is a standard part of liberal theorizing. Agency is a gradual concept, and the same is true of the capabilities for agency. Agency needs to be developed and this implies that citizens will have navigational agency-deficits, either globally (across the board) or in a more targeted area, with respect to some subset of capabilities. In these cases, justice may require of governments, in addition to trying to bring people up to the threshold level, to promote citizens' functionings directly. This is in line with Joel Feinberg's defence of 'soft paternalism' as part of liberal theory: when individuals are unable to exercise autonomous choices themselves, governments may have reason to make choices on their behalf (Feinberg 1986). Paternalist measures on behalf of vulnerable or dependent individuals may be warranted. Given the gradual and local nature of agency-deficits, we may all be insufficiently autonomous in some contexts to make choices. Not to intervene may then be a form of serious neglect. It is a big question how to conceptualize these deficits and how far to take this in concrete contexts. Nonetheless, the general line is clear enough, and I will not enquire into the countless practical questions of border-drawing here. On the other hand, within the logic of liberalism, 'hard paternalism' is ruled out. When agents are sufficiently autonomous, they cannot legitimately be interfered with. How to bring these general ideas to bear upon the problem of adaptive preferences and the cases we distinguished from it earlier?

Let's start with a forceful argument made by Khader who has criticized autonomy-based theories of adaptive preferences for licensing paternalist interventions of a coercive sort. If people are non-autonomous, there is, according to such theories, no harm in coercively imposing the good on them. But this would risk being disrespectful, especially in the context of oppressed persons whose capacities for critical reflection, as mentioned above, may tend to be overlooked by outsiders (Khader 2011, 103). While this risk is real, there is no reason to assume that an autonomy-based theory of paternalism must be uniquely committed to coercion, especially where less intrusive means are available (Stoljar 2014, 250). The term 'intervention' can be understood as covering a full range of policy options, from improving legal guarantees to education and providing information, from facilitating real exit-options (see next section) to, in extreme cases, coercion. Moreover, neither need intervention always be paternalist. Let's run through the four cases distinguished earlier.

The case of the *incompetent reasoner* is indeed a classical case which would qualify for some form of paternalist action. The goal would be to bring the reasoner up to the level of competence in terms of capacities for autonomous deliberation, if possible. If this would be durably impossible, a case would arise for long-term involvement to help the person reach certain levels of well-being. Also relatively straightforward is the response to cases of *adaptive choice*. Here a diagnosis is necessary of the legal protections and material facilities made available by a society to check if they effectively guarantee a set of basic capabilities for each citizen. If not, action to remedy these defects is called for. More difficult are cases where adaptive choice occurs because of coercion by a third-party, as within a group of which the victim is a member. Then an assessment of the situation from the outside is necessary – as when the doctor is enquiring: 'were these bruises the result of physical abuse by one's family member, or, as the patient claims, a fall from the stairs?' This may potentially be intrusive and coercive, but rightly so. Intra-group coercion then is responded to by public coercion to prevent the former. In all cases of adaptive choice, the response is *not* paternalist interference (on grounds of 'harm-to-self'), but interference on grounds of harm to others (harm understood in terms of violations of access to the basic capabilities).

Most difficult is the question how to distinguish cases of *adaptive preferences* from cases of voluntary submission. Here the first guideline for public intervention would be to find out. Hence if there is any preferred strategy for intervention to start with, it is communication and deliberation with those who may be oppressed. We may have hope that most oppressed people, upon intensive engagement and interrogation by outsiders (and effective outside protections) will be inclined to recognize their own oppression and change their preferences. In the context of human development worldwide, such a deliberative strategy may be very effective (Conradie and Robeyns 2013). Coercion then is not needed. On the other side, there may be situations where it is impossible to find out whether consent was truly voluntary without coercive interventions. If one wants to know whether a woman doesn't appear in public because of her husband's manipulation, or out of her own will, then, on the model of adaptive preferences described above, she will have to be brought in a situation where she effectively enjoys the capability of free movement. But this requires counteracting manipulating actions and social norms (assuming they are the effective obstacle keeping her home). If such a change doesn't happen after awareness-raising efforts which create the prospect of such a change by imagining it *in thought*, then only an outside interference *in the reality* of their family life, which coerces both husband and wife into a new pattern of mutual expectations (imagining such a thing could be done) can guarantee the capability for the woman – after which she can then choose whether or not to continue living as she did before or stick with the new pattern. This coercive 're-set' to a state where capabilities are open, so that they can then voluntarily be closed off, is a merely theoretical idea. In practice public authorities will face a choice between soft measures changing cultural norms or breaking up private practices entirely and continuously. But if the freedom to forgo a basic capability is to remain more than a theoretical option, the latter must be a bridge too far. For some suspect preferences, a liberal society will – after probing, persuading and deliberating – have to conclude they are formed under conditions of sufficient autonomy and a sufficient availability of basic capabilities to act otherwise.

This brings us to the last category, of cases of *voluntary submission*, where the political stance will have to be to accept submission on grounds of its being autonomously chosen in the presence of all the basic capabilities to choose otherwise. It may be hard to get one's head around these voluntary choices, but some have suggested that gendered patterns of actions and other cases of submission do persist even when all forms of coercion and manipulation have been cancelled (Levey 2005; Baber 2007; Stoljar 2014). This prohibition of hard paternalism may be, to some, problematic in cases where the oppression takes on extreme forms – such as those of voluntary slavery, torture or maltreatment. Sometimes we may feel that such practices should be interfered with no matter what the victims themselves claim. Would such an attitude be inconsistent with a liberal framework based on procedural autonomy? While this is a hard case, I think that it remains important to make a distinction between a position which claims that such forms of oppression are incompatible with autonomy by definition and a position claiming that a categorical prohibition of such practices is based on the practical presupposition that 99 per cent of the cases will turn out to be ones where manipulation and/or coercion is involved. The latter policy consciously errs in 1 per cent of the cases so as to be able to have an effective policy response to the 99 per cent. Possibly expressive arguments about the possibly contagious effect such practices may have on others, or arguments about the impossibility of reversing one's decisions to give up one's autonomy, may also be admissible within a framework based on procedural autonomy. I cannot discuss these matters further here.

In conclusion, adaptive preferences are one major obstacle to the full enjoyment of the empowerment capabilities in society. There may be a legal framework and other formal guarantees that one can move about freely, express one's opinion, associate freely with others and choose to practice a religion or not. But if cultural and social norms claiming that certain of these options should not be exercised by some categories of people become accepted by these people themselves, then these capabilities are not truly guaranteed. Such norms need to be countered, and how to do this without disrespecting those who cooperate in reproducing these norms in their daily practices is the challenge adaptive preferences pose.

5.4 Freedom of Association and the Right to Exit

The agency-based capability theory requires that citizens are able to voluntarily enter and exit practices and/or have a voice in them. I will consider the question what it actually means to have these abilities in focusing on one particular empowerment capability: the ability to associate, or freedom of association. While I would not go so far as to grant the freedom of association a privileged theoretical status (Kukathas 2003), it does have an important place given my definition of agency in terms of the participation in social practices. Many discussions about the freedom to practice one's culture or religion, about non-discrimination and rights to education are strongly related to the freedom of association. In discussing the freedom of association, the incorporation problem will emerge again as a key challenge: Can this capability be specified without an appeal to other values? In this section, I will argue that we can: the reference to the set of basic capabilities as a whole is sufficient to operationalize one key demand of the freedom of association: the 'right to exit'.

There are two sides to the right to freedom of association. On the one hand this right would give everyone the right to exit associations when she or he wants to, while on the other hand it would give associations the right to exclude individuals when they want to. The former right can be pretty straightforwardly related to the interest in personal autonomy (L. Green 1998); to be able to lead an autonomous life, one has to be able to choose one's own attachments with others.[13] The latter right is related to autonomy more indirectly, the rough idea being that for individuals to be able to associate with others in groups, they need the power to decide with whom to associate, hence also with whom *not* to associate. For both rights, a similar tension arises, hence we can roughly discern two competing positions: a more individualist position which grants strong, effective rights of exit, and tends to restrict the power of groups to exclude versus a more associationist position which grants merely formal, weak rights of exit and tends to leave groups ample powers of exclusion (S. White 2013). In this section I will deal with the right to exit, and in the following section I discuss the right to exclude.

To orientate our minds, let's consider a paradigmatic case of exit. Imagine a member of an orthodox religious community wants to leave this community out of dissatisfaction with the norms it imposes on believers. However, such a decision imposes costs on her: (1) she will no longer be able to attend its religious meetings; (2) members of the community – including long-standing friends – will break off contact with her; and (3) members from the community will refuse to hire her for jobs. The right to exit is assumed to guarantee that navigational agents are voluntarily engaged in whatever practices they choose themselves. However, as this example highlights, there are always costs to leaving a practice. Some of these costs may be so heavy that we may judge that these costs make us unfree to do so. If so, the right to exit is violated. The suspicion is that in making these judgements we tacitly need to rely on other values than freedom itself. For example, in discussing when we call something a constraint on our freedom, David Miller argued that this ascription depends on whether someone bears moral responsibility for this constraint. But this judgement on moral responsibility cannot in a circular vein point back to freedom, hence 'judgments about freedom cannot be wholly value-neutral' (D. Miller 1983, 68). How to respond?

The case above was loosely inspired by a similar example used by Brian Barry who introduces three types of costs of exit in his discussion of multi-culturalism. One is what he calls 'intrinsic costs', which relate directly to the practice itself. Not being member of the practice simply implies foregoing these benefits which are internal to the practice.

---

[13] Weinstock (2004) argues that exit rights can be defended not just by autonomy-defending liberals, but also by liberalisms based on value pluralism or associationism.

The cost of missing religious meetings is of this kind. A person may regret missing the spiritual experience these meetings brought her, but this kind of cost needs to be borne by individuals. The right to free association includes the right for the community to set its own rules, and to exclude members who do not agree to these rules. Second, Barry distinguishes 'associative costs' which members of the community in a liberal society may freely impose on others. This includes breaking off contacts with former members. However painful, this too falls under freedom of association. Finally, he distinguishes 'external costs', which impose a 'gratuitous loss' on former members. These the state may try to curb. Here he gives the example of commercial relations, such as buying goods from or hiring the work of the former community member.

Barry considers the idea that we should define voluntariness so as to exclude only external costs. Any act would then count as voluntary which incurs only intrinsic and associative costs. However, he rejects this idea himself, because it is counter-intuitive: after all, a person may incur great intrinsic or associative costs and be heavily coerced as a result (he mentions parents who threaten to abandon their child when she marries someone against their wishes). All three types of cost may lead to make the person's choice involuntary. However, from this Barry does not conclude that the state may intervene in all these cases, because he believes practical difficulties stand in the way. It is practically very difficult for the state to interfere with the forms of coercion practiced by group members under the heading of intrinsic and associative costs. Hence he concludes that there is an enduring conflict between the freedom of association of the group members and the voluntariness of the decision of the individual who considers to exit (Barry 2001, 150–2).

The navigational agency theory would give a different analysis of this problem. There are really two questions here which need to be kept distinct: one is about the *type* of costs and the other about the *size* of these costs. The former is most important. Barry's distinction is not entirely satisfactory because for him the line between external costs on the one hand and intrinsic and associative costs on the other hand lies in the fact that the state can influence the former but not the latter. The practical impossibility to regulate all the internal aspects of the social life of groups is doing the normative work in accepting intrinsic and associative costs as unavoidable by-products of the freedom of association. I would like to suggest that a more principled reason must lie elsewhere. In discussing the question when people can be said to 'have a capability', Jonathan

Wolff and Avner De-Shalit have pointed out that this depends on the reasonableness of the costs they face when acting upon the capability: 'Someone has a genuine opportunity to do x only if doing x is reasonable for them, in the sense that the costs of doing so are reasonable for them to bear. The relevant costs are the impacts on other functionings, and what is reasonable depends on the context' (Wolff and De-Shalit 2007, 80).[14] In this proposal, the *type* of cost is related to people's other functionings. I propose to understand this as referring to *basic* capabilities to function. Whether or not the cost renders the act involuntary depends on whether it has a negative impact on their other basic capabilities to function. This is familiar from the fact that the offer 'your money or your life!' leaves the person facing the choice without a real choice. The *size* of the cost is in Wolff and De-Shalit's proposal to an unspecified 'reasonableness' standard. This I propose to understand by reference to the *threshold* value to be specified for each of the basic capabilities (see Chapter 4 on thresholds).

Putting both elements together, a choice which has as its cost that people fall below the threshold of one or more of their basic capabilities renders that choice unfree. The right to exit requires the state to ensure people do not face such costs when leaving social practices. The required specification of the capability to exit social practices can refer back to the set of basic capabilities for agency as a whole to determine which costs/constraints are an unjustifiable burden upon an individual's capability to exit. In terms of our illustrative case, under this standard intrinsic and associative costs are painful for the individual, but other things being equal, the person can still enjoy basic education, freely express her or his opinion in public, associate with other people, vote in elections, etc.[15] These costs are hence to be borne by the exiting individual, not because state interference is practically difficult, but for this principled reason following from the theory. External costs are an interesting and more difficult matter. It is, I think, no coincidence that Barry here chooses a commercial context. In contrast to relationships in the personal sphere (family, friends and the home) or in civil society (religious communities),

---

[14] Similarly, Olsaretti argues people act involuntarily when they lack 'attractive alternatives' (Olsaretti 2004, 119), which is worked out by reference to a criterion of basic needs: 'choices made so as to avoid having one's basic needs go unmet are non-voluntary ones' (Olsaretti 2004, 140).

[15] Indeed, those like L. Green (1998) who have argued in favour of effective rights of exit have also stressed how the right of exit necessitates other rights, such as those to freedom of mobility, freedom of religion, etc. For a pessimistic view of what exit can accomplish on its own, see Reitman (2004). For a critique of the economistic overtones of the terminology of costs of exit, see Borchers (2012).

the marketplace seems to be an area of social life where private and public elements are mixed. It will depend on many factors (such as the availability of alternative commercial opportunities) whether a person's navigational agency – especially her or his access to the subsistence capabilities – is threatened by a former community's refusal to maintain economic relations.

In closing, I want to reflect upon two potential objections to this position. The first one is that this position is too harsh on vulnerable individuals because by leaving all the intrinsic and associative costs to fall on them, it denies them an *effective* right of exit. In response, I should say that the fact that intrinsic and associative costs should be borne by individuals themselves does not mean that there are no duties of the state to interfere within groups to make sure these individuals have effective access to these outside options. Here the points made in the previous section on (paternalist) interference apply. Some internal arrangements will amount to such pressure on individuals that – even if outside options to practice other religions, etc. are guaranteed in the sense of legally and effectively open to all – they cannot conceive of themselves as making such choices. If so, there is a reason to interfere to make the right to exit effective (Okin 2002). Barry may be right to be pessimistic about the possibilities for the state to interfere in private relations in order to make individuals escape these costs once they exit, but it doesn't follow that we have to be pessimistic about possibilities to interfere to make exit possible in the first place.

The second objection is that exit rights are inappropriate protections for individuals in some groups, especially those groups which one is born into and/or which are strong markers of identity and affiliation. Exiting these is nearly impossible for most members given their psychological attachments. Hence they would be better served with more opportunities for voice within these groups (Newman 2007) or a political stance which does not emphasize exit but rather accommodation of the group to the larger (liberal) society (Weinstock 2004). In response, I would claim first of all that the right to exit remains important as a fall-back option for individuals who try to fight for their view internally, next to other possible political strategies to support them. Given its central importance to individual agency, exit cannot be rendered superfluous by such other strategies. I would therefore not agree with the general view that, since voice can be a substitute for exit in terms of protecting autonomous agency, we should therefore put all our cards on such substitution, especially when dealing with identity-heavy cultural or religious groups. Second, however, nothing I have said would prohibit following such other strategies in addition to exit. Indeed, some of these strategies might be very worthwhile exploring.

This much, hopefully, suffices to show how the navigational agency theory takes a convincing position on the exit problem, which is also in line with the response given to the incorporation problem in Section 5.1, not to bring in other – perfectionist – values in the specification of the basic capabilities (such as freedom of association) themselves. Let's now address the other side of the associative coin.

5.5   Association and the Right to Inclusion

As a mirror image of the individual's wish to exit a group that the group wants to retain as a member, what to do when individuals want to enter (or continue to be part of) a social practice but the group refuses them? On a standard view, the freedom of association seems to include the prerogative for groups to arrange for their own membership rules – how otherwise can one maintain the integrity of a group? If it is important that there are possibilities for association, then one cannot deny this basic prerogative because otherwise the group cannot control its own functioning. In line with this, from the individual's perspective, it seems that the freedom of association does not entail a claim-right to associate, to which others would then have duties. It takes two to tango, so that most individuals have a liberty (i.e. no duty not) to associate, subject to the consent of others. However, the question is whether things are so clear-cut as this standard view assumes.

There are two debates here. One debate is about the *right to exclusion*: can groups exclude individuals as members, because of a conflict between their purposes and the choices or ascriptive traits of these persons? Cases here include groups banning homosexuals, men or women, people from other races, etc. The question here is whether we should recognize a limit to the right to exclude. This question basically points to a conflict between the freedom of association (of the group which excludes) and non-discrimination (of those excluded). Some have defended wide latitude for groups to exclude on the basis of such characteristics (L. Alexander 2008) while others argue that there should be a balancing act between the interests of the group and the interests of the excluded individuals (S. White 1997). The latter position is plausible and could be reformulated and accepted by an agency-based capability theory. However, I will not pursue this question any further. Instead, I want to focus my attention on the other issue, which can be framed as the *right to inclusion*. It is one thing for persons to be excluded by a group on the basis of a specific trait, but it quite another thing not to be included in any group at all. As mentioned above, the standard view of the freedom of association does not recognize such a right. However, is that a justified position?

If we define agency as I have done, as taking place within social practices, then persons must have some right to *enter* social practices just as much as to exit from them. There seems a perfect parallelism here; both are equally necessary to have a meaningful right to navigational agency. The standard view recognizes only a liberty to associate, and takes mutual consent of both parties to a putative association as a necessary and sufficient condition for a legitimate association. However, as Kimberley Brownlee has argued, this is too course-grained and can be a default position at most which must allow for exceptions. Sometimes it is morally obligatory to enter into a relationship with particular others, such as the relationship between parent and child, or the relationship between the mineworkers who got stuck together for 69 days in Chile and depended on each other for survival. In the opposite direction, sometimes a consensual relationship is morally problematic, such as a relation between teacher and student (Brownlee 2015, 272–4). Hence a better approach is to see the general agential need for associative interactions as a starting point and then consider, as a separate matter, what this means in terms of allocating concrete rights and duties. This raises the question: for which (types) of association do people have a right to inclusion and under which conditions?

In the logic of the agency-based capability theory developed here the answer to the question would be: there is minimally a right to inclusion in those social practices which reproduce the conditions of navigational agency themselves (the 'mandatory practices' discussed in Section 2.3). So, if participation in social practices which produce conditions for empowerment, subsistence and political decision-making should be possible at all, individuals have to be able to become participants in firms, unions, political parties, media outlets which cover political debates, etc. By contrast, it is not necessary to grant a generic right to inclusion for 'optional practices' in which individuals do not develop the necessary conditions for their agency, but merely exercise their agency, such as in sports clubs, arts associations, religious organizations, etc. Thus, my position on the right to inclusion is instrumentalist. Only where association is necessary for agency development itself, it is a right. Where association is intrinsically enjoyable, or merely instrumental to the realization in cooperation with others of a personal conviction, it doesn't generate a right. The liberty to decide with whom (not) to associate trumps the (felt) need to associate with particular others in the latter, but not in the former, case.

Compare this with Brownlee who has argued for the recognition of a 'human right against social deprivation'. She claims there is such a right to 'minimally adequate opportunities for decent or supportive human contact including interpersonal interaction, associative inclusion, and interdependent care' (Brownlee 2013, 199). She does make it clear that persons do not have a right to friends or loved ones, since feelings of friendship or love cannot be produced on demand. Nonetheless, the focus is on the intrinsic value of human interaction as such, and she does include some concern for the quality of these relations where she stipulates these must be 'decent' or also 'non-threatening' (Brownlee 2013, 206). This is a very broad description of the right, which resembles Nussbaum's generic capability for affiliation, the ability 'to live with and toward others, to recognize and show concern for other human beings, to engage in various forms of social interaction' (Nussbaum 2000b, 79)(see also Section 2.2). Both contrast starkly with my instrumentalist proposal. The problem with such broad descriptions is both that it is unclear which aspects are to be seen as *politically* enforceable rights (for Nussbaum, see also Appendix 3 on this) and also questionable whether such a right can be convincingly justified.[16] By contrast, on an instrumentalist approach, the justification is clear: as for the other basic capabilities, it is to develop navigational agency.

In a later article, Brownlee specifies the rights-claim in a narrower sense. Here she argues for accepting two types of positive claim-rights relating to association: (1) a right 'to have associates (not necessarily of our own choosing) during periods of abject dependency or risk of abject dependency' and (2) a right to 'have meaningful opportunities to form associations when we are not abjectly dependent' (Brownlee 2015, 275). This proposal is more in line with the spirit of an instrumentalist approach and the distinction between the two clauses mirrors the mandatory/optional practices divide which I have proposed. In relation to Brownlee's first claim-right, my approach would actually be broader. Interactions during periods of dependency in

---

[16] Nussbaum-I sees affiliation as constitutive of human flourishing, hence offers a perfectionist justification. Brownlee refers in one sentence to a justification on the basis of the Kantian duty to treat persons as ends in themselves, and then goes on to offer the 'intrinsic value' of social interaction as itself a justification (in a teleological sense?).

childhood, illness and old age which Brownlee describes when fleshing this out, are captured in my approach under the capability to be cared for, which is part of the subsistence capabilities (see Section 6.1). As stated, my approach goes beyond this specific situation to include social interactions instrumental to *other* basic capabilities as well. Brownlee's second claim-right does not include a right to have associates (as the first one does), but only to the opportunity to form associations. This seems to refer to a liberty, an opportunity to try to find companions. It is not clear why Brownlee thinks this is a claim-right, unless she makes it refer to a positive duty on government to establish a (legal) framework for associative activity. The latter of course is included in my approach as well.

Finally, a brief word about the conditions under which this right to inclusion is to be honoured. The right is conditional in exactly the same way in which other positive rights are conditional, which will be spelled out in Section 6.2. The two main conditions are (1) that persons have a primary personal responsibility to try to fulfil the right themselves – the duty on others to help them are conditional on failure by persons themselves to fulfil the right; and (2) that others only must help as far as this can be reasonably demanded from them. These conditions give quite some leeway for associations to exclude obnoxious stalkers and other over-demanding personality types, but also for removing under-performing members in competitive associations or persons who do not share the convictions of the association (here the right to exclusion mentioned but bracketed earlier would need to be more fully fleshed out). At the same time, these conditions on positive duties point to the need for an institutional system which guarantees that every citizen is able to find a place somewhere. In most cases there will not be a need to invoke such a right, since individuals who have civil liberties to associate will create a civil society that offers plenty of opportunities to find associations which are willing and open to new members. However, there may be exceptions. For example, if all political parties in a society refuse a particular individual entrance, she doesn't have a real capability to political participation. In the economic sphere, if an individual has a duty to find a job to earn income by himself, but cannot find a job because no work organization wants to hire him, the duty may fall back on the state to provide income. What would the analogous state duty be in the case of political participation? For example, would the right to create a new political party be sufficient? Such questions would need to be answered if we want to provide a full specification of these conditions on a positive claim-right to inclusion for all types of mandatory practices. Here I will not attempt to do this, but merely flag the issue.

This finishes our discussion of one set of basic capabilities, the empowerment capabilities. These capabilities (corresponding to the traditional civil liberties) are not particularly controversial, especially when compared to the socio-economic capabilities and the political capabilities which I will deal with in the coming chapters. However, what is controversial is whether such capabilities can be specified in a non-perfectionist way, thus responding to the incorporation problem which is an important challenge to the type of moderate perfectionist liberalism I develop in this book. At various points I have argued that this challenge can be met, mainly because the set of basic capabilities as a whole is itself an important reference point when specifying conditions for freedom and autonomy. It is now time to study a second set of basic capabilities, i.e. subsistence capabilities.

CHAPTER 6

Subsistence Capabilities and Socio-Economic Justice

Introduction

What does justice in its socio-economic dimension require? In this chapter I will argue for two claims: it requires a right to subsistence capabilities and a redistribution of income and wealth that goes beyond subsistence capabilities. The bulk of the chapter will be devoted to the defence of the inclusion of subsistence capabilities on the list of basic capabilities, while in the final part I will sketch the reasons for also going beyond subsistence.

The idea that socio-economic justice requires rights to subsistence is widespread, inside and outside of capability theory. Whatever else justice would require, surely alleviating poverty in the sense of being deprived of food and water, shelter, clothing and basic (health)care, is a core demand? Feelings of compassion in the face of those suffering from deprivation seem to go hand-in-hand with a rational endorsement of this idea; after all, subsistence is a necessary condition for human life, almost disregarding one's specific normative view of what is worthwhile in or about human life. If there is no right to such necessities, what other rights could there be? Nonetheless, the idea remains controversial among principled opponents who reject anything going beyond negative liberty rights (i.e. most libertarians). Moreover, many of those who are more sympathetic to the idea of a socially guaranteed level of subsistence wonder how far such rights stretch. For example, should subsistence be defined so as to include more and more expansive resource claims as the general wealth of a population increases? Are such claims to subsistence unconditional, in the sense of not requiring any performances in return from those citizens who claim access to these resources from their societies? And what does such a claim imply for the basic organization of an economy, in terms of the recognition of property rights?

In this chapter I will address these questions, simultaneously giving a principled defence of subsistence rights and giving shape to the conditions of such rights in response to the more particular worries about their scope. As far as I know, there is no encompassing political-philosophical treatment of subsistence rights in capability theory that addresses both these questions of justification and scope. There is literature about subsistence rights (or social rights – I will use the terms interchangeably) in the field of theories of fundamental/human rights. By engaging with that literature from my own agency-based capability perspective, the chapter aims to contribute something to capability theory, but also to this wider literature on subsistence rights. In particular, I will argue for three principles which taken in tandem should govern the distribution of subsistence capabilities:

(1) A *sufficientarian principle*, according to which every citizen is entitled to a threshold level of subsistence capabilities (Section 6.1);

(2) A *reciprocity principle*, according to which agents should contribute to the realization of their own subsistence capabilities as far as they are able to and be entitled to receive them from others as far as they are unable (Section 6.2); and

(3) An *efficiency principle*, according to which the most efficient property arrangement should be selected for each subsistence capability (Section 6.3).

The defence of these three principles will go hand in hand with the defence of some further important philosophical implications. Most notably, consideration of the sufficientarian principle will lead to the conclusion that we should understand subsistence as *social subsistence*, a level of subsistence calibrated to existing social practices. The justification of the reciprocity principle will be based on a detailed defence of the idea of *positive duties*. And the consideration of property arrangements will also lead to the defence of a basic right to a *capability to hold property* as an addition to the list of basic capabilities. All of these claims will be grounded in the theory of participational and navigational agency.

This leaves us with one final, pressing question: even if the protection of subsistence rights is its core, are there also socio-economic requirements of justice *beyond* subsistence? What about the widespread inequalities in the distribution of the income and wealth, even in advanced capitalist societies where some threshold level of subsistence seems to be (more or less) effectively accessible to (almost) all? This question, put on the agenda again by Thomas Piketty and others, cannot be ignored. I will argue that a case can be made for a dispersal of wealth for two main reasons. The first is that having a cushion or buffer against economic misfortunes is a requirement of subsistence itself. The second is that a dispersal of wealth may be necessary to prevent concentrations of economic power spilling over into the political sphere. I discuss the scope and limits of both of these reasons (Section 6.4).

6.1   Social Subsistence and the Sufficientarian Principle

Subsistence capabilities are capabilities to nourishment, clothing, shelter and basic health. When interpreting them as demands of participational agency, however, I will argue we have to understand them as conditions of *social* subsistence. Subsistence capabilities are subject to a *sufficientarian principle* of distribution, but the threshold itself may shift over time depending on shifts in the average requirements for effective participational agency in a society.

To start off, what is included in the category of subsistence capabilities? There are several standard items included on lists of fundamental rights, which can be divided into two categories. Henry Shue makes a distinction between 'physical security' and 'economic security' (Shue 1996, 23):

(1)   *Economic* security refers to the standard social rights from the human rights literature: adequate nourishment, shelter, clothing and basic health.

(2)   *Physical* security encompasses capabilities to one's life (hence a prohibition on murder) and physical integrity and security (hence a prohibition on torture, rape, etc.). These are normally classified as civil, not socio-economic rights.

Based on this distinction, Shue reserves the term subsistence for the rights to economic security. In principle, however, physical security rights – just as much as economic security rights – primarily serve the function of human beings' subsistence. To continue to function over time as a human being, one needs to maintain one's life and physical integrity as much as have access to socio-economic living conditions. In my capability theory, therefore, agents have rights to subsistence in both of these dimensions.[1] Notwithstanding this principled inclusion of physical

---

[1] Other rights traditionally classified as civil rights (freedoms of association, religion, movement, etc.) fulfil a different function: the 'empowerment' of agents (Section 5.1). In the subsistence/empowerment dichotomy, physical security (while normally classified as civil right) is part of subsistence. My other point of divergence from the traditional classification would be education. In terms of its function, it is best classified as serving empowerment, even though in theories of fundamental/ human rights, with their dichotomy of civil versus socio-economic rights, it normally lands on the latter side.

security on a list of basic capability rights, in this chapter I will leave them out of consideration given my focus on socio-economic justice.[2]

The main items on the list of subsistence rights I will take (following many others) to be nourishment (food and water), clothing, shelter or housing, and (health) care, where the latter refers both to access to medical care interventions against mental and physical diseases and day-to-day care-taking which sustains life for those who cannot do so by their own efforts. In resourcist theories these rights are interpreted as rights to the *resources* needed for subsistence, but I will here interpret nourishment, shelter, etc. as *capabilities* (the ability to nourish oneself, etc.) and the rights as pertaining to these capabilities. This will allow variations in the resource bundles necessary for different persons to have these capabilities, depending on characteristics of themselves and their environment, as well as allowing choice whether to exercise or forego exercising such capabilities. All of this is familiar from theorizing about capabilities.

The concept of subsistence thus delineated, however, needs to be understood in light of the theory of participational and navigational agency. Subsistence for agents requires whatever it means to subsist *as* free and autonomous participants within social practices. This theory can guide our choice between three competing understandings of the subsistence threshold.

The understanding favoured here is subsistence as *social subsistence*. This covers those levels of nourishment, housing and (health) care that enable persons to participate in the social practices of their society. This entails a clear reference point to the typical or average demands made on citizens by their societies.[3] A primary consequence of this is that subsistence may require more in wealthier societies, if (and only to the extent that) the higher demands for participation these societies put on their members necessitate these higher levels of subsistence.[4]

---

[2] Also, physical security rights, which are normally treated as part of criminal justice, raise different types of philosophical questions. Like the other civil rights, they are classified as negative rights, while social rights are positive rights. The latter, but not the former, raises the specific problem of positive duties central to my chapter here (see Section 6.2).

[3] This answer does presuppose that justice refers to demands within internally coherent societies which are bounded; otherwise why not defend a global threshold for participation in the world society? I will leave this dimension of global justice out of consideration here, but see Chapter 7 on the boundary problem.

[4] I assume average capability and resource levels for the average person move up and down together. For example, when health-care resources improve, all other things being equal, health levels improve as well. Alternatively, one could say that when resource levels improve the threshold level in terms of capabilities stays the same: one still has 'adequate access to health', albeit that what is adequate differs in resource terms before and after. This is a matter of presentation.

For example, modern working life has raised to prominence mental health care challenges (such as burnout and depression) which were unknown before; hence adequate levels of care have to take account of these. Transportation opportunities have created labour markets which go far beyond one's village, necessitating expenditures for transportation formerly unknown. Isolating oneself from such rising demands is impossible without risking social exclusion.

This kind of relativity has long been accepted in the literature on poverty measurement. Poverty can be approached from an absolute perspective, relating it, for example, to biologically determined absolute standards of sufficient food intake. While we can acknowledge an absolute core for most subsistence capabilities as a minimal baseline, a relative perspective, however, holds that we should go beyond that core: for many goods whose lack constitutes poverty what is relevant is how much one has in a certain social context. When focused on income, for example, the poverty level is often calculated as a certain percentage of the median household income. Thus, if a society's average living standard increases, the poverty line needs to be upwardly adjusted to take this into account. This taking into account of relative deprivation is familiar in the capability approach. For example, Amartya Sen often quotes Adam Smith's example of the labourer who cannot appear in public without shame if he couldn't wear a linen shirt (Sen 1983, 161), which is a key example for the importance of relating resource inputs to the demands of participation in a social context. The conception of agency as participational agency serves as a theoretical explanation and justification for why such intuitions about social participation need to be accepted.

Such an interpretation of subsistence is to be distinguished from two rival understandings. A first one relates subsistence to an asocial concept of agency. An example is Henry Shue's definition of subsistence as 'to have available for consumption what is needed for a decent chance at a reasonably healthy and active life of more or less normal length' (Shue 1996, 23), which does not provide any reference to social standards (or it should be implicit in the reference to an 'active life'). As some have argued, a conception of agency built around an individualist feature such as purpose-fulfilment, or the realization of a plan of life is ambiguous between an absolute and a relative threshold (Bilchitz 2007, 40–5). Such conceptions, therefore, at least leave open an absolute interpretation according to which the subsistence level could sink to very low levels compared to the levels enjoyed by others in the society in which one lives. That these very low levels – which admittedly still lead to people 'subsisting' in some sense as long as they don't immediately die – would still be just levels, is something a defender of an asocial conception of agency would then have to defend. As stated above, we may accept such an absolute core as a minimum baseline, i.e. the lowest possible subsistence threshold across any conceivable society; but a just society should not allow citizens to fall below a higher threshold where participational demands dictate the latter.

Finally, we may distinguish a third understanding of subsistence which errs in the opposite direction by relating a person's subsistence needs *too much* (or in the wrong way) to his or her social context. On such an understanding what persons require would depend on the specific practices in which they participate. Thus, a millionaire would require much more for subsistence than a middle-class family, which would lead to very high levels of subsistence, depending on the person's personal circumstances. This introduces the expensive tastes problem (familiar from welfarist views) into capability theory, through the back door of a person-specific interpretation of the notion of participation. If a person chooses to participate in expensive practices, then this will define such a person's subsistence level. This highly undesirable understanding of subsistence can simply be rejected by reminding ourselves that justice requires treating all persons equally, and equality has been referenced throughout to those citizens within the society in which justice is to obtain. Justice requires a threshold calibrated as some percentage of the average living standard in that society, as a proxy of the average requirements to participate in the practices of that society.

Hence we arrive at the sufficientarian principle of distribution: *each citizen is entitled to a socially calibrated threshold level of subsistence capabilities.*[5] This is an admittedly general rule, and one would need to set separate thresholds for different subsistence capabilities. These thresholds need not be low, they may sometimes be high, depending how much of a specific capability is needed to achieve equality of participation. For the sake of simplicity, I will abstract from such qualitative differences between the different subsistence capabilities. Let's imagine that we need systems of socio-economic provisioning in which housing, health

[5] Some may wonder whether sufficientarianism is compatible with adjustments for social relativity. Isn't this introducing an egalitarian rather than sufficientarian distributive principle through the back door? I would agree, however, with those who argue that the relativity of deprivation can be taken into account *within* a sufficientarian framework by shifting the threshold upwards (Huseby 2010, 182–4). Only positional capabilities represent a genuine challenge to the sufficientarian framework (see Section 4.3). I here assume, as seems reasonable, that (most) subsistence capabilities are non-positional.

care, food, shelter and clothing are produced so that the subsistence threshold refers to an 'adequate standard of living' (Article 25 of the UN Declaration on Human Rights), which covers the basket of subsistence capabilities as a whole (see Section 6.4).[6] With these definitional matters covered, we can now address the normative question: is there a right to subsistence capabilities?

6.2 Positive Duties and the Reciprocity Principle

The justification of a right to subsistence capabilities hinges on the question of positive duties. Agents may need subsistence capabilities, but does this mean they have enforceable rights, hence other agents have duties to help them realize such capabilities? This question, widely addressed in the literature on fundamental and human rights, is central in this section (Copp 1992; Beetham 1995; Fabre 1998; Griffin 2000; Nickel 2005).[7]

Objections to positive duties often target the presumed direct link between the needs-based rights of some people (recipients of aid) and the duties to fulfil those needs by other people (donors). The fact that one person has a claim grounded in an urgent need cannot itself ground a duty of others to help that person, for such a direct link disregards the reasons duty-bearers may have for *not* helping. When establishing rights and duties of justice, one cannot merely look at the 'demand side' of the equation, but must also consider the 'supply side'. *Reciprocity* seems to be an important consideration in justifying rights and duties, and welfare rights – in contrast to liberty rights – generally do not meet this criterion. Whereas the rights and duties of donors and recipients with respect to liberty rights are exactly equal, with respect to welfare rights donors have a larger moral burden to shoulder than recipients (Lomasky 1987, 2000, 108). This general objection against positive duties has also been launched against capability theories by resourcist theorists who claim that a focus on rights to capabilities merely takes into account demand-side considerations without regard for the costs of realizing these capabilities on duty-bearers (Pogge 2002; Kelleher 2015). How to respond?

---

[6] Note that the living standard as a (monetized) aggregate of all necessities also includes necessities related not to subsistence but to the material basis of the political or civil capabilities to the extent that these are not delivered as public goods, but paid for out of private consumption (e.g., the subscription to a newspaper which is necessary to stay informed to be able to participate in public debates; or the transport costs necessary to exercise one's freedom of movement).

[7] Doubts about whether positive duties can be justified have led authors such as Thomas Pogge to propose a theory of justice which does not need an appeal to them (Pogge 2008). Whether or not such circumvention strategies are successful, I deem it better to confront the challenge directly.

The most influential argument in favour of positive duties is probably the one given by Shue: that the distinction between positive and negative rights breaks down in light of an analysis of what governments must do. Call this the *equivalence thesis*.[8] Shue argues that many rights normally classified as negative also require governments to actually do something. For example, the right to physical security requires governments to maintain systems of policing, courts and prisons. Conversely, many rights normally classified as positive also require individuals to refrain from interference. Shue gives the example of a farmer who signs a contract that brings his employees into destitution. Should the farmer have refrained from signing the contract, he would have avoided this positive rights violation (Shue 1996, 35–40). Every basic right has three corresponding types of duties: to avoid depriving a person of the interest protected by the right (negative), to protect people from deprivation by others and to aid the deprived when necessary (both positive) (Shue 1996, 52). Others have also emphasized the equivalence of positive and negative rights in terms of the positive duties (and their costs) both impose upon governments (Holmes and Sunstein 2000). Note that this argument plays on a *supply-side* consideration. According to the equivalence thesis, the position of duty-bearers in both cases is not as different as is claimed by opponents of positive duties.

The equivalence thesis seems to run into a problem. One can accept – as a matter of fact – that negative rights also require positive duties. Nonetheless, positive duties incurred by governments with respect to negative, but not positive rights are justified by reference to the negative rights of the rights-bearer. For example, the government's actions to prevent citizen A from violating the physical security rights of citizen B are grounded in B's negative right not be interfered with. The negative duty to non-interference is primary, the positive duties to protect it are derivative, to be invoked only to guarantee that violations will not occur (deterrence) or otherwise will be punished (revenge). This is different for a genuinely positive right that requires a positive duty to help ('aid the deprived') from the start. To the extent that one believes, as libertarians typically do, that these negative rights have a firmer moral grounding (because of the reciprocity considerations mentioned above) this still commits us to positive duties necessary to safeguard negative rights, but

---

[8] I leave out of consideration other arguments that positive and negative duties cannot be meaningfully distinguished, namely because each can linguistically be rephrased in terms of the other (Fabre 1998, 271–3) or because there would be no meaningful way to distinguish actions from omissions given arbitrariness about how to define the baseline (Pogge 2007, 20–1).

not positive duties to safeguard positive rights. Hence, even if Shue's observation is correct, a real difference may seem to remain in place, and a separate moral argument is needed to ground positive rights (Fabre 1998, 274–5). The equivalence thesis as an argument for positive duties is incomplete.

An additional argument would need to show that positive and negative rights are in the same boat with respect to their moral justification. There are two promising candidates here. One is to provide a linkage argument, and show – as Shue himself tried to do – that accepting positive rights is necessary for the effective enjoyment of some *other* basic rights that are uncontroversial (i.e. some classical negative rights). Whether these linkages can be established has been disputed. I will leave this type of argument out of consideration here and focus on what I consider to be the more straightforward type of argument, which is to ground positive rights directly in the same normative source as negative rights. For theories of autonomous agency, the idea would simply be that positive and negative rights alike are justified to the extent that they are necessary for the effective realization of everyone's autonomous agency (whatever the exact concept of agency used) (Gewirth 1996, 39; Fabre 1998, 267; Griffin 2000, 29). Call this the *moral similarity thesis*. Note that this is a demand-side argument: it rests on the rights-bearer's claim to both sets of rights and says nothing about the claims which are made by these rights on duty-bearers.

This seems to be roughly the state of the current debate. We have an argument relying on a combination of two insights: positive and negative rights are morally similar (both are justified as necessary for agency) for recipients and impose an equivalent burden on duty-bearers (they both require positive duties). Objectors seem to have no ground left to stand on. However, I will now argue that this conclusion proceeds too quickly. Closer inspection reveals that it still seems there is an important asymmetry between positive and negative rights.

To see this, the first observation we need to make is that authors defending positive duties always (as far as I know) qualify their scope in two respects. First, with respect to duty-bearers, a limit is imposed on what can be expected as a performance. This limit is not only a matter of 'ought implies can', so that positive duties to provide aid can only stretch so far as the budget of a government allows.[9] It is also a matter

---

[9] Cf. the 'progressive realisation' formula that is used to operationalize many socio-economic rights, in order to account for the scarcity of resources in developing countries.

of the balance between duty-bearers and rights-bearers. Alan Gewirth expresses this by saying individuals have moral duties to help only if doing so doesn't come at a 'comparable cost' to themselves (Gewirth 1996, 40; similarly Griffin 2000, 36). This move is meant to assuage worries about over-demandingness on the supply-side. Second, on the demand-side, positive duties are always qualified by asking what rights-bearers can do themselves. Gewirth expresses this by saying that agents should first try to acquire the conditions of agency 'by their own efforts' (Gewirth 1996, 42). This introduces personal responsibility. Positive rights are conditional in a sense in which negative rights seem not to be. I will take these restrictions to be justified. Although much controversy exists around their exact scope, let's assume that (up to some level which would need to be specified) cost-considerations of duty-bearers and considerations about the efforts of rights-bearers can lead to restrictions on positive rights claims.

Based on this observation, someone could object that if both sets of rights are really equally necessary to autonomous agency, then it is mysterious why positive but not negative duties are conditional (in the double way just explained). Put in terms of reciprocity, negative rights seem to be based on a straightforward conception of reciprocity as requiring equivalent performances from all parties, while positive rights are based on a conception of reciprocity in which the performances of both recipients and duty-bearers are hedged with qualifications about what they can reasonably do given their circumstances (S. White 2003, 50–9). The objection could be put most forcefully by claiming that this is an inconsistent position. Either one has to make positive rights as unconditional as negative rights; or to give up on the moral similarity thesis, acknowledging that positive rights are morally less firm, in need of the two types of scope restrictions. The former strategy is unattractive because it leads to an implausibly wide-ranging set of positive duties, the latter strategy because it undermines the normative force given to positive rights by the moral similarity thesis. Can one maintain that positive rights only lead to conditional duties and still hold that they are morally on a par with negative rights? Is there a way out of this dilemma?

In my view, there is. The third way I will defend is that negative rights and positive rights really are on a par, not because positive rights should be taken as unconditional as much as negative rights, but on the contrary, because the (positive) duties corresponding to negative rights are conditional, just as the duties to safeguard positive rights are. As long as we do not make this move, the restrictions on positive duties seem arbitrary concessions motivated by the force of an imaginary libertarian opponent who stresses the individual responsibility of rights-holders (along the lines of 'take care of yourself, instead of claiming your basic necessities from the state'). Instead, I propose to see these restrictions are part and parcel of the same moral structure which also characterizes negative rights. To make this argument, a theory of autonomous agency (like the one defended in the previous chapters) offers an indispensable framework.

Agents face two types of threats to their freedom and autonomy (see Table 6.1, row 1). One is that other persons interfere with their agency; negative rights are to provide a bulwark against these *social* threats. The paradigm case is physical aggression. The threat here is one of the *violation* of agency. The other type of threat comes from *natural* causes, either external (e.g., a drought) or internal (e.g., an illness) to agents. These are threats to the basic living conditions (food, shelter, clothing, health) which all protect necessary conditions for the *constitution* of agents: our bodies need food and healthcare to survive. Subsistence doesn't come naturally to agents. If nobody does anything, we will die pretty quickly after birth. True, this natural lack, this non-automaticity of our constituting and sustaining ourselves as agents, points to the need for creating socioeconomic systems of provisioning, hence we often perceive social systems as the causes of misery when something goes wrong. But this does not take away the fact that the threat to our agency originates in nature.

From the perspective of rights-bearers, both types of threat can lead to incapacitation and both are threats to a person's agency that are not

Table 6.1. *Rights and duties: Negative and positive*

	Negative rights	Positive rights
1. Origin of threat	Social: other agents interfering with agency already constituted	Natural: agency needs to be constituted
2. Primary duty – on others (negative)	Non-interference (i.e. don't form a threat)	–
3. Secondary duty – on rights-bearer (positive)	Self-help, individually and collectively (voluntary systems)	Self-help, individually and collectively (voluntary systems)
4. Tertiary duty – on moral community/government (positive)	Help: interfering to counter the threat of other agents	Help: helping the agent who is not succeeding in self-provisioning

of their own making. While the origin of the two types of threat is different, the mix of responses is similar (see Table 6.1, 3rd and 4th rows).

First, agents can by their own efforts try to ward off the threat – I call this a positive duty of 'self-help'.[10] With respect to negative rights we tend to overlook this duty. But for the negative right of physical security, for example, citizens can take responsibility themselves for protecting their homes and possessions against threats; the literature on crime-control long recognizes the importance of such responsibilization efforts. This is no different from citizens' personal responsibility to provide their own food, shelter and health care where they can, through activities of production and exchange in markets (both presuppose a public authority which defines rights and creates the structures within which individuals can 'help themselves'. For subsistence rights, this raises the question of what systems of socio-economic provisioning should be like; see the discussion of the right to property in the next section).

Second, when this is not effective enough, though, governments – as the collective representative of all duty-bearers – have positive duties to help. The rights-character ascribed to positive and negative rights implies that, even when governments rely in the first instance on voluntary social systems against these threats (self-help by individuals and groups, possibly supported by governments, such as when they supply the public conditions necessary for markets to arise) they need to monitor and jump in where self-help fails to effectively respond to the threat. What can be done by governments for protecting a certain negative or positive right, however, remains conditional in the sense that what can be reasonably demanded depends on circumstances, such as the wealth-level on which government taxation can draw and the competing duties governments need to fulfil (this supply-side conditionality is the political equivalent of Gewirth's 'no comparable cost to oneself' condition, mentioned above).[11]

---

[10] The category of 'self-help' discussed in this section should be taken to include help by others who are in a care-taking relation to the needy person (e.g., parents' responsibility to provide for their children). The contrast is with others who have no such pre-established relation to help the person.

[11] The inclination to think that the duties necessary to discharge negative but not positive rights should be unconditional perhaps arises because of two factors: (1) while we have seen that negative rights are also costly, positive rights are usually much *more* costly for governments – hence considerations of cost are more quickly invoked to limit expenditures for the latter. But this doesn't prove that they play no role for negative rights (2) similarly with respect to personal responsibility, while there is some responsibility for individuals to help protect themselves against interferences, this condition is more quickly exhausted and the role of the state comes in more quickly. For example, its monopoly on the use of force presumes that the primary duty to self-help is restricted to non-violent preventive measures of citizens; hence the tertiary duty of governments is indispensable to discharge the duties to prevent or react to violent interferences.

In conclusion, the moral similarity between negative and positive rights still holds at the level of moral principle. Both are justified as a necessary reaction to an external threat or lack (either natural or social) to one's agency (of course there remains a difference in that negative but not positive rights are grounded in a primary right to non-interference, which goes back to the fact that negative rights are rights of already-constituted agents while positive rights protect conditions for the development or constitution of that agency. This difference should however does not obliterate the moral similarity). What my argument adds and clarifies compared to existing accounts, is that negative and positive rights both lead to duties conditional in scope (with the exception, of course, of the primary duty with respect to negative rights not to form a threat to others, see row 2 in Table 6.1). Both require governments to take considerations of cost for the duty-bearers (here, tax payers) and personal responsibility for the rights-bearers into account. This is because all capabilities have a threshold structure, where the threshold marks the point where sufficient agency is achieved (Section 4.2). Below the threshold, agents have a right to assistance wherever they cannot bring themselves above the threshold. From that point onwards, agents do not have such rights and are deemed to be capable of taking responsibility for their own lives. In a sense, this shows how political morality, when it is grounded in considerations of agency, has a *remedial* structure. One can only claim that others have a duty to protect one's agency conditions to the extent that they are really needed to realize these conditions (whether by helping or not interfering). Anything more than that cannot be a claim of justice since the agent doesn't need this more from others in order to be an agent. In addition, one can only claim what can be reasonably asked from others, given their circumstances, since anything more violates the condition of 'ought implies can'.

We can now formulate the reciprocity principle with respect to subsistence capabilities: *agents should contribute to the realization of their own subsistence capabilities as far as they are able to and be entitled to receive them from others as far as they are unable.*[12] As mentioned above, this is a different type of reciprocity compared to quid-pro-quo reciprocity, where the performances of both parties to the exchange are to be strictly equal (or equivalent in value). Stuart White calls the alternative a 'fair-dues

---

[12] The use of the term 'their own subsistence capabilities' assumes that the required resources are private goods. Where these are more efficiently realized as public goods, the formula should be read as requiring contributions by the able-bodied to the public funds to pay them, to realize 'their own and other people's subsistence capabilities' collectively.

conception of reciprocity' (S. White 2003, 59), which nicely captures the tailoring of performances on both sides. Admittedly, this leaves many details unspecified. Here different subsistence capabilities require different considerations to put the principle into practice; think only of the debates about work requirements for welfare entitlements, or debates about the delineation of medical need and personal responsibility for certain lifestyle diseases. Moreover, some variation between societies as to what a person is considered to be 'able' to do may also be expected. Here I only have attempted to bolster the egalitarian framework for these debates, by reconstructing the basis in rights-theories on which it relies, to defend it against scepticism about the acceptability of positive duties.

The reciprocity principle requires distinguishing the extent to which citizens are able to contribute. This introduces a seemingly luck-egalitarian element into the theory (see Section 4.4). Those who do not contribute out of their own choice, while they could do so (i.e. display unwillingness) violate the reciprocity principle. On the other hand, those who do not contribute because of circumstances beyond their power (inability) do not commit such a violation. The theory requires being able to distinguish who is in which camp – however difficult it sometimes is to draw this line in practice. I accept this practical predicament, but we should remind ourselves that the rationale for the distinction here is not luck-egalitarian, but agency-based. Two types of necessity are at play which should not be confused. Having access to a subsistence capability x is strictly necessary for every agent P (in order to be able to act as an agent). However, getting help from agents Q, R, S, etc. in getting this access is *not* strictly necessary for P in the case of unwillingness, while it is in the case of inability. It is because of this failure of necessity-to-agency, not because of a judgment that inequalities due to people's circumstances are inherently unfair, that the capability theory needs to rely on distinguishing the able from the unable, and tailor the positive duties of others towards them in accordance with this distinction.

My formulation of the reciprocity principle may be understood as a variation of the familiar Marxist slogan 'from each according to his abilities, to each according to his needs' (Marx 1978, 531), which many may think has lost its relevance. However, the approach developed here shows it does not – as long as three restrictions on its application are kept in mind. First, its application is restricted to the context of the resources required for subsistence capabilities. This leaves it open that more 'capitalist' requirements may be more suitable for non-subsistence contexts (see Section 6.4 hereafter). Second, the principle is restricted to the area below the sufficientarian threshold level of these resources defended in Section 6.1. Both principles should be read in conjunction. No claims of justice can be made about above-threshold quantities of subsistence resources. Third, the principle is mediated by the demands of a third one, which is about the efficiency of economic production. This leads us to the question of property.

6.3   Property and the Efficiency Principle

The subsistence capabilities roughly cover what in human rights systems is called 'social rights' as opposed to 'economic rights'. While the category of economic rights includes somewhat more than the right to property, this arguably is the pivotal economic right.[13] Should a capability theory of justice acknowledge a right to a 'capability to hold property'? Building upon – and partially revizing – an earlier attempt (Claassen 2015), I will give a positive answer, but one that diverges from the usual focus on *private* property. Persons should be seen as having a right to a system of various forms of property. This will pave the way for an introduction of the efficiency principle, which establishes the link between property and subsistence capabilities.

Two tendencies have been prevalent in liberal thinking about property: to equate justice with the protection of property, and to equate property with private property.[14] For the first tendency John Locke is a particularly prominent example, holding that people have joined in society for the 'mutual preservation of their lives, liberties and estates, which I call by the general name, property' (Locke 1960, 250). His theory of property through labour-acquisition has been hugely influential in the liberal tradition. David Hume defined the problem of justice in terms the search for a convention which is able 'to bestow stability on the possession of those external goods' (Hume 2000, 314), and declares 'our property is nothing but those goods, whose constant possession is established by the laws of society; that is, by the laws of justice' (Hume 2000, 315). Immanuel Kant, when attacking the question of how to define a 'rightful condition' among people, sets up the problem in a slightly broader fashion, but for him too, the first task in establishing such a condition

---

[13] See the account of economic liberties as basic rights proposed by Nickel (2007, 125), which was prominently defended by Tomasi (2012), and attacked by, inter alia, Gourevitch (2015) and von Platz (2014).

[14] For a more detailed exposition of the content of the following two paragraphs, see Claassen (2018a).

is to have rules for the legitimate acquisition of external things, as our property (Kant 1996, 413–21). In these and other cases, moreover, the preoccupation is with private property. To be sure, the background for many authors is one of original common ownership of the earth, but the question is how to justify the transition to a state in which everyone has private ownership rights. These assumptions are carried over into contemporary libertarian theorizing, both in its right-wing and left-wing variants. For however much they differ in their views of world-ownership, both left- and right-libertarianism define the problem of justice as a problem of ownership – i.e. how to understand and combine ownership of the self and ownership of external goods.

By contrast, egalitarian theories start from a completely different set-up of the problem of justice. The primary consideration is a conception of the person, and property structures are derivative. The fairness of ownership shares is determined by whatever – instrumentally – best realizes the normative ideal embodied in the conception of the person. John Rawls's theory of justice is a primary example of such an instrumentalist attitude. His primary aim is to arrange social institutions so that they realize the 'two moral powers' of citizens. A secondary consideration is which property structures fit this bill. Rawls, indeed, discusses on empirical grounds whether capitalism or socialism could be compatible with his principles of justice (Rawls 1999a, 239–42, 2005, 298). The question of property, then, is an *instrumental* question. However, Rawls makes an exception for 'personal property', which is included in the basic liberties 'to allow a sufficient material basis for a sense of personal independence and self-respect' (Rawls 2005, 298). Indeed, including personal property but not any other forms of property (such as property in the means of production) as a basic liberty is the hallmark of the liberal-egalitarian position. An *intrinsic* relation between property and the person is recognized, but only in this limited area. As a basic right, agents need 'control over personal belongings and security of one's living space', nothing else (Freeman 2011, 19).

Here I accept the egalitarian way of conceiving the problem of justice (a direct defence against the libertarian alternative would take us too far afield.[15] The whole book, with its grounding in a view of the person as a navigational agent, does so). Instead I will concentrate on the second issue, liberal theory's focus on private property. In the following I use the

---

[15] A quick-and-dirty one: from the egalitarian perspective, one can always ask a libertarian 'why should a person x have ownership rights in him/herself?' The answer will likely point to some substantive ideal about the person (e.g. self-determination) which is distinct from and hence more fundamental than self-ownership itself (Kymlicka 2002, 122–5).

theory of navigational agency to suggest that this position is problematic, and that – if there is a basic right to property on intrinsic grounds – it should be extended to other categories of property, and be detached from the object of 'personal' belongings. Only after that, I will return to the instrumental side of the argument.

A three-fold distinction in types of property is customary in much of the (legal) literature: private, common (sometimes: communal) and public (sometimes: state/collective) property. Private property refers to the right of individuals to control assets (which includes the right to exclude others from use). When an asset is held publicly, then a designated public official or public body controls the asset for a public purpose (in practice the asset may be offered to the public on a non-exclusionary basis or be used by a selective individual or group for a specific public purpose, such as an airplane for national defence). Common property is more complicated. Sometimes it is defined as a system in which everyone has a free right to use, and nobody has a right to exclude others. On such a definition, no one stands in a privileged control relationship to the asset in a common property arrangement, in contrast to what is the case for private and public property (Macpherson 1978, 4; Waldron 1988, 41; Heller 2001, 84). However, this definition needs to be rejected. It is better to call the structure described above one of 'open access' and confine the term common property to property by a group of individuals who each have these rights of control and exclusion towards non-members of the group (Ostrom 1990, 48; Rose 1998, 155; Eggertsson 2003). Garrett Hardin's famous 'Tragedy of the Commons' actually was a tragedy of an open access arrangement. Open access is a limit-case of property, some classify it as a situation of 'no-ownership'. To make matters even more complicated, on top of these four types of ownership we also have the question of non-profit and for-profit corporations. They are artificial persons created by law, which own assets themselves (corporate property), but are not owned by anyone. Several stakeholders – among which are shareholders of for-profit corporations – do have several types of limited control rights, but no one owns the corporation itself. This type of arrangement is obviously highly important for groups forming themselves in civil society and the market sphere (Stout 2012; Ciepley 2013, 146; Strudler 2017, 111).

Against this background, let's now explore the argument for private property as a basic (or human) right. In Rawls, we see its justification in the idea that property-ownership fosters personal independence and a sense of self-respect. Similar ideas have been defended by many liberal political theorists, both egalitarian liberals (Waldron 1988, 298–307;

Munzer 1990, 90–8; Christman 1994, 167; Gewirth 1996, 173;) and classical liberals (Lomasky 1987, 120; Tomasi 2012).[16] Each draws an intrinsic connection between a certain view of individual freedom – either more negative or positive – and the ability to hold items as one's personal property. For example, Waldron discusses the link between private property and privacy, arguing that if all material resources were in public hands then we would constantly be dependent on the permission of others to use resources which would be 'morally exhausting and individually debilitating' (Waldron 1988, 295). Also, people need a 'refuge from the general society of mankind', a place into which they can withdraw and be alone, or with those with whom they chose to be intimate (Waldron 1988, 296). Finally, people need to have the feeling that the plans they make, the accommodations they reach with others and the choices they make in shaping their environment are somehow their own. This, too, requires private property because without it we cannot trade with others (Waldron 1988, 297). Whatever of the details of these specific linkages, the general picture is one in which private property is held to be constitutively important for becoming an autonomous agent, in some dimension or aspect of our agency.

If such linkages are strong enough to establish a basic right, then similar linkages between agency and other forms of property would have to lead to a similar conclusion. Accepting this means we arrive at a basic right to property covering *all* forms of property, rather than only its private form. However, at the same time, drawing in these other forms of property also gives reasons, or so I would argue, to be cautious with granting *any* one of them the status of a basic right. To illustrate these claims, I will only use common property as an example, but parallel arguments could be – indeed have been – made for public and corporate property and open access regimes.

Research and public interest in common property arrangements has seen a boost. They have been investigated in contexts such as the internet and cyber-based production (Benkler and Nissenbaum 2006), the management of environmental common pool resources (Ostrom 1990), and the sharing economy in which apartments and other personal items are shared with strangers (Zale 2016). Several legal authors have researched their characteristics and argued that common property should be taken more seriously, as well as mixtures between private, public and common property (Rose 1998; Dagan and Heller 2001; Lehavi 2008). Two points emerge from this

---

[16] This is also true for the literature dealing with the question whether property should be seen as a human right, such as Hayward (2013) and Dagan and Dorfman (2017).

literature. First, with respect to the instrumental question of which types of property arrangement leads to the most efficient use of resources, the standard economic argument that private property is most efficient should be relativized. Although private property remains most efficient for many resources, there are also many exceptions. These relate to the size of group using a resource, its homogeneity or heterogeneity, the scarcity or intensity of use, the cost of setting up and enforcing a private property system, etc. Second, the literature also argues for intrinsic connections between other forms of property and agency. Let's mention two examples. Dagan and Heller in their article on the 'liberal commons' argue:

> Our relationships with spouses, children, friends, neighbours, coworkers, and other types of potential commoners have intrinsic value that we often strive to promote. Participants in a group with a joint commitment may perceive themselves as members of a 'plural subject'. This perception stimulates a sense of unity, even of intimacy or closeness, that human beings tend to find gratifying. Liberal commons settings are particularly suitable for furthering these types of social relationships because certain tasks, like the common management of a given resource, provide an opportunity to enrich and solidify the interpersonal capital that grows from cooperation, support, trust, and mutual responsibility. Indeed, in certain settings, such as in some religious and cultural communities, the commons resource may even form the center of a way of life that profoundly affects the commoners' self-identity. (Dagan and Heller 2001, 573–4)

From the perspective of the theory of participational agency, opportunities to engage in common activities are indispensable. If agency is the ability to act within social practices, then there have to be social practices in the first place. Many practices in which agents join together are situated in a setting in which assets are either common property or the property of (non-)profit corporations, as mentioned above. Moreover, as Dagan and Heller make clear in the remainder of their article, legal provisions are crucial to ensure these practices can be established. If people have a right to a legal infrastructure allowing them to interact with others, then they have a right to a more varied menu than private property alone.

   This only touches upon the participational side of agency. One may wonder, however, whether there is not a privileged connection between private property and navigational agency. Doesn't the latter require *independence* in thinking and acting, and doesn't the nurturing of such independence merely require *private* property, as suggested by Rawls, Jeremy Waldron and many others? Here an article by Yochai Benkler and Helen Nissenbaum who argue that web-based 'commons-based peer production' fosters three sets of virtues, is instructive. First there are virtues of 'benevolence, charity, generosity and altruism' (this set roughly overlaps with Dagan and Heller's characterization). Another set of virtues is that of 'creativity, productivity, industry'; the argument there supports those – mentioned above – who argue that common property can also be economically efficient by triggering entrepreneurial virtues. The third set is most interesting for my purposes here, including 'autonomy, independence and liberation'. They write:

> In the first place, individuals have chosen freely to participate and are free to continue or cease to participate as they please. Usually, they are able to contribute when and how much they want, and can select aspects of production according to their own criteria. In the typically decentralized, non-hierarchical settings, even if participants seek to please and impress peers, they need not cower to a boss or any other such authority. As volunteers, they exercise independence of will, initiative, even self-reliance, discretion and free-spiritedness. No matter what other demands constrain their lives, participation in peer production constitutes an arena of autonomy, an arena where they are free to act according to self-articulated goals and principles. In this arena, they manifest, in Charles Taylor's terms, the virtue of 'liberation', manifest in bearers 'directing their own lives…deciding for themselves the conditions of their own existence, as against falling prey to the domination of others, and to impersonal, natural, or social mechanisms which they fail to understand, and therefore cannot control or transform.' (Benkler and Nissenbaum 2006, 404–5)

Here we see activity in a common setting fostering exactly the characteristics of individuality and autonomy for which authors – throughout the tradition of Western philosophy – have extolled private property.[17] In the absence of empirical analysis establishing exactly how much which form of property is likely to contribute to the development of agency (an exercise that would be fraught with difficulties), we would do well to acknowledge the potential of all property forms to the development of agency.

Two conclusions can now be drawn. First, citizens have a basic right to a capability to hold property, understood as a right to a legal system which organizes and protects a variety of forms of property (private, common, public, open access, and corporate), making it possible for them to act as holders of property. This is based on the considerations establishing constitutive linkages between property and agency. Without a property

---

[17] To safeguard true independence, this enjoyment of common property settings may well require private property as a fall-back option when individuals choose to withdraw from collectives. Thanks to Lisa Herzog who pointed me to this link.

system it would be impossible to organize many types of social practices and develop many of the personal abilities belonging to participational and navigational agency. Subject to constraints mentioned hereafter, citizens are free to make use of this legal system as they wish, and exercise their agency in a variety of property settings. This basic right is itself a right to empowerment, not to subsistence.

Second, there also is an instrumental justification for accepting a right to a system of property rights, connected to its function in realizing the production of the resources at the basis of subsistence capabilities (this would by itself not make property a *basic* right, but only a right functionally necessary to protect basic subsistence rights). Without such an organization and protection of property rights, economic activity would be severely hampered, rendering fulfilment of subsistence capabilities near-to-impossible. This can be interpreted as an application of Leif Wenar's role-based theory of rights introduced in Chapter 3 (see Section 3.1), in which duties are prior to rights. If individuals have a duty to help themselves to create the resources for their subsistence (see Table 6.1 and accompanying text), then they need to have the rights to be able to do so. Property rights, by creating a legal infrastructure for setting up socioeconomic systems of provisioning, do so. This instrumental case is independent of and parallel to the case for a basic right to such a system on constitutive grounds. The instrumental case is important, for it sets the stage for the introduction of a third and final principle for the fair distribution of subsistence capabilities, the 'efficiency principle'.

The variation in property forms guaranteed by the right to a system of property rights makes it possible to search, for each subsistence capability, for the most cost-efficient way to produce subsistence resources. For example, in some situations, food will be produced by the market based on exchanges of private property-entitlements (subject to public regulations), while there can be a case that health care can be provided most efficiently in a public system of insurance (Heath 2011). Given this diversity, it is a requirement of justice to accept the efficiency principle: *choose the most efficient property-arrangement for each subsistence capability.* The reason for this is simply that – in conditions of scarcity of resources – wasteful or inefficient production of subsistence resource A for group K will potentially contribute to the nonfulfillment of the subsistence capabilities of either another group L or another subsistence resource B for group K (or both). Waste is a moral notion, although only derivatively: for the reason that it detracts from the possibilities for fulfilling the morally required subsistence capabilities.

The efficiency principle may conflict with the reciprocity principle. The conflict comes in the familiar guise of the incentive problem. Market-production may be in many contexts the most efficient option to realize subsistence capabilities. But where it is, honouring efficiency may require relaxing the redistributive implications of the reciprocity principle. If in a two-person market economy with one subsistence resource, person A produces above-threshold levels of resources and person B produces below-threshold levels (due to some incapacity), then A may be inclined to produce less, knowing that he or she will have to share the surplus with B. She may even be inclined to produce so much less that B may remain stuck at a below-threshold level. The extent to which this is a real problem empirically speaking, depends on the strength of self-interested versus altruistic motivations for person A (note that the fact that A may shirk by lowering productivity runs parallel to the problem that B may shirk by pretending incapacity – reciprocity may be undermined from both sides). I won't delve into the complex empirical literature on this question, nor about the normative question what a fair balance between both principles would look like. Suffice it to say that the capability theory of justice cannot wish this familiar conflict away.

This concludes my discussion of the principles governing subsistence capabilities. But are there any other requirements of justice in the socio-economic sphere? Most notably, given its huge importance in economic and political life, what should we think about the distribution of income and wealth above threshold levels of subsistence?

6.4   The Distribution of Income and Wealth

There have been many public debates about income and wealth inequality in recent years, inspired by publications of prominent economists such as Stiglitz (2012), Piketty (2014), and Atkinson (2015). In political philosophy, the issue of 'property-owning democracy' has received renewed attention, following James Meade and Rawls (Meade 1964; Rawls 2001a; M. O'Neill and Williamson 2012). Others have made proposals for a basic capital grant (S. White 2003, 176–200) or a basic income (Van Parijs 1995 and many others), with many variations as to their weight and conditions and how to finance them. Abstracting from the details, would there be a justification to redistribute wealth beyond whatever is necessary to guarantee every citizen's subsistence capabilities?

The practical complication in answering this question, from the capability perspective defended here, is that 'the socio-economic system' is an abstraction in which the production of resources satisfying subsistence capabilities (hereafter: 'subsistence resources') and other resources (hereafter: 'luxury resources') are intermingled. For example, employers producing subsistence resources compete in the same labour market with employers producing luxury resources for the same pool of employees. Employees may consider taking a job in either of them, depending on pay and other conditions. Similarly, capital markets and investment for both types of resources are connected. Also, there are no separate product markets for the same resource in its subsistence and its luxury variants. While simple apartments are a condition of subsistence and upper-segment houses or villas are luxury resources, they form one housing market in which supply and demand in different segments are interconnected. As a result, the income and wealth distribution have an impact on people's ability to pay for their subsistence resources, and for their ability to pay for luxury resources. Only analytically can we separate the 'subsistence economy' and the 'luxury economy' and then ask the question about wealth distribution separately for both. Imagining that the subsistence economy is fair (i.e. obeys the three principles defended in this chapter) the question we now face is: are there – from a capability perspective – any reasons to redistribute the remaining luxury wealth? Or does subsistence exhaust socio-economic justice? I will defend that there is a justification for redistribution for two reasons that both, however, have a different justificatory logic and would lead to different conditions and restrictions.[18]

The first and more modest function of wealth redistribution is to provide every person with a financial buffer. To orient our minds, let's take Thad Williamson's concrete proposal for a property-owning democracy. He defends a scheme which would be gradually phased-in over thirty years, guaranteeing every household US$100,000 in assets – i.e. US$50,000 per person, divided over cash assets, housing-based assets and stockholdings (subject to various conditions). Such a scheme could be funded solely by

---

[18] Some have used the term 'pre-distribution' to mark off the difference between a welfare-state which redistributes ex-post, and a property-owning democracy which carries out an ex-ante dispersal of capital so that all have truly equal opportunities. However, the temporal difference is shallow, since every end of a period is also the start of a new one. Taxation to establish a capital grant is also 'ex-post'. The only real difference is in the focus on the redistribution of income, in contrast to capital (M. O'Neill 2012, 90). Welfare state arrangements and capital dispersal can go together anyhow and the Rawlsian opposition between welfare state capitalism and property-owning democracy as regime categories is unwise and unnecessary (Jackson 2012, 47).

taxing the wealthiest 1 per cent, in which case, at least in the American situation, the 1 per cent would still retain 70 per cent of their level of wealth
(2012, 227). Obviously, even this modest proposal may still be difficult
to achieve in the current political climate, and less progressive forms of
taxation would then have to be used. Whatever the details, such a scheme
would give every household a sizeable budget, while still leaving large
wealth disparities intact.

A financial buffer can be justified in the subsistence capabilities framework, by emphasizing, as Shue did, that subsistence serves 'economic
security'. It provides security against life's misfortunes and calamities,
from sudden illness to the costs of moving, from divorce to unexpected
household expenditures. Of course, one could argue a buffer is superfluous when such misfortunes are already covered by separate arrangements
to provide subsistence capabilities (e.g. health insurance covering illness). Nonetheless, to the extent that it is improbable that other separate
arrangements seamlessly cover all calamities, there remains a function
for a buffer of one's own.[19] Beyond such a subsistence-related argument,
one could also argue that a buffer may be needed to cover investments
in one's life projects (from education to starting a business) thus making
possible a life of one's own choosing. The buffer would then also fulfil a
function to making possible a life characterized by navigational agency
(not merely subsistence). Here, too, not everything may be covered by
existing arrangements (such as those for obtaining personal credit at reasonable terms at existing financial institutions) and to the extent that it is
not, a positive case for a financial buffer exists.

A second and more wide-ranging justification for some measure of
wealth redistribution lies in the argument – made famous by Rawls – that
wealth dispersal is needed for maintaining the fair value of political liberties. Citizens can only have equal access and influence within systems of
democratic political decision-making if the rich are prevented from buying
themselves privileged access to political influence (Rawls 2001a, 148–50).
On the assumption that a case for the inclusion of political liberties can be
made within the agency-based capability theory (see Chapter 7), such an
argument as to the fair value of the political liberties could also be made
in this theory. It would be an application of an egalitarian distributive
principle being warranted in the case of positional goods – with political

---

[19] As an extension of the case for subsistence capabilities, the buffer would be subject to the same reciprocity requirement, hence conditional on individuals not being able themselves to create such a
buffer. This creates huge incentive problems.

power here functioning as the positional good which needs to be distributed equally, in turn requiring a (not-too-unequal) distribution of another positional good which influences political power, money (see Section 4.3). Such an argument is focused, not – as the financial buffer argument – on the needs of those at the bottom of the wealth distribution, but at the excess-resources of those at the top (Robeyns 2017a, 6–10). Whereas the buffer-function could be realized by wealth redistribution in the order of magnitude of Thad Williamson's proposal, here much more would be needed. As Williamson stated, his scheme will leave the richest with 70 per cent of their current wealth. Given that most normal citizens will not be able to use their US$50,000 fund for buying political access, the richest 1 per cent can continue to do so. Imagining that a much more radical redistribution of wealth is feasible, would this be required by the fair value of the political liberties?

One objection may be that there are *other* ways of preventing the spillover from economic wealth into political power. For this reason, Martin O'Neill argues that Rawls does not provide a compelling argument for why wealth redistribution is necessary for protecting the political liberties, in contrast to 'insulation strategies' such as the regulation of political speech, campaign finance reform, etc. In particular, O'Neill points to the fact that on Rawls's own understanding property arrangements are conventional, so that in the legislative stage societies can legitimately put limits on those exercises of property rights by individuals and corporations which gain them political influence (M. O'Neill 2012, 81–84). I agree with O'Neill that the issues here are largely empirical and that Rawls's suggestion is inconclusive. I do, however, feel that there is an inconsistency in expecting that democratic societies that allow large wealth inequalities can nonetheless implement effective insulation policies, because *ex hypothesi* such policies would have to implemented by a system which is itself in the grip of an economic elite buying itself political power to prevent such measures from being implemented. Their implementation seems to be the more unlikely to be feasible the more they are actually needed. If anything, this would suggest that attacking the root of the problem – economic power concentrations themselves – makes more sense.

In closing, I want to contrast this second with a third justification for wealth redistribution. According to this justification, wealth redistribution would be necessary to prevent inequalities of social status and domination. This justification was made popular by Wilkinson and Pickett's theory that status anxiety is the empirical explanation for why relative inequalities are bad for everyone in society (Wilkinson and Pickett 2010). Republicans and relational egalitarians have also put non-domination forward as the main rationale for economic redistribution (Lovett 2009; Schemmel 2011). In Rawls, the connection is via the idea of the social basis of self-respect. In an economically unequal society, the worst-off would start to look upon themselves with contempt and their sense of self-worth would diminish, leading to attitudes of servility on their side and dominating behaviour by the economically best-off (Rawls 2001a, 139; M. O'Neill 2012, 88).

I must confess being sceptical about this as a separate argument. Obviously, self-respect, or an effective sense of self-worth, is important to autonomous agency. But the content of this 'social basis' in Rawls refers back to the other primary goods: the social basis is formed by basic liberties, opportunities and income/wealth (Rawls 2001a, 60). One can, therefore, wonder whether he is really consistent in also presenting the social basis of self-respect as a separate primary good. But if really nothing more is at stake than the fair provision of these other primary goods, then the conclusion seems justified that implementation of policies guaranteeing each person – in my theory – subsistence capabilities (and other basic capabilities) is already sufficient to guarantee each person's sense of self-respect. Similarly, now against republicans, the actual occurrence of dominating behaviour between rich and poor would already be prevented by the implementation of subsistence capabilities for all – these guarantees should give everyone the independence needed to resist efforts to be dominated by others – if not, the threshold has not been put high enough.

Why do many seem to have the intuition that inequalities in social status would be wrong in themselves? This intuition is much less widespread with respect to status differences between artists, football players, or for that matter, philosophers – call these 'local' status differences, arising in a specific social practice. It is an intuition many do have about society as a whole; or more precisely, about general social status as it is indicated by economic status – i.e. given the contingent fact that income and wealth, in our type of society, functions as an all-purpose marker of social status. I would speculate that the only reason can be because many people believe that in a society marked by (strong) economic inequality, dominating behaviour actually *will* occur, hence (counter-factually) subsistence capabilities will apparently *not* have been guaranteed for all. But the only credible explanation for this, in turn, is that the wealthy will be able to rig the political process. Hence the status argument is underpinned by a causal link from economic-inequality-cum-social-status-inequality to political inequality, and then from political inequality to sub-threshold realization of subsistence capabilities, and from the latter to forms of domination in private relations and lower levels of self-respect. The latter phenomena are themselves a violation of our right to navigational agency, of course, but they are explained by the violation of the conditions earlier in the chain. Social status inequality, as a by-product of economic inequality, does not do any separate work here. The picture of a society in which economic-cum-social inequality would lead to domination and lower self-respect *without* the intermediate phenomena (political inequality and violation of subsistence capabilities) is unintelligible.

If this is correct, then the argument from the fair value of the political liberties can do the job, provided it is extended, compared to the version presented above. The fact of people enjoying differential value from their political liberties is not only unjust in itself (a violation of their right to these political liberties) but also has knock-on effects on *other* capabilities which are supposed to be guaranteed by this political process. This should include the effect, not only on the subsistence capabilities, but also on the empowerment capabilities. When the political process is captured, this can have detrimental effects on citizens' civil as well as their social rights. With this extension, the argument as to the fair value of the political liberties seems to be the best justification for redistributing wealth beyond what is needed for a financial buffer for all. This puts more weight on the empirical uncertainties surrounding this argument and the question whether there are other, more effective means for protecting the integrity of the political process.[20] These might include the insulation strategies mentioned above, but also measures which challenge economic inequality even in an 'earlier' stage than wealth redistribution does – i.e. measures challenging the power relations within economic life, through economic or workplace democracy.

In making the arguments above, let's once more stress the social relativity of the subsistence threshold. The rise of populism in many western countries has often been linked (apart from complaints about the loss of national identity and immigration) to stagnating levels of income and wealth, leading to a justified feeling of being left behind. I would interpret these matters in terms of a violation of their subsistence capabilities. Whereas the

---

[20] One important factor I have omitted is Rawls's emphasis that property-owning democracy is about the dispersal of financial *and human* capital – i.e. also about education and skills. That the combination of more financial wealth and better education does lead to more political influence is taken as a given by Jeffrey Green, discussing the empirical evidence from political science (J. Green 2016, 89–90).

threshold for these capabilities rises, given the prosperity for the upper parts of society (not just the 1 per cent but also a larger group of upper middle-class professionals), the lower classes cannot keep up. Theirs is not a complaint about social status per se, but about the unfairness of not sharing in the fruits of society's progress, leading to higher standards of living (hence participation) that they do not have access to. This is not meant as a full explanation of the populist vote (which is arguably more complex) but only as an indication of how to interpret the charges of economic unfairness in these political debates in terms of the theory developed here.

The main result of this chapter is to have provided a justification for accepting a set of subsistence capabilities as well as some redistribution of wealth in light of maintaining the fair value of political and other basic capabilities. What I have not been able to do is to spell out the relation between both of these results. Most noticeably, the right to subsistence capabilities was embedded in a structure of reciprocal rights and duties, conditional on one's (in)ability to contribute. Wealth redistribution to prevent concentrations of wealth spilling over into politics is, however, subject to a different logic, unconditional with respect to specific individuals' abilities to contribute. The latter argument is a macro-level argument for redistribution, focusing on systemic effects between the economic and the political sphere as a whole. The former argument obeys a micro-level logic of individual contribution. When the two are implemented together, this may create conflicts; rendering entitlements which should be conditional unconditional or vice versa depending on which argument one gives priority. I cannot deal with these complications here, but at least they should be noticed. While there is nothing inconsistent in accepting both an unconditional and a conditional argument for redistribution within one egalitarian theory, this doesn't make it easier to determine, in practice, which set of policies will make a society just in the socio-economic sphere.

CHAPTER 7

Political Capabilities and Democracy

Introduction

The waves of democratization in Eastern Europe and elsewhere at the end of the twentieth century heralded an era of optimism about the future of democracy. Nothing much of that seems to be left today, given the continuing democratic deficit of the European Union in the face of economic crises, the rise of populism and the election of leaders such as US President Donald Trump, the marginalization of opposition voices within countries with a formally democratic system of elections (Russia, Turkey) and the seemingly stable adherence to autocracy (despite economic development) in countries such as China. Against this background, philosophical questions about the fundamental nature and justification of democracy, the boundaries of its authority and its contested relation with related norms such as the rule of law, remain highly pertinent. Does (capability) justice require democracy?

The core feature of democracy, as I will understand it, is to give all citizens an equal say – i.e. rights to equal capabilities to participate and hence influence the content of the decisions made (Kolodny 2014a, 197–8). In contrast to unequal power-distributing political regimes, such as monarchies or oligarchies, in a democracy it is not one person or a small class of persons who rule, but all, and all to an equal extent. Of course actual participation will not have to be equally intense for everyone, but all have an equal capability to participate. The core is thus made up of two elements: equality between citizens and a substantive notion of the respect in which citizens are deemed equal, their freedom to participate. One can, thus, contest both elements. Is equality really intrinsically important and always best when it comes to the best way of running a political community? One could also argue that some citizens should have more opportunities for political influence, for example by allotting political influence in proportion to the stakes a person has in a decision

(Brighouse and Fleurbaey 2010). Is substantive participation by engaging in activities such as deliberating, protesting, bargaining and voting really necessary? One can also argue that while citizens should be equal, we can use procedures such as tossing a coin to express their equality (Estlund 2009). Both of these challenges will have to be kept in mind.

Given this definition, the question whether democracy is justified is equal to the question whether equal rights to political participation capabilities are justified. Should political capabilities be added to the list of basic capabilities? I will assume a fairly standard list of several types of political capabilities. A political practice is a special, 'overarching' kind of social practice that concerns the exercise of authority to set norms on other social practices and activities to legitimize and contest that authority. Participation in this practice requires appropriate rights to political participation that relate to the legitimation, contestation and exercise of that authority. The most direct ones are the rights to active and passive participation in elections – i.e. to vote and stand for office. Moreover, the civil rights mentioned as part of the empowerment capabilities have an important function as well, especially the rights to free speech, assembly and association – hence, there is some overlap between civil and political capabilities. Similarly, education is an important condition since one cannot participate on an equal footing without having sufficient knowledge of how political practices function. Also, there has to be effective access to channels of influence; this requires access to the media and other public platforms to make one's voice heard (for similar characterizations, see Rawls 1999a, 195–200; Christiano 2011, 146). Finally, although not my focus here, legal capabilities should also be included: rights to an effective remedy, fair trial, safeguards against arbitrary arrests, etc. The application of law in courts is itself an overarching practice in the same sense as the practices of making and executing the law. Both political capabilities in a narrow sense (identified with the legislative and executive functions of government) and legal capabilities (identified with the judicial branch of government) are, therefore, to be included on a list of basic capabilities. In working with this core understanding of democracy and corresponding list of capabilities, I will remain agnostic about the correctness of more specific understandings compatible with this core, such as specific forms of participatory democracy, deliberative democracy, etc. We can imagine a case for any of these specific forms and the list of capabilities would then have to be modified and enlarged to accommodate such a specific understanding. For example, if some form of deliberative democracy would turn out to be the most justified all things considered, addition of specific deliberative capabilities to the list would be warranted. I neither exclude nor argue for such conclusions here.

This chapter starts with an overview of liberal justifications for democracy. I briefly discuss arguments on instrumental grounds which claim that democracy is a necessary condition to advance the realization of other rights. I also discuss intrinsic arguments which claim that equal participation is a necessary component of each citizen's freedom as self-determination. I argue both types of arguments are problematic (Section 7.1). This opens the way for a novel defence, grounded in the agency-based capability theory. My argument ties equal participation rights to a duty to create a just political system. Given that all citizens are equal in having a duty towards others to create such a system, I argue they must have equal rights to a share of the political power which makes such a system run (Section 7.2). Having established this duty-based argument for democracy, the second half of the chapter turns to applications of this argument. I discuss the objection that the argument would be over-demanding and asking for direct-democratic participation of everyone. My argument can deflect such worries by accepting a system of representative democracy. Then I discuss whether the argument should exclude inegalitarian participants and how to deal with the possibility of a tyranny of the majority (Section 7.3). Finally, I consider the so-called 'boundary problem' which asks if boundaries between states can be democratically legitimated. I argue that existing responses to this challenge fail, but that a combination of a cosmopolitan starting point and statist substantive conditions can provide a satisfactory answer, which legitimizes a world divided into separate political communities (Section 7.4).

7.1   Liberal Arguments for Democracy

Discussions within liberal-democratic theory about the justification of democracy are conducted both in the context of 'domestic justice' (Rawls-inspired discussions about the inclusion of 'political liberties' on a list of basic liberties) and in the international context where acceptance of a 'human right to democracy' is at stake. Since the question is structurally similar, I will draw from both discussions.[1] Often a distinction

---

[1] Authors denying the human right to democracy (J. Cohen 2006; Beitz 2009, 174–86; Reidy 2012; Peter 2013) are often inspired by Rawls's rejection of such a right, when he proposed in his *Law of Peoples* a much shorter list of basic rights (Rawls 1999b). These authors claim we should make a distinction between justice-based moral duties and human rights-based duties, which the theory of

between two types of argument to justify democracy is made: instrumental and intrinsic (e.g., E. Anderson 2009). Both link democracy's justification to individual freedom – as one would expect from liberal theory – but in different ways. In this section I will argue that both types of argument cannot do the job.

One important and representative type of *instrumental argument* is that democracy is a necessary requirement for the reliable realization of *other* human rights (Shue 1996, 75–7; Sen 1999a; Griffin 2008, 247–55; Christiano 2011) or domestically, other basic liberties (R. Dworkin 2000, 186; Arneson 2009). The thought is that other, uncontroversial human rights – such as against torture and rape and other violations of physical integrity – are best realized when governments are required to take their subjects seriously. Democratic mechanisms of accountability will ensure, in a way that no other political system can, that governments feel compelled to protect and respect these rights. One example of this is Amartya Sen's famous claim that famines do not appear in countries which are organized democratically (Sen 1999b, 180, 2009, 342). The instrumentalist argument is empirical in nature. Sometimes it relies on mere conjecture (as in James Griffin and Henry Shue), but there are also serious attempts to link the available empirical evidence about the democratic nature of states with their human rights records (Christiano 2011). I have nothing against these types of argument as far as they work. Their weak spot obviously is that they assume a large burden of proof. It is difficult to establish the causal linkage between democratic governance and human rights protections. For example, Christiano's empirical case has been repeatedly attacked by critics arguing that there are conceivable scenarios of non-democratic societies protecting human rights just as well and that positive human rights records can be traced back to other correlated factors, such as respect for the rule of law (Beitz 2009, 174–86; Reidy 2012, 198–201; Buchanan 2013, 164–7).

The instrumentalist position is predominant throughout much of liberalism. When the existence and authority of the state itself is considered to be justified to the extent that it respects and/or realizes an individual's private freedom, then it is a wholly different and secondary question whether the state's decision-making processes should be arranged democratically. Giving each citizen an exactly equal say in

---

navigational agency does not accept. Although I have mostly used the term 'basic rights' instead of human rights in order to simply circumvent this problem, I concur with those who want to be able to use the term human rights as well since, after all, the basic rights are rights belonging to all humans *qua human beings* (see Introduction to Chapter 3).

the political process (hereafter, 'public freedom') will only be the correct answer if this is what happens to maximize the realization of equal private freedom. Some have been critical – echoing long-standing suspicions in political philosophy about the wisdom of the masses – of the extent to which democracy could ever be the best procedure for reaching justice, given widespread incompetence of voters in making informed, unbiased decisions (Arneson 2009, 200–3; Brennan 2012, 21–5). As a threat to instrumental arguments, there always lurks the – at least theoretical – possibility that a benevolent dictator or enlightened aristocracy might do better. John Rawls in his earlier work was also drawn to an instrumental perspective on political participation. He argued that in some circumstances a case may be made for John Stuart Mill's famous proposal for plural voting, in which knowledgeable citizens get more votes (Mill 1991) than others. Assuming they are better able to guide the polity to the common good, Rawls says, 'the ship of state is in some way analogous to a ship at sea, and to the extent that this is so, the political liberties are indeed subordinate to the other freedoms that, so to say, define the intrinsic good of the passengers. Admitting these assumptions, plural voting may be perfectly just' (Rawls 1999a, 205). These doubts about democracy's ability to realize justice will remain relevant even when a sound intrinsic argument can be made, because in that case a tension between justice (demanding maximally competent government in order to realize justice) and democratic equality will arise, and trade-offs may be necessary.

Let's see if an intrinsic argument can be made in favour of equal participation rights. I will categorize them in two main camps: direct and indirect intrinsic arguments.[2]

Direct intrinsic arguments argue that an individual's exercise of democratic participation rights (her public freedom) contributes to – or is even constitutive of – her individual freedom in a direct sense, just as much as her exercise of private freedom rights. Starting from the normative ideal of individual freedom as self-determination, these arguments try to show that this ideal must not only guide us in our personal lives (as private freedom) but also in our common life in society (as public freedom). Freedom as individual self-determination should be equally realized as a

---

[2] Brennan (2012) discusses seven different types of argument; Arneson (2009) discusses four types (with little overlap). Some historically important arguments, such as those based on the personal development of character (Rawls 1999a, 205–6; Brennan 2012, 20) I must leave out of consideration here, as also Gewirth's argument from civil liberties (Gewirth 1978, 308–10), and Benhabib's discourse theoretical argument (Benhabib 2012).

private ideal and as a public ideal (Gould 2004, 31–7; R. Dworkin 2000, 201–3). When choosing to buy white instead of black shoes, marrying this rather than that man, or voting for one rather than another political party, isn't one in all these cases exercising one's freedom? Aren't private and public acts of freedom on a par? If so, it seems that there is a case for requiring equal freedom in the political sphere just as much as in other spheres.

However, the soundness of this extension (or analogous reasoning) from private freedom (i.e. what is covered in my theory by the rights to subsistence and empowerment capabilities) to show that the same should hold in the public sphere, has been widely criticized (Kolodny 2014a, 210–18; Rostbøll 2016, 802–3). As James Griffin remarked, 'to have one vote among millions does practically nothing to protect one's being able to pursue one's chosen ends' (Griffin 2008, 247; similarly Talbott 2005, 140). The difference is that one's choices with respect to private decisions such as shoes and marriage partners are (more-or-less) decisive, while one's choices with respect to public decisions are not. Achieving one's preferences in politics depends upon the cooperation of countless others, so that one will often be frustrated. Hence the political arena doesn't offer a very promising arena of individual self-government given that power has to be shared with so many others. And even to the extent that the political arena is valuable for individual self-government, it surely doesn't offer the only, or a privileged, place for such an autonomous life. Since this is so, it is hard to argue that public participation for individuals is an indispensable component of everyone's equal individual freedom (Brennan 2012, 17–20).[3]

Indirect intrinsic arguments try to circumvent these problems, by relating the value of political participation not to the individual's freedom directly, but to her or his social standing, which in turn may influence her or his freedom. Equal standing or equal respect between citizens is the most basic requirement and equal political participation rights are an expression of that complex ideal. A number of very different and influential arguments fit into this category, but I will focus on Rawls's to make a critical point which, I think, will apply to all of them.[4] The later Rawls

---

[3] Cohen reads Rawls as making this type of argument (Rawls 1999a, 181) and criticizes it for the same reasons (J. Cohen 2003, 104–7). Wall attributes a 'moral agency' argument to Rawls and also criticizes it for similar reasons (Wall 2006, 255–6).

[4] Most notably, Christiano's argument from the equal advancement of everyone's interests belong in this category (Christiano 2008). Christiano's theory may collapse into instrumentalism, see Valentini (2013, 195) and Rostbøll (2015b, 271).

argues that equal participation rights are necessary to secure each citizen's self-respect. Self-respect requires the respect of others, as part of the social basis of self-respect, and this is violated when others do not grant me equal political rights (Rawls 2005, 318–19). Here political equality acquires an expressive meaning, it marks the public recognition of one's equal social standing in general towards others (J. Cohen 2003, 107–11; Gutman 2003, 179–80).

The problem with this type of argument is that, depending on how it is interpreted, it either collapses back into a direct-intrinsic argument or into an instrumental argument. On an *individualist* interpretation, the argument is mainly a variant of the direct-intrinsic argument. Self-respect is a phenomenological or psychological condition which can be acquired in a number of ways. It is questionable whether there are no other ways to acquire self-respect than through political participation, for example by providing everyone with a fair share of wealth and all the civil liberties (Wall 2006, 259). Some even question whether this kind of tight connection, would it exist, would not be morally problematic itself, glorifying the importance of political power for one's self-image in a way that can be socially pernicious (Brennan 2012, 6–9). To avoid these problems, one could instead adopt a *systemic* interpretation which holds that giving unequal power to different individuals and groups will lead to situations of sub-ordination and domination. Their self-respect will tend to get harmed, in all other (non-political) dimensions as a consequence of power inequalities. The postulation of such causal links, however, means that we are back at an instrumental argument: non-democratic regimes tend to undermine their citizens' other basic rights.

Based on this admittedly all-too-brief overview of a complex literature, I surmise that liberalism has a problem justifying democracy. This is not surprising. If the justification of the state is understood along liberal lines, through its role in protecting everyone's equal *private* freedom, then any argument for democracy will tend to collapse into either an instrumental argument or a direct-intrinsic argument. Either political participation rights are seen as necessary conditions for safe-guarding other individual liberties or as themselves on a par with them. In the first case, one can doubt whether ascribing them equally is really always necessary to the protection of these other rights. In the second case, one can doubt whether these public freedoms are really as necessary as private freedoms for the exercise of our individual autonomy. Political junkies who happen to value political agency as their conception of a good life may value them highly – but if that would be the leading criterion, one would be led to distributing political power unequally as well, giving more to the politically active than to the politically passive citizenry. In both cases, one cannot get the required *equality* of participation – which distinguishes democratic from undemocratic political systems – out of the argument.

If all such arguments for democracy fail, one may wonder whether this predicament can be overcome. In the following I will argue that it can, by making use of the resources of my agency-based capability theory developed so far.

7.2 A Duty-Based Argument for Equal Political Capabilities

Rational participational agents have a valid claim – so I argued in Chapter 3 – to basic rights protecting their standing as navigational agents. This imposes a corresponding duty to respect these rights for all others. Here I will argue that this duty, in turn, justifies rights for all to participate in the creation and maintenance of a political system that respects these basic rights. The novelty of the argument is in the introduction of a duty to participation as a mediating concept between private rights and political rights. This will prevent the argument from sliding back into pure, contingent instrumentalism. Instead, the argument can be characterized as making democracy *categorically-instrumentally* valuable.[5] But this is running ahead. The argument has four steps.

In the first step we recognize that the political practice has a different function than other social practices. In line with other liberal theories, its function is understood as *instrumental*: to realize rights to exit and co-governance within all other social practices (i.e. my rights to subsistence and empowerment – the private basic rights). Taking seriously its overarching location in society, it cannot be put on the same level as other social practices; politics must ensure, through its law-making function, that individuals can participate in these other practices freely and autonomously. Whatever organization of the political sphere works best in guaranteeing these private rights for individuals, should be adopted. It could be guaranteeing agents equal political rights or by some unequal political arrangement. At this step, the theory only demands the creation of a political practice as a third party (arbiter) to avoid oppressive and coercive relations between agents within social life. Shouldn't we be

---

[5] I borrow the term from Beyleveld, who uses it in the explanation of Gewirth's argument. See e.g., Beyleveld (2015, 584).

pragmatically committed to whatever is the most functional organization of the political arbiter, democratic or otherwise? In designating this function to politics, it seems we are back at the instrumentalist argument criticized earlier.

If the argument in Chapter 3 is sound, then I as a navigational agent can claim from others that they respect my rights to navigational agency. Corresponding to this, these others have a duty to respect my rights. Assuming a political community with an identifiable set of other agents (see Section 7.4 for a discussion of this assumption) all these others have such a duty towards me *equally*. With respect to the duties of non-interference, some may have more intensive contact with me, so that these duties have more practical consequences for them. Not interfering with me is a heavier burden on their life than on that of others. Nonetheless, this should not distract from the fact that all in the community have this duty equally in principle, for if they would come into contact with me, the duty would be triggered just as much. More importantly for the argument here, positive duties are also born equally in principle by all in the community. One new positive duty now enters the argument. The whole idea of negative rights and duties already presumes that there already is an effective legal infrastructure in place which promulgates, specifies and enforces these rights so that these others know what their duties are, which is not (necessarily) the case. Implementing rights to each of the basic capabilities in a concrete society requires countless decisions as to their specification, which will depend on the circumstances, history, culture and other factors of that society. Since all of this will not come about unless human agents make it come about, all other agents in the community have a *duty with respect to me to cooperate to create a political-legal system which determines, enforces and specifies my rights* to navigational agency. Recognising the necessity of this duty is the second step of the argument. This step basically borrows Immanuel Kant's view that there is a duty to get out of the state of nature (Kant 1996, 451). The need for a public authority arises out of the three defects mentioned: we need an authority to determine otherwise merely provisional rights (legislative function), to enforce them (executive function) and to specify them in concrete cases (judicial function) (Ripstein 2009, 145–7; Pallikkathayil 2010, 134–41).

So far, the argument has only established a duty to create a public authority or state. But the creation of a state which protects each citizen's rights is not a one-time affair. It is itself a complex social achievement which needs to be socially reproduced each day through countless efforts.

The duty of others towards me continues to hold up after the creation of the state. To discharge their duty, others need to participate in the political practice which can create this system. *Participation rights* for them are necessary means to be able to discharge their duties to me. Recognising these rights is the third step of the argument. The argument here makes a – perhaps unexpected – use of Leif Wenar's theory of rights as derivative from prior duties that I also used earlier when explaining the role of rights in social practices more generally (Section 3.1). Rights help us to discharge our duties, as Wenar puts it: to fulfil our social roles. This general thought can be applied here. In our role as citizens, we have a duty to political participation and we need rights to discharge these duties otherwise we would be incapable of doing so (Wenar 2013, 221).

All of this is true for me with respect to all others as well: I too am under a duty to respect the rights of all others, hence I too am under a duty to cooperate to create the legal system respecting their rights as well, hence I too need political rights to be able to discharge my duty towards them. All citizens are symmetrically placed with respect to this duty, hence the conclusion that participation rights must also be granted *equally*. Thus arises a system of reciprocal positive duties to participate in a political practice which creates and upholds that legal system. Recognising this equality and reciprocity is the fourth and final step of the argument. We ought to do our part in ensuring others' rights to navigational agency. The very first step we can and, therefore, ought to take to ensure this is to make sure that there is a system defining and protecting these rights in the first place. Since all have these duties to the same extent, all have the rights to political participation to the same extent. It expresses a common-and-equal responsibility for all in the relevant political community.

Unlike other arguments for democracy, political participation rights in this argument are not based on my own rights to navigational agency, as an extension which is necessary to be able to effectively defend these rights to navigational agency in the public sphere and/or have my equal standing vis-à-vis others respected in the public sphere. Such an extension from private freedom to public freedom, as we have seen, can only lead to a contingent instrumental case or an implausible intrinsic case for political participation rights. By being based upon my duties to respect your rights to navigational agency, the argument is instrumental (in the sense of not valuing democratic participation intrinsically) but the instrumentality is categorical instead of contingent, because the ascription of the duty to every citizen does not depend on an empirical causal link, but on the fact of their being situated as co-members of the same political community. There is an analogy with the case for subsistence capabilities, which are also instrumental for agents as much as political capabilities are (Section 5.1). The difference is that subsistence capabilities refer in the first instance to attributes of individuals (health is a state of my body, the food is consumed by my body) whereas political capabilities refer to individual performances which are contributions to a *collective good*. However, the difference should not be over-stated, for the realization of subsistence capabilities also requires the creation and maintenance of collective systems (of property rights and where necessary, of public provisioning). This is where positive duties came in, but only as conditional duties to the extent that individuals could not provide for themselves. Since individuals can never create a system of legislative, executive and adjudicative powers for themselves, the positive duties in the political sphere are, however, unconditional. The taxes one pays for social security and the taxes one pays for the proceedings of parliament both are justice-based positive duties. Both are morally on a par, and the duty to participate is morally on par with the duties to contribute financially to the state.[6]

To the best of my knowledge, a duty-based argument for democracy has not been made before.[7] The question is why? As we saw, it builds on Kant's argument about the duty to leave the state of nature. His argument, however, was about the creation of a public authority and not about the democratic character of that authority. Similarly, many have accepted, following Hart and Rawls, a 'principle of fairness' which states roughly that if one benefits from participation in an institution one has a duty to contribute to that institution as well (Rawls 1999a, 96). Also, in Rawls's theory one has a natural duty to uphold justice, which sometimes overlaps with the principle of fairness (Rawls 1999a, 99). Similarly, most republicans recognize that politics is a collective good and that we have duties to participate in politics to maintain that good. But in each of these cases, while the argumentation could have been easily extended to reach the conclusion about democracy that I have drawn, it hasn't. I cannot see whether the fact that this didn't happen is

---

[6] A variation on my argument would be to first establish monetary duties to contribute to the state, and then – via the slogan 'No Taxation without Representation' – to justify equal participation rights as corollaries of these duties.

[7] I lately found one place in the literature where something like my argument is suggested, in two sentences: Waldron (1999, 234). Unfortunately, Waldron's own defence of democracy doesn't follow up on this suggestion.

due to an oversight on the part of Kant, Rawls and others, or a weakness in my argument which I have not yet discovered.

This concludes my presentation of the duty-based argument. There are several possible objections to it, some of which I will consider in the next section. There is one more general objection which I want to take up here. It is not so much a strict refutation of my duty-based argument as a judgment that a rights-based theory of the republican sort in the end is more convincing. Indeed, one may think that – by focusing on liberal arguments in the previous section, I have overlooked what is the more promising category of arguments for democracy.

There are basically two types of republican arguments. One is the *classical republican* argument, associated with Aristotle (1984), Arendt (1998) and others that defends democratic (or at least political) participation as a part of the good life itself. This type of argument basically is the same as the liberal direct-intrinsic argument and suffers from the same flaws. Betraying a specific, comprehensive view of the good makes it perfectionist in a strong sense, which even my moderate perfectionist liberalism would not accept (see Chapter 1). More recent *neo-republican* arguments, such as those of Philip Pettit (Pettit 1997, 2012) on the other hand, do not rely on this kind of elevated picture of political activity but instead argue for a link between a conception of individual freedom as non-domination and a democratic system of government. These seem to me to share the fate of what I have called indirect-intrinsic arguments. Either one argues that democracy is instrumental to securing relations of non-domination in the private sphere, in which case the argument collapses into instrumentalism (Celikates 2014; Rostbøll 2015a), or one argues that non-dominated, equal relations in the political sphere are themselves important. In the latter case the argument becomes a direct-intrinsic one and one can ask: in the absence of private domination, why would equal political relations be a requirement of justice? We stand in justified relations of hierarchy in many contexts, without being insulted or denigrated. Why would this be problematic in the political sphere – in the absence of knock-on effects in the private sphere?

It seems, then, that republican arguments basically suffer the same fate as liberal ones. However, I do think that some of them may be able to escape this fate. Some authors advance what I have classified as a categorical-instrumental argument, by positing a *necessary* connection between the possibility of enjoying private basic rights on the one hand, and relations of equal standing (or non-domination) in the political sphere on the other hand. If one is really to be secure in the enjoyment of one's private rights, one needs to stand in relations of political equality. In Rousseauian terms, we leave behind our natural freedom (independence) in a state of nature and strive to regain civil freedom in a civil state. But we can only do so if we create a system of political decision-making in which no one is dependent on the arbitrary domination of a set of specific others ('masters'), but all are dependent on all others as equals. This is a form of dependence which is impersonal, as embodied in a system of law legislated by a general will which aims to protect everybody's interests equally (Rousseau 1997; Stilz 2009, 64). In Kantian terms, we cannot really enjoy our innate right to freedom if we are dominated politically. For whatever we enjoy under a (benevolent) dictatorship, it is not a set of rights, but some *privileges* which can be revoked at the will of the dominator (Rostbøll 2015b, 2016). In relational egalitarian terms, we cannot enjoy social equality in its non-political dimensions if we do not stand in relations of social equality in politics which are able to moderate non-political inequalities of standing (Kolodny 2014b, 303–7).[8] Taking these arguments together despite their important differences, they suggest that democracy is at least a *necessary* condition for the protection of private basic rights. Even if it is not a sufficient condition, because of the possibility of a majoritarian tyranny emerging within a democratic process (see the next section) these arguments rule out, by definition, the possibility of a benevolent dictatorship as a condition in which private rights are guaranteed. They do so in the name of a substantive idea of what it means to actually stand in a rightful relation to others at all in the private sphere; inegalitarian relations in the political sphere, by virtue of the arbitrary dominance they allow, are incompatible with such rightful relations.

Coming with rights to political participation, republicans also recognize duties to political participation. The emphasis on civic duty is characteristic of the republican tradition throughout and survives the transition from classical republicanism to neo-republicanism. The political sphere is seen as a public good (as it is in my duty-based argument) but duties to participation are derived from the necessity of having a system protecting private rights. The case for political rights necessitates political duties, both being based on the same necessity vis-à-vis private

---

[8] In addition to these authors, a part of Waldron's argument for democracy may also fall into this category, especially the crucial passage arguing for the right to justification on the basis of respect for the status of rights-bearers (Waldron 1999, 249–52). This is combined, however, with a stress on democracy as the only neutral procedure in the face of disagreement, which is a wholly different argument.

Private rights   - - - - - - - - - ->   Political rights
(subsistence, empowerment)   to participation

Private duties   Political duties
(subsistence, empowerment)   to participation

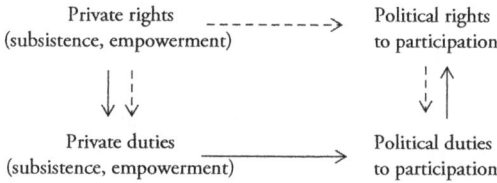

Figure 7.1   Rights-based (discontinuous lines) versus duty-based (continuous lines) justification of political rights

rights (see Figure 7.1 where the discontinuous lines illustrate the republican route to the justification of political rights).

The republican argument gains its strength from the powerful intuition that an equal right to a say in democratic procedures belongs to citizens as a right. The fight for democratic inclusion by sub-ordinated groups ('they owe it to me to listen to me') seems inspired by a rights-based claim for equal standing, not by a claim that, as suggested on my theory, one is withheld the tools to make true upon one's political duties to others. Against this, however, I think should be weighed two considerations. First, that intuition goes back to the wish to have one's social standing as expressed by *other* basic rights recognized, e.g. one's civil rights (cf. the Black civil rights movement in the United States), one's rights to work and equal treatment (the feminist movement), etc. For that, one needs to fight in the political arena and, hence, have the tools (rights) to engage in that fight. Second and more offensively, the duty-based theory does justice to other strong intuitions people have, namely about political duties. Most people recognize at least a moral (and sometimes advocate a legal) duty to vote, keep oneself informed and participate in politics, etc., wherever that is compatible with the moral duties arising from private life. Along these lines, citizenship is often thought of as a package of rights and duties (especially by those decrying a one-sided focus on rights). The duty-based argument stresses these duties and the package-deal nature of citizenship upfront.

Going beyond these intuitions, the theoretical challenge for the republican argument, it seems to me, is that it remains vulnerable to contingencies. In particular, to argue that one's private rights are only securely guaranteed ('robust') in a democracy presupposes that the level of reliable protection against violations is predictably higher in a democratic state than in any benevolent dictatorship. But given the possibilities for a majoritarian tyranny this is an empirical consideration, which could be falsified under particular circumstances. There cannot be a 100 per cent guarantee that under a democratic regime, everyone's basic rights will be protected, hence relations of non-domination are secured. To the extent that republican arguments commit themselves to such a tight causal link between democratic governance and private relations of non-domination, they promise too much (on the other hand, if they revert to a quasi-conceptual link, by stating non-domination constitutively implies having egalitarian social relations in public and private spheres, they are back at an intrinsic argument). Democratic protections may or may not be more robust than the ones offered by benevolent dictatorships, depending on the circumstances. Although this may sound provocative, one's basic rights are also privileges when granted by a democratic political system in the sense that they can always be revoked or violated by a majority. The duty-based argument by contrast does not make the outcome of a robust protection of private rights the linchpin of its categorical-instrumental argument; it doesn't promise any outcome in this respect. The only thing it argues is that if we are going to try, as private persons, to fulfil our duties (to respect their private rights) to others, we need a right to the only set of tools that may get the job done: political participation rights. Whether and to what extent the tools succeed, is a different matter and remains a contingent matter.

These are not decisive considerations and the debate will continue. If my reflections have shown that there is a serious duty-based contender to these republican arguments which deserves discussion, then this section has succeeded. In the remainder of this chapter I will elaborate on this perspective by taking up some further issues of democratic theory which have particular salience in contemporary societies.

7.3 Representative Democracy and Majority Rule

In this section, I want to ask if we can get from a justification of democracy in general to the type of democracy we know in modern advanced democracies. I highlight two features and discuss them in response to two objections one may launch against the duty-based argument. The first objection is the over-demandingness objection, which will allow me to introduce the issue of representative democracy. The second objection is the exclusion objection and it will allow me to introduce majority rule and discuss the problem of the tyranny of the majority.

The over-demandingness objection questions whether we really have an equal duty to political participation since it would be over-demanding for all citizens to participate in politics. Since ought-implies-can, we ought not to attribute an equal duty to all (and hence we need not give all an equal right). The objection assumes that the duty-based argument is committed to some form of direct democracy in which all citizens participate actively in politics on a regular basis to establish the laws. It argues that under modern conditions where political communities have a much larger scale than the idealized city-states of Ancient Greece, medieval Italy or Rousseau's Geneva, and where there is an extensive division of labour that doesn't allow many citizens time for active participation, such a direct democracy is unachievable.

Addressing this objection will allow me to clarify an important aspect of the argument. The rights to participation on my account come with strings attached: one gets these rights in order to use them in a particular way – i.e. to create a system of basic rights. This gives a republican flavour to the argument since it introduces a civic duty or responsibility to exercise one's political rights and to exercise them wisely.[9] Establishing a liberal political community is a common responsibility. However, the argument does not prohibit citizens to delegate this responsibility. The duty is to ensure a system of basic rights comes about, but the argument doesn't specify how. Whether this happens through permanent direct democratic engagement of all citizens or through a system in which representatives do much of the actual work, is a secondary matter. Similarly, parts of the work could be outsourced to officials, experts and bureaucrats. These possibilities are compatible with the argument so far, and are matters up for further discussion.

The only thing the argument requires is that in the final instance all political decisions are legitimated as being an expression of 'the will of the people', the collective of citizens discharging their duties towards each other. While citizens can choose a system in which they authorize specific others (officials and/or representatives) to do much of the work in practice, they must remain, in the final instance, those who are the authors of the law. Authorization must remain conditional, and all citizens must remain in a position to supervise these officials and representatives – and revoke their decisions. The reason for this is that citizens, finding their rights violated, should always be able to complain to all others of such a violation. All remain accountable and cannot hide behind the back of those who were authorized. In terms of responsibility,

---

[9] While recognizing such duties as important for making a political system function well, republicans do not seem to have realised (like those defending a duty to uphold just institutions, see Section 7.2), that this provides a basis for justifying democracy itself.

the actions of those authorized remain 'done by' the authorizers. To be able to assume accountability vis-à-vis such complaints from victims among our fellow citizens, all citizens need action possibilities for assessing and remedying these complaints. Hence they all need rights to oversee and correct the officials or representatives who actually committed a rights violation. Equality of rights for participating in such a system of mandated responsibilities remains necessary to discharge our inalienable duties to others, hence justified.

These considerations point to the fact that the duty to participation – as a duty to cooperate to create and uphold a legal-political system – may have practical implications which vary in intensity depending on how many others participate and on whether there is a crisis (widespread threats of rights-violations) or not. A certain level of political complacency in a well-ordered democracy may not be problematic. While in times of acute crisis the duty may become more demanding, it is precisely under such circumstances that the objection that the duty would be over-demanding (because not all citizens have the same time, will or knowledge to participate in politics) loses much of its moral force. Finally, we should also note what it means if we would accept the objection from over-demandingness and hence allocate the duty and accompanying political rights unequally. This would mean to relieve some citizens from their duties and burden others more heavily with the tasks of politics. While the selected group may actually like to bear that burden (for instance, because it would allow them to gain advantages for themselves) there is no normative ground available to justify such a distinction between citizens.

The *exclusion objection* argues that attributing political participation rights equally is instrumentally harmful to the achievement of other basic rights to the extent that there is the risk that some will abuse their participation rights by trying to have political decisions adopted which violate the basic rights of others (presumably, to their own private advantage). Hence, the structure of the duty-based argument makes it committed to withholding political participation rights from racists, sexists, defenders of caste-systems and others with inegalitarian aims (hereafter, inegalitarians), because not doing so would be instrumentally dangerous. The objection would have some force both in case we adopt consensual decision-making (unanimity rule) and when we adopt a majority rule. In the former case, even one inegalitarian could block all political decisions aiming to protect basic rights. Hence it seems the duty-based argument must exclude them categorically under such a decision rule. However, even under a majority rule inegalitarians pose a threat, since when they achieve a majority they can exercise what is famously called the tyranny of the majority, not only violating basic rights but also at the limit overthrowing the democratic system as a whole. Historical and contemporary examples show that this is not an imaginary danger. In short, the objection is that the duty-based argument ought to exclude inegalitarians from participation rights, but can't do so on its own terms.

On the (reasonable) assumption that there will always be inegalitarians in any sufficiently large population, the duty-based argument indeed cannot be committed to a unanimity rule. Consensus has the advantage of superior legitimacy since it ensures that everybody agrees with every decision. However, it is another (true) cliché of democratic theory that under modern conditions where political communities are large and political disagreement is unavoidable, consensus is an unworkable method. Pragmatic considerations dictate some form of majority rule. That need not be a large concession, indeed convincing arguments can be made that majority rule treats everybody with equal respect and is, therefore, a (or even the most) justified method of decision-making in the circumstances of politics (Waldron 1999, 113–16). Let's then accept majoritarian decision-making as a consequence of the duty-based argument both for these familiar pragmatic reasons but also because it allows us, in the first instance, to avoid the damaging implication that inegalitarians must be excluded, hence participation right unequally allocated.

Accepting majority rule, the exclusion objection reasserts itself at least in those circumstances where a party of inegalitarians is threatening to gain a majority position in the relevant decision-making bodies. The tyranny of the majority is not just a problem for my duty-based theory, of course, but for every theory of democracy. It is often phrased as a tension between the 'constitutional' element (protection of constitutional rights) and the 'democratic' element (protection of popular sovereignty) in constitutional democracies. As soon as a non-elected constitutional democracy would cancel the result of an election or otherwise disenfranchise a group which would otherwise reach a majority position, one horn of the dilemma is chosen. Where such a group gains the majority and engages in massive violation and annulation of basic rights, we reach the other horn of the dilemma. In itself the possibility of this dilemma is unavoidable under majority rule (indeed, at the limit it can arise even under unanimity rule if all are in favour of a non-constitutional, inegalitarian regime). The only question is how a theory can interpret and deal with it.

I cannot here give this issue anything like the treatment it deserves (which would require, inter alia, delving into long-standing debates about judicial review and constitutionalism). What I do want to suggest is that the duty-based theory could interpret the dilemma along the following lines.

Protecting basic rights from a justice-based point of view is not a constraint on democratic decision-making but its very aim. The legitimation of the creation of a political-legal practice in Section 7.2 was in terms of realising this aim. This leaves it an open question whether a part of the work of protecting these rights is allocated to non-elected bodies or whether the whole work is left to (indirectly or directly) elected bodies themselves. Hence the conflict between democracy and constitutionalism is better seen as a conflict between the justice-based legitimation of democracy and the actual political views of a justice-violating majority. The purpose built into the democratic ideal is like the purpose built into a complex piece of machinery, such as a car. An inegalitarian group can abuse democracy and try to use it for another purpose than the rights-protection for which it was designed, just as a driver can use a car not for the benefits of efficient transportation from A to B, but instead for deliberately wounding strangers in the street. Once someone is determined to abuse the system, there are no good options left. Both courses of action – forcing the driver to stop his or her abuse and allowing him or her to wound the strangers – would not lead to the salutary use for which the car was designed (efficient transportation). One can only stop the abuse by bringing to a halt the whole practice the abuser is engaged in.

The response of a duty-based theory to the possibility of such abuses is not that those who seem committed to abuse must be excluded. The exclusion objection is wrong in assuming that the duty-based theory *must* be committed to an exclusion strategy in every case of abuse. The theory is committed to two things: (1) equal political participation rights for all and (2) equal duties to political participation for all. The latter element should be interpreted, I suggest, substantively, not formally. Not just any type of action in a political forum counts as political participation. Participation presupposes sharing the collective goal for which one participates with others in the common endeavour. Hence the duty is a duty to participate in bringing about a rightful condition – i.e. a society in which everyone's basic capabilities are protected. As we saw, these rights are abstractly formulated and require specification (as well as enforcement and adjudication). That is the task participators face. If they go beyond the bounds of the duty thus specified, they violate the duty itself. But what counts as working within or beyond the boundaries of this pre-set purpose of democracy, thus conceived, cannot be decided in the abstract – and must itself be left open to democratic debate. Hence it is not very democratic to exclude those who play the game at the edges. Only in clear cases of violation could a case be made that the assignment of rights cannot be allowed to be self-defeated by exercises of these rights which defeat their purposes. At least by specifying these purposes in advance, a justice-based theory (in contrast to a pure proceduralist theory) has the resources to make such judgements.

These reflections have hopefully cleared up some potential misunderstandings and shown some of the implications of the duty-based argument for democracy. Much more needs to be said, but here I will address only one final issue.

7.4 A Democratic Solution to the Boundary Problem

The justification of democracy so far has not *eo ipso* solved the legitimate delineation of the people (*demos*) among whom democratic mechanisms of decision-making are to be applied. Who to exclude or include within the people, and on what basis? In this section I will argue for a solution to the boundary problem which reconciles aspects of so-called cosmopolitan and statist positions on this issue.[10]

Within the tradition of social contract theory, instead of referring to an external source (such as the will of God), the social contract refers to the will of the people as the legitimating ground for establishing a political authority and endowing it with specific powers. A democratic criterion – the unanimous consent of all individuals to the contract – is doing the work of legitimation. However, this contract cannot itself legitimate the delineation of the set of individuals who are to belong to 'the people', since that would require that a democratic procedure is already established through which the will of the people is exercised. In the absence of a democratic forum to decide on the boundaries of the people (hence, the exclusion of others as not belonging to this people), it seems that this question can only be decided pre-politically, hence non-democratically. Therefore, it fails to have legitimacy. This is the boundary problem.

---

[10] In this section, I concentrate on the territorial side of the boundary problem, leaving aside internal boundaries (who should be included and enfranchised among those living on the territory, e.g. minors, non-citizens, animals as well?).

In the history of social contract *theory* this legitimacy problem was often ignored by imagining – counter-factually – that there was only one set of individuals living together in the state of nature in one proto-community without any problems arising from the existence of other external communities. However, such a presupposition is hard to sustain in a globalized world where there are real questions about the reconfiguration of nation-states. Globalization similarly throws into doubt the historically prevailing *practical* solution to the boundary problem since the political revolutions of the seventeenth and eighteenth centuries: nationalism. The identification of 'the nation' as a pre-politically existing community in which the relevant members are united rests on a set of cultural characteristics (language, religion and history) constituting the unity of a group. However, these characteristics fail to demarcate a group of individuals consistently given the overlap in shared characteristics between nationals and non-nationals. To remedy these inconsistencies, cultural nationalism always risks sliding into ethnic nationalism, based on a mythic ethnos from which foreigners can be excluded by definition. However, to draw the boundaries of an ethnic people in an unambiguous way also relies on the political use of force and hence fails to qualify as a pre-political solution which escapes the charge of circularity (Abizadeh 2012, 868–73).

The most common response in political theory has been that the boundary problem is unsolvable. A solution in terms of democratic legitimacy simply is impossible. The boundaries of the demos can only be determined by whatever *historically contingent process* has happened to lead to the formation of separate peoples. Democracy is a criterion which specifies a decision mechanism within a group already formed; it cannot decide about the boundaries of the group itself. The historical position is widespread in political philosophy, appearing in democratic theorists as diverse as Schumpeter, Dahl, Habermas and Rawls (Näsström 2007, 625). However, such an appeal to historical contingency has conservative implications. It privileges the historically grown status quo of power relations over alternative arrangements which would require reconfiguring these relations (Näsström 2003, 818–19, 2007, 643–4). This seems to lead to the tragic conclusion that while boundary decisions do call for legitimate solutions, every solution can be criticized as illegitimate. There is a legitimacy problem, but there are no criteria to resolve it (Näsström 2007, 644–6, 2011, 126–31). Can we do better?

One prominent position which one may want to consider is the so-called 'all-affected principle'. It says that all those who are affected in a certain decision should be enfranchised (Arrhenius 2005; Goodin 2007).

When applied to territorial communities this would lead to giving all world citizens a vote in the US elections, since all are affected by its outcomes. However, this would be absurdly over-inclusive (the US government makes many decisions which do not influence the typical Asian or African citizens). The principle, therefore, naturally pushes to the conclusion that different policy proposals will affect different constituencies and hence to a need for assembling a different demos for every new proposal (Whelan 1983, 19; Goodin 2007, 57; Song 2012, 56). However, that seems unworkable. In the following, I will therefore assume that territorially bounded political communities applying democratic methods to their common life once constituted will remain a basic feature of political life. Functional integration may be a supplement to territorial integration but cannot completely replace it. People who live in each other's physical proximity tend to have more and more intense interactions with each other and hence influence each other's interests across a broader spectrum of issues than people who do not live in proximity. The fact that human life takes place in a spatial dimension means we bring our children to a school around the corner, go to the hospital nearby and participate in local traffic when commuting to work. This basic feature seems unlikely to change however many layers of globalized activity are added to our modern lives. Applying the all-affected principle, then, leads us to a need for a political community through which to organize and legitimize these interactions with those in our proximity, even if we accept more flexible, supplementary mechanisms for decision-making to structure less intensive interactions with distant others.[11]

More promising is a *cosmopolitan* position.[12] The boundary problem calls for the construction of a global demos, not through the expansionary

---

[11] In addition, there are two other considerations militating in favour of territorial integration: (1) Decision-making in one issue-area affects decision-making in other areas. An exclusively functionally integrated political system would have no mechanisms for dealing with these cross-over effects, or for prioritising some issue-areas over others, and channeling people's time, resources and attention to where attention is most needed from a larger, holistic perspective of life in the community as a whole. The need for integrated decision-making on the basis of a formulation of a 'common good' also militates in favour of territorially based communities. (2) A world without territorial integration may be politically chaotic, violent and insufficiently stable to fulfill the first function of any political system: providing predictable, publicly known, reliable rules on the basis of which people can organise their day-to-day interactions.

[12] I leave out of consideration that the all-affected principle can also lead to a cosmopolitan position. Goodin has argued the principle should be understood as calling for the inclusion in the demos of all *possibly* affected by a decision. Since it is never sure who will be included, 'virtually (maybe literally) everyone in the world – and indeed everyone in all possible future worlds – should be entitled to vote on any proposal or any proposal for proposals' (Goodin 2007, 55). This leads him to endorse something like a 'world government', at least in the form of a global appeal possibility

logic of identifying the circle of all possibly affected (as argued by Goodin), but on more principled grounds. The boundary problem only arises on the assumption that political communities are bounded and based on the actual (even if implicit) consent of a specific subset of all people on earth. However, these are assumptions inherited from a nationalist framework. When we reject them, we arrive at the idea of an in principle unbounded demos (Bartelson 2008; Agné 2010; Abizadeh 2012). If all of humanity is included in the act of establishing the boundaries of territorially defined communities, then the boundary problem – as a paradox of democratic theory – dissolves. We can democratically decide, after all, how to constitute communities which can then be democratically organized by including all, as a matter of principle, in that decision. A decision legitimated by all does not run afoul of the problem that motivated the boundary problem – i.e. that the drawing of boundaries is an historically contingent exercise of power which is unjustified towards those who are excluded (Agné 2010, 389). The global demos, then, is the only demos which enjoys 'prima facie democratic legitimacy' (Bartelson 2008, 171) and all other demoi can only be derivatively legitimated, through an exercise of political will of the global demos. This cosmopolitan position is supported by my agency-based capability theory. In Section 7.2, I argued that people in the same political community owe each other duties of justice. To the extent that those living within closed boundaries affect each other's lives but not the lives of those living in other communities, such an assumption was warranted. But in a globalized world, where complex interactions among communities take place and boundaries are contested, we have to shift upwards, consider all agents as members of one community and legitimize particular communities and the boundaries between them from this most inclusive, global point of view.

The consequences of this cosmopolitan position, however, do not necessarily point in the direction of a global demos functioning in the way a national demos does within states, as the legitimising constituency of a fully-functioning territorial government at a global scale, a world government. Instead, they point to a legitimation of a state-system as we know it. The reason for this is given by statists who point to the substantive preconditions for well-functioning democracies. Thus, Sarah Song has convincingly argued that a democratic system requires political

---

against decisions of territorial states which affect interests across states (Goodin 2007, 64). Others, reasoning from a coercion principle reach similar conclusions, given the ubiquitousness of cross-border coercive effects of state action (Abizadeh 2008). However, the problems with a world government are well-known, so I will not rehearse them here.

equality, equal opportunity for political influence and some solidarity between members of the political community (Song 2012, 43–8). Song argues that the track-record of successful modern states show that these conditions can be realized in the context of a state, while there are good reasons to believe this will be more much difficult to realize in a global context (Song 2012, 58–62). These are Song's estimations about the comparative chances of implementing democracy at a state or global level and one might not exactly share them and be more optimistic or pessimistic than she is. However, the focus on substantive conditions suggests a promising method for thinking about a legitimate state-system. David Miller similarly proposes a method which identifies democratic theory with a set of normative ideals and then asks what the conditions are for the successful realization of these ideals. Miller distinguishes two types of democratic theory (liberal and radical ones) that portray an ideal democracy differently, and then shows how this may lead them to different answers to the boundary problem. For example, liberal democrats favour a pluralism of voices within a political community and, hence, may be more open to an 'inclusionary push' while radical democrats favour cohesion among members of the public and will, therefore, be more sensitive to an 'exclusionary pull' (D. Miller 2009).

The details of these accounts are less important for my purposes. The method, however, is a promising way to identify a substantive framework of criteria for whether or not to upscale or downscale the size of currently existing democratic communities. Statists like Song and Miller convincingly show how these considerations can be derived from democratic theory, in thinking about its substantive preconditions. My agency-based capability theory would similarly be a basis for offering such considerations. The boundaries should then be drawn in such a way that this best respects the substantive normative demands articulated by this theory. Such considerations must then be treated as the input of the deliberations of a global demos, for cosmopolitans have rightly shown how that is the only truly legitimising framework for state boundaries (or any boundaries, for that matter). This solution combines the cosmopolitan position and the statist position on the boundary problem in a coherent – and I would claim attractive – way (Ypi 2008).

Some will object to such a solution. Thus, Arash Abizadeh argues that to reach 'a completely global social contract establishing differentiated political jurisdictions (if any) and the distribution of individuals among them' we require unanimity, which is 'astronomically improbable' (Abizadeh 2012, 875). It is true, of course, that the decision requires controversial judgements about which type of democratic theory to use, how to derive substantive conditions for a well-functioning democracy from this theory and how to apply these conditions to the real world. However, instead of imagining a world-assembly of all humanity reaching unanimous decisions on the precise location of all borders on the planet, one might also take a more deflationary approach. One could work from the assumption that the borders of the state-system as it exists are legitimate to the extent that they are undisputed. When there are controversies (e.g. new states due to secessions) one could then think about practical ways to solve them which can be treated as the expression of a global demos. For example, Agné argues that we could have a system where new states are recognized by international law not when other states recognize them unilaterally, but when global democratic institutions do and where such institutions resolve border disputes between existing states (Agne, 406). To the extent that the current state-system does not adhere to such procedures, it is illegitimate. However, this is not an objection to the theoretical position defended here. To imagine a global system of legitimate boundary determination is 'realistically utopian'. It is not a requirement for solving the boundary problem that it must be realizable today or tomorrow.

To finish up, I want to draw attention to two features of this position. First, there may be *several* ways of drawing the world's boundaries which might be legitimated in the sense of satisfying the substantive democratic criteria. While physical proximity creates territorially more intense interactions, this doesn't dictate a unique solution as to who should band together with whom (Simmons 2013, 335). If so, there is no unique solution and historically contingent facts may help make a decision in favour of one of them. Imagine there are four territories A, B, C and D that each organize a range of internal public goods (say, garbage collection) but are each too small to organize high-end health-care services, given the specialized knowledge and scale for doing so. The territories are roughly arranged as four squares and each combination of two of them would be the optimal scale for organising the health service. Whether they divide up one way (A–B and C–D) or the other (A–C and B–D), doesn't matter from the point of view of democratic legitimacy (all else being equal). This is the only way in which contingencies may enter the argument. However, this is not different from countless other decisions made within political communities where justice-respecting solutions to practical problems may incorporate cultural, historical and other local considerations to prefer one solution over the other.

Second, one may question whether the need for integrated decision-making provides an argument for a state-system. Within a state-system, integrated decision-making primarily takes place at the state level. Functionally organized integration above the state level is the exception, an 'add-on' to the primary political community which is the state. Hence the primary responsibility for realising the demands of social justice (basic capabilities) also lies with the state. But what if the number of exceptions – due to globalization – becomes so large that a need for integrated decision-making arises at a higher, supra-national level? A lot of important issues of global justice – climate change, immigration, global trade and finance, world poverty – call for their solutions by adding to territorially bounded communities functionally specialized global *demoi* to alleviate these problems. Instead of having a large number of supra-national organizations each dealing with specialized issue-areas, at some point clustering these into one organization will be not just more efficient, but also indispensable in light of the conflicts between these issue-areas (e.g., think of how global trade regulations interact with global environmental concerns). Arguably, exactly this is the experience of European integration in the European Union and something similar could happen at the global level – then we would have a case for something resembling a world state. My position can accommodate this limit-case since it justifies going in this direction when the inclusionary pushes are radically stronger than the exclusionary pulls (in Miller's terminology). We should keep in mind, however, that in such a territorially and functionally integrated world-state there will be subdivisions (as in any federal state) and the same questions about the borders between the sub-units will arise as we have concerning the borders between states.

Conclusion

In a just society citizens should each have an equal right to a set of basic capabilities. This claim, familiar from other capability theories of justice in political philosophy, has been developed in a particular direction in this book. By tying the concept of basic capabilities to an ideal of navigational agency, I have hoped to strengthen the liberal character of the capability theory in the direction of what I have called a 'moderate perfectionist liberalism'. Simultaneously the introduction of the concept of navigational agency aims to accomplish an innovation in liberal theory. By tying the concept of action itself to the social context in which individuals act, stressing how action is a form of participation, liberal agency could be determined more precisely as a specific type of agency: that type which allows those who possess it to navigate between different social contexts, choosing where and how to participate freely and autonomously. This is a form of empowerment that requires capabilities for either exit or voice (or a combination of both) to gain a critical distance from existing social practices. I have tried to justify this conception with an agency-based transcendental argument and shown the consequences of adopting this conception for adopting distributive principles and selecting capabilities.

All of this leaves work to be done. In conclusion, I want to briefly mention three issues which each deserve a chapter-length treatment (or more) of their own. I cannot adequately deal with them here, but saying nothing about them at all might raise serious misunderstandings about the implications of the navigational agency theory.

First, there is the question of *conflict between capabilities* which has been mentioned in passing. It is one thing to draw up a list of capabilities, but assuming this can be done, it is quite something different to show how such capabilities need to be traded off in case of conflict. How to trade off one person's capability to free expression against another person's free association (when they would conflict)? To take a stance on that issue requires resolving at least two issues. One is the difficult philosophical issue of commensurability. Should one, on the model of a utilitarian theory, assume that all capabilities to agency can be measured on a single scale? Arguably, this would then be an agency-scale, where each capability represents a certain amount of agency (the talk of amounts and scales is quantitative; but even if one takes the position that exact quantification is impossible, one is confronted with the fact that conflict resolution requires some activity of weighting or balancing, hence determining relations or ratios). Second, we need to consider whether there is a hierarchy between capabilities, so that some get a greater *a priori* weight (or even at the limit, lexical priority) than others. I have to leave both of these matters for some other day.

Second, there is the question of extending the capability theory beyond the standard case of presently living mentally healthy adult human beings within one's political community. One extension is to accept rights to capabilities for *future generations*. Elsewhere I have argued that rights to capabilities can also be attributed to members of future generations, pace several standard objections against such rights attributions. I have also explored what this implies in terms of sustaining critical resources for future generations, in contrast, for example, to John Rawls's just savings principle, or the economist's way of arguing about sustainability (Claassen 2016). Another extension relates to those who seem to lack rational agency in a radical sense: young children, animals and severely mentally disabled persons, sometimes lumped together as so-called *marginal agents*. It is often thought that theories giving preeminent status to rational agency cannot present a credible treatment of these categories of agents. I think, but cannot argue this here, that such a conclusion is much too hasty. The work by Christine Korsgaard in animal ethics, for example, attests to the fact that non-rational agency can also be valued from a rational point of view (Korsgaard 2004, 2011). While not without its own problems, such theories are at least as promising as other theories in animal ethics. Finally, there is the extension to the *global level*. While I have argued that duties of justice are primarily owed within political communities (paradigmatically, in modern times, nation-states) I have also argued that the legitimacy of the boundaries between these communities requires a global assessment (Section 7.4). This position should not be thought to exclude the possibility that in addition there are duties of global justice. To the contrary, where states create a shared global order, duties pertaining to their interactions within this order arise. And even in the absence of such an order, political communities may have remedial positive duties when political communities fail to protect their own citizens' basic rights. These matters I have treated elsewhere as well (Claassen 2019b).

Third, there is the question of the completeness of the account in terms of justice. One may wonder whether there are also grounds to act for political communities which go *beyond justice*. The present book, focused as it is on requirements of justice as the ground for government interventions, may give the impression that no other grounds would be possible in this respect. However, this need not be the case. My theory leaves open the possibility that governments provide certain public goods which are not necessary for attaining social justice. In the literature this problem is discussed as the problem of 'discretionary public goods' (Klosko 1990; Miller 2004). Assuming one has a theory of justice which defines which goods governments need to provide as a matter of justice, the question in this debate is whether governments are allowed to do more. A famous example is the question whether state support for the arts is legitimate (presuming it is not a necessary condition for justice). Elsewhere I have defended the position that democratic majority rule, under certain constraints, may be a legitimate way of allowing for discretionary public goods provision (Claassen 2013). Whatever one thinks of this position, we can here leave it open and recognize that this category of public goods needs to be debated on separate terms.

All of these and other questions remain to be discussed. A theory of justice is work in progress, as much as realizing justice in society is. The hope (or the consolation of a professional philosopher) is that the former may contribute to the latter, however indirectly. Anyhow, it belongs to the deep structure of a liberal society to strive not just for justice, but also for maximal self-clarification and self-understanding about what it is we are doing and why, when we try to achieve a just society.

Appendix 1: Amartya Sen on Agency, Capabilities and Rights

This appendix discusses two important potential criticisms of my agency-based capability theory that one could raise on the basis of Amartya Sen's work. The first one pertains to the relation between agency and capabilities; the second one to the relation between capabilities and rights.

A1.1 Agency, Well-being and Capabilities

The argument about the connection between agency and capabilities in Chapter 2 may raise the question how I see the relation between my definition of agency and Sen's use of the same concept.

Sen has used the concept of agency in different ways (Crocker 2008; Crocker and Robeyns 2010). A first usage of agency is common to Sen and other capability theorists: to refer to the individual's capacity to make choices from a capability set, which lead that person to achieve certain functionings. This usage represents the core idea of the capability approach: to guarantee a set of freedoms from which the individual can choose for herself. This use of agency, however, does not remove the interpretation of the concept of functionings as bringing the possessor of a functioning 'well-being', but it brings us a theory which combines well-being and agency: the agent chooses herself between functionings which give her well-being.

A second usage is more distinctive of Sen – he uses agency to denote a space of evaluation that is *not* captured by the conceptual pair of capabilities and functionings. Sen often made a distinction between four terms, all parts of what he calls a person's 'advantage': well-being freedom and well-being achievement, and agency freedom and agency achievement. Well-being refers to the well-being one derives from achieving and being able to achieve one's personal goals. Agency (in both its freedom and achievement aspects) is meant to reflect a wider range of goals, not necessarily relating to one's personal well-being, but also, say, to the well-being of others or not to anyone's well-being at all (Sen 1985b, 1992, 59–62, 2009, 286–90). Sen furthermore associates his own capability notion exclusively with the well-being pair of notions: functionings for him are well-being achievements, and capabilities are well-being freedoms. Capabilities for him are a metric of well-being, introduced in contrast to utilitarian interpretations of well-being. The need for going beyond well-being is introduced by the wish to acknowledge that we sometimes have goals that do not form part of our well-being at all.[1]

This conceptual apparatus has been very influential. Following Sen, many have thought of capabilities as necessarily being indicators of 'well-being', not of 'agency'. However, Sen's fourfold framework is confusing, because we need to exercise our agency in converting any freedom into an achievement (the first usage of agency), whether the content of this freedom relates to one's own well-being or not. The positioning of agency as opposed to well-being wrongly suggests that the exercise of agency is absent from the well-being freedom/well-being achievement part of Sen's structure. The framework is also unhelpful where it identifies only 'non-well-being goals' with the term agency. One way of recasting Sen's scheme in less confusing language would be to say that he recognizes agency for the sake of one's own well-being goals and agency for the sake of 'non-well-being goals', and both of these goals can, in turn, be achieved when our agency is successful. But, even then, there is a more fundamental objection.

Nussbaum has argued that Sen himself has already introduced a very broad notion of well-being by using capabilities instead of utility to characterize well-being. Given that redefinition, the idea of a 'non-well-being goal' does not make much sense. Capabilities can have as their object *any* goals we set ourselves (whether or not they are related to our own well-being). So the well-being freedom/well-being achievement pair of notions is superfluous and should be abandoned (Nussbaum 2011b, 197–201). Similarly, capabilities in my use of the term encompass both Sen's broader agency pair of notions and his pair of well-being notions: they may serve to enhance our own well-being or that of others.[2] I have stressed a wide concept of an agent's goals, in which we only assume that the chooser values (the realization of) his or her goals as good; for otherwise he or she

---

[1] Carter maintains that in later work it becomes less clear whether Sen restricts capabilities to the well-being pair of notions because he talks about capabilities 'we have reason to value'. See Carter (2014, 80). My argument is directed against any position making the restriction Sen made in earlier work.

[2] I would also object to the word 'achievement' in Sen's account: we do not only function in a certain way when we achieve a goal, but already when we pursue it (whether or not we are successful). Unsuccessful action is also action.

would not have a reason to choose these goals in the first place. Thus there is a necessary orientation to well-being in every action. But it is an entirely different question whose well-being the agent aims at: his or her own or that of someone else (or impersonal well-being, whatever that may be).

This latter question moved Sen to introduce agency freedom and agency achievement. He was worried about the narrowness of the egoistic assumption that people would only be motivated by their own well-being (Crocker and Robeyns 2010, 76). This however is important only when we are concerned with a descriptive or explanatory theory of agency, which wants to give a correct account of the fullness of human motivation in setting goals. But if we are concerned with normative exercises (such as theorizing justice) all of this is irrelevant. In making claims like 'citizen *a* should have a right to a set of capabilities (x, y, z)', the capabilities (x, y, z) refer to characteristics of the relevant individual *a*. Whether the goals he or she sets him/herself once he or she has obtained that set are egoistic or not, is besides the point. For evaluative purposes, we are only interested in whether we are justified in claiming that he or she should be entitled to this set with these elements. The evaluative exercise aspires to an impartial, third-person standpoint. In such exercises the content of the justified set for citizen *b* is determined separately, by a parallel exercise, not by thinking about whether *a* could use his or her capability set to altruistically further *b*'s well-being.

A1.2　Capabilities and Rights

Now let's consider an objection explicitly raised by Sen against those who – like me – want to capture all human rights in terms of capabilities. Sen argues that the capability approach can only constitute part of a theory of human rights because some human rights cannot be captured in the language of capabilities. According to him, the capability approach is well able to cover the 'opportunity aspect' of human rights but would miss their 'process aspect'. He introduces the distinction between both aspects by way of three examples.

First, assume that a girl, Rima, wants to go out in the evening. If now an authoritarian guardian decides that she must not go out, he is violating her freedom. If, however, he decrees that she must go out (so that she is forced to do what she wants to do anyway), this is a violation of the process aspect, but not the opportunity aspect, of her freedom. Sen immediately relativizes the force of this distinction, for he adds that her opportunity freedom may also be violated, even though the violation is not 'substantial'. He says that it would be more substantial if Rima would be forced to do something she had not chosen anyway (Sen 2004b, 331, 2009, 371). Second, Sen uses a health care example. He notes that when given 'symmetric care', women tend to live longer than men. Focusing on the opportunity aspect (i.e. men's and women's capability to live long) would entail giving more care to men. But there may be reasons of 'process equity' to give equal care in this situation, even if this leads to unequal capability outcomes (Sen 2004b, 336). Third, Sen states that 'a denial of "due process" can be the subject matter of human rights (no matter what the outcome of the fair trial may be)' (Sen 2004b, 331–32, 2009, 371). Here too, capabilities would only be able to capture the outcome, and not the process aspect. What to make of this critique?

First, Rima's example does not show the usefulness of distinguishing a process aspect from an opportunity aspect. Both are violated when Rima is forced to go out. Contrary to Sen's statement, her opportunity set *is* restricted substantially, from (go out, not go out) to (go out). That she wants to go out anyway is inconsequential in assessing her opportunity freedom.[3] If we reject Sen's way of accounting for opportunities, then it seems to me that the capability approach does not have to accept a separate process aspect. Every restriction in an agent's process of choosing (process aspect) is brought about by a restriction in the options that an agent is able to choose (opportunity aspect). The nested structure between agency-as-a-capability and lower-level capabilities (see Section 2.1) helps to understand this point. Having a concrete capability (say, to move around freely) means being able to make a choice (between moving to A or B, or not moving at all), so it presupposes the capacity for choosing (agency) itself. There is no way of interfering with a person's process of free choice between these options which does not also, at the same time, affect the size of the available option set (and the intensity of the interference can be measured, inter alia, by how many options it blocks).

The second example is also problematic. Let's modify it and look at Ann and Ben who are both eighty years old. If given no care, Ann will continue to live. Although we can't predict exactly for how long, according to the standard statistics, she will have five more years. Ben however has contracted a standard old-age disease and will die if given no care. Who would say that we should withhold care to Ben? In terms of opportunity sets, 'process equity' here reduces Ben's set to one element (to die), while Ann remains free to choose between two options (to live, to die).

---

[3] That Sen judges otherwise is caused by his preference-based conception of opportunity freedom. For a discussion on this, see Carter (1996).

Ben's freedom of choice is heavily interfered with. The only reason why Sen's example seems to have some intuitive force is because he focuses on an ex ante allocation of resources between two groups (women, men) instead of an allocation of resources between individuals, which is made at the moment when they do or do not fall ill (e.g., according to medical need). This seems a flagrant misapplication of his own capability approach. Of course men will have a right to receive more care (as a group), if there is some conversion factor (whatever it is) which makes it the case that women need less care to reach the same longevity.

We should note that the 'process aspect' refers to very different things in these two examples: to the process of an individual's free choosing (Rima's example) and to a specific distributive outcome (i.e. strict equality in the distribution of health care resources). In Sen's third example (due process), apparently a fair outcome of the trial refers to one's opportunities (capabilities) while the guarantees of due process refer to the process aspect. Here the process aspect refers neither to the process of an individual's choosing, nor to the process of reaching a specific distributive outcome, but again to something else: to certain processual guarantees that are neither under the individual's control, nor reduce to a specific outcome. This interpretation of 'process aspect', too, can be captured in capability language (Nussbaum 2011a, 28). After all, being able to have a fair trial is a specific opportunity (besides the content of the verdict). Anyone who has lost a trial but is nonetheless content that he or she has been heard and fairly treated will consider the value of that capability. If one considers that this capability cannot be left to people's free exercise in judicial practice, one might also conclude that the appropriate goal for due process rights is functioning, not capability. This still remains within the capability-to-functionings metric.[4]

I conclude that the concept of process aspect in Sen is elusive, but the examples he uses do not point to a defeat of the capability metric with respect to its ambition to capture the nature and content of human rights.

---

[4] Linda Barclay has argued that capabilities cannot capture non-discrimination rights in particular and the demand for equal status that motivates human rights lists in general. The capability approach must rely either on ad hoc introducing a capability to equal standing, or to allowing functionings (instead of capabilities) to be the policy goal. See Barclay (2016, 11–12; similarly Liao 2015, 91–3; Richardson 2000, 323). Against this, I would argue that my agency-based capability theory introduces the idea of equal standing in the idea of equality of agency, from the beginning (not ad hoc). Second, functionings promotion is no embarrassment for the capabilities approach, since its metric is capabilities-to-function, and it may recognize that where agency is lacking, functionings must be the goal (see also Section 5.3). This does not undermine the capability approach's claim to be the right metric for human rights.

Appendix 2: Philipp Pettit's Republicanism and the Capability Approach

Philip Pettit has argued that the capability approach uses a notion of freedom that is close to his republican concept of freedom as non-domination (Pettit 2001, 2010). In this Appendix I discuss his debate with Sen, and argue why my concept of free and autonomous agency should be preferred over republican freedom.

Pettit starts by making a distinction between two ways in which a person can be free. First, his preferences can be decisive for a choice independent of the content of these preferences: 'I am free in relation to A or B only if, depending on how my preference may go, I get A or I get B' (Pettit 2001, 5). Pettit attributes this notion of 'content-independently decisive preference' to Sen, but claims it is not enough for an adequate understanding of freedom. In addition, I can be free only if my preferences are what Pettit calls 'favour-independently decisive' (Pettit 2001, 11), independent of any arbitrary decisions of others who may happen to hold power over my decisions. This is republican freedom as non-domination by the arbitrary will of others (Pettit 1997). He also calls this an idea of 'status-freedom', since it focuses on the status of a person as a free man, not a slave (Pettit 2010, 108). Pettit claims this kind of freedom is implicit in Sen's concept of capabilities. The most attractive interpretation for what it is to have a capability to a functioning is to enjoy content-independently as well as favour-independently decisive preferences. This means that the capability approach should endorse the republican view of freedom.[1]

Sen's response to this can be characterized as a friendly 'thanks but no thanks' (Sen 2001, 52–56, 2009, 304–9). He emphasizes that republican freedom and the freedom offered by having capabilities still capture two distinct aspects of freedom. Both can have merit but it is not a good

---

[1] A similar plea for merging republicanism and the capability approach can be found in (J. Alexander 2008). See my review in Claassen (2009b).

idea, he claims, to subsume the capability approach's concept of freedom under republican freedom, for then something is lost. He uses an example to explain this. Imagine a disabled person in three types of situations:

> Case 1. Person A is not helped by others, and she is thus unable to go out of her house.
> Case 2. Person A is always helped by helpers arranged either by a social security system in operation in her locality (or, alternatively, by volunteers with goodwill), and she is, as a result, fully able to go out of her house whenever she wants and to move around freely.
> Case 3. Person A has well-remunerated servants who obey – and have to obey – her command, and she is fully able to go out of her house whenever she wants and to move around freely. (Sen 2009, 306)

Sen claims that from the perspective of the capability approach Cases 2 and 3 are equal: person A is able to reach the same level of functioning either way. The republican approach, by contrast, judges person A unfree in both Cases 1 and 2; in Case 2 because she depends on the arbitrary favours of others for reaching that functioning level. The capability approach focuses on what a person can actually do, while the republican approach focuses on the robustness of certain freedoms. The capability approach remains important as a separate perspective, Sen argues, because 'we live in a world in which being completely independent of the help and goodwill of others may be particularly difficult to achieve, and sometimes not even be the most important thing to achieve' (Sen 2009, 308).

Sen, in my view, overestimates the differences between republican freedom and capabilitarian freedom. His position is understandable to the extent that he talks about the capability metric as such. The metric does not include robust protections of freedom but only focuses our attention on the actual attainment of capability levels. But this restriction is somewhat artificial, since Sen himself has *also* argued that the capability approach should form the basis of a theory of human rights (Sen 2004b, 2005). To the extent that citizens have rights to capabilities they do receive robust protections against the arbitrary will of others. One could object that this robust protection is the result of embedding the capability metric in a rights-based approach, which is only one possible way of using the metric. I do not find this reply particularly convincing. For, as Sen himself has repeatedly stated, the capability approach as the mere endorsement of a metric is incomplete and therefore *must* be embedded in a more general theoretical framework to be operationalized. Therefore, *any* defender of the approach cannot escape the task of 'completing' the metric, and proposing her or his favoured larger framework, if she or he wants to be able to actually put the approach to work. Once this is done, we arrive at full capability *theories*. Embedding the capability metric in a rights theory is a very important application of the general approach. Such a capability-rights theory does offer the robust protections of capability levels that Pettit argues are the advantage of republicanism (note that the pure 'metric' of republican freedom also needs to be translated into politically protected rights to be able to offer robust protections against domination).[2] Both theories do not differ in this respect.[3]

The real difference between both theories, in my view, lies elsewhere. Pettit positions republican freedom between negative and positive freedom (Pettit 1997, 27–31). Negative freedom is about freedom from interference, republican freedom is about freedom from domination by others and positive freedom is about self-mastery (Berlin 2002). The capability approach is most-often associated with positive freedom, since it would be about protecting effective, not merely formal freedoms (Olsaretti 2005). The latter observation is correct, but the link to positive freedom is too quick, for it all depends on *which* capabilities are selected as basic (again, the metric needs to be embedded in a full theory). One can imagine a libertarian capability theory that restricts itself to protecting effective freedoms to non-interference with private property. An ideal of self-mastery is only realized in capability theories which also recognize rights to functionings that are necessary to overcome internal deficiencies, e.g. in their mental (education) and physical (health care) constitution.

Such capability theories that aim to protect positive freedom are more demanding than a theory of freedom as non-domination. Following Pettit's own positioning of republican freedom, there remains a crucial difference between a person who is not dominated by others and a person who is a master of him/herself (Dagger 2005, 181–7; Qizilbash 2016). In focusing so much on external threats to persons (the masters to the slaves) Pettit has little regard for internal threats to full personhood. This

---

[2] It remains a separate question how robust the protection must be (note how one might question the strong difference in robustness between Cases 2 and 3, by questioning the security of the disabled person's fortune which allows him or her to have servants in the face of variable government taxation policies, or by upgrading the robustness of the volunteer system).

[3] Qizilbash offers a different (complementary to mine) diagnosis of the Sen-Pettit exchange: he suggests they can be brought together if the capability approach includes a capability for self-respect, something which would be thwarted by the dependence on volunteers in Case 2 (Qizilbash 2016). Yet another answer to Pettit would be to stress that the capability approach can be centrally concerned with the security of functionings (Wolff and De-Shalit 2007, 63–73).

difference would be obliterated when one imports the capabilities and resources necessary for positive freedom into the theory as *necessary conditions* for reaching republican freedom, as Pettit sometimes suggests (Pettit 1997, 81–2). But if one's theory does in fact include all the conditions necessary for positive freedom then it can better be described as a theory defending positive freedom instead of a theory defending republican freedom (given the uncontested idea that republican freedom is in between positive and negative freedom, hence less extensive than positive freedom, such a theory would have to carry the name of the more extensive ideal, not the lesser one). If, on the other hand, one restricts the theory to conditions necessary for republican freedom only, then there remains a real difference between both theories. The defender of positive freedom could then ask Pettit what the worth is of a life free of domination from others, if one is not able to master oneself. As Richard Dagger states: 'the desire to be free from domination is rooted in the desire to be in some sense self-governing' (Dagger 2005, 185).

In conclusion, a rights-to-capabilities theory can have the robustness the republican approach advocates; these rights should give one abilities independent of the favours of others. But the rights covered by this metric should not only include those which secure non-domination by others, but in addition cover those securing domination by oneself, in the relevant respects.

Appendix 3: The Anthropological Method of Justifying Rights

Nussbaum's early theory is exemplary for the anthropological method of justification. We seek capabilities belonging to a life that is 'truly human'. When Nussbaum's work is taken as exemplary, the capability approach gets qualified as a 'naturalistic' human rights theory, in the sense that it uses a list of invariable human characteristics which are to be the object of human rights protection (Beitz 2009, 62). In this Appendix I discuss what I see as the main problem this anthropological method raises when one wants to *justify* a set of basic rights.

Nussbaum explains that her capabilities list is an answer to the question: 'What are the features of our common humanity, features that lead us to recognize certain others, however distant their location and their forms of life, as humans and, on the other hand, to decide that certain other beings who resemble us superficially could not possibly be human?' (Nussbaum 1990, 219). Whatever features are identified as an answer can then be qualified as worthy of moral and political protection, in terms of all humans having a right to them. Can this work as a justification of human rights? To explain the problem with this argumentative strategy, let's make a comparison between Nussbaum's list of basic capabilities and the list of human rights from the Universal Declaration. We can discern three distinct types of relations between the items on these two lists (see for overview Table A3.1).

Table A3.1. *Human rights lists: Nussbaum and the UDHR*

Nussbaum's capability list (adapted from 2011, 33–4)	List of Human Rights (UDHR)[a]
1. Life: being able to live a life of normal length, not dying prematurely	Life, liberty and security (art. 3) including prohibitions on slavery (art. 4), torture and cruel inhuman or degrading treatment or punishment (art. 5)

Nussbaum's capability list (adapted from 2011, 33–4)	List of Human Rights (UDHR)[a]
2. Bodily Health: good health; adequate nourishment and shelter	Right to an adequate standard of living and social security (art. 22, 25)
3. Bodily Integrity: freedom of movement; security from domestic and sexual assault; opportunities for sexual satisfaction	Right to freedom of movement and residence within a state (art. 13); right to marry and found a family (art. 16)
4. Senses, imagination and thought: adequate education; ability to enjoy artistic, religious works and events; freedom of expression, freedom of religion	Rights to education (art. 26); right to participation in cultural life (art. 27); right to freedom of thought, conscience and religion (art. 18)
5. Emotions: to love, grieve, experience longing, gratitude and justified anger (entails: support for institutions that foster human associations which develop this)	—
6. Practical reason: being able to form a conception of the good and engage in critical reflection about the planning of one's life (entails: freedom of conscience and religion)	Right to freedom of thought, conscience and religion (art. 18)
7. Affiliation (A): being able to live with and towards others (entails: protecting institutions that nourish affiliation, freedom of assembly and political speech)	Protection from arbitrary interference with one's privacy, family, home or correspondence (art. 12); plus rights mentioned below at 10A.
7. Affiliation (B): social basis of self-respect and non-humiliation (entails: non-discrimination)	Recognition as a person before the law (art. 6), equal protection for the law (art.7)
8. Other species: being able to live with concern for and in relation to animals, plants and the world of nature	—
9. Play: being able to laugh, play and enjoy recreational activities	Right to rest and leisure (art. 24)
10. Control over one's environment (A) Political: having rights of political participation; free speech and association	Right to freedom of expression and opinion (art. 19), right to peaceful assembly and association (art. 20); right to political participation and universal suffrage (art. 21)

Nussbaum's capability list (adapted from 2011, 33–4)	List of Human Rights (UDHR)[a]
10. Control over one's environment (B) Material: ability to hold property; right to seek employment; freedom from unwarranted seizure; humane work conditions, meaningful relationships with other workers	Right to own property 'alone as well as in association with others' (art. 17), rights to work, free choice of employment and other work-related rights (art. 23) no subjection to arbitrary arrest, detention or exile (art. 9) and related legal rights (art. 8, 10 and 11)

[a]The table omits three rights from the UDHR, which have as their object international relations (art. 14, 15 and 28).

First, some of Nussbaum's capabilities are almost equivalent to the human rights formulations: the capability to life, parts of the capabilities of bodily health and bodily security, and most strongly the capabilities to political and material control over one's environment. In these areas there is substantial overlap if not similarity between the lists. A second group of Nussbaum's capabilities does not have any analogue in the lists of human rights at all: her capabilities for the emotions and contact with other species, and some subparts of other capabilities, e.g. the capability to enjoy sexual satisfaction (included as part of the capability of bodily integrity) or the opportunity (included under material control) of 'entering into meaningful relationships of mutual recognition with other workers'. Third, there is an intermediate group that is only marginally covered by human rights protections: the capabilities of senses, imagination and thought, practical reasoning, affiliation and play. Here much more is needed than what is covered under the human rights clauses. For example, Nussbaum notes that practical reasoning entails protection of the liberty of conscience and religion. But surely a lot more is needed to realize that capability. Similarly, to make sure that everyone has a capability to play, much more will be needed than a legal right to time off from work. In conclusion, Nussbaum's list is much more expansive than this canonical list of human rights (Dorsey 2008, 431; Richardson 2007, 404; Beitz 2009, 67).

Nussbaum herself, in her explicit statements, denies this. She sometimes argues as if there is a *one-to-one relationship* between the content of her capabilities list and the content of what lists of human rights *should* prescribe. This is clear from her frequent statements that the capabilities should be taken to form the basis of a list of fundamental constitutionally guaranteed entitlements (e.g., Nussbaum 2000b, 74). It also is clear from statements such as, 'If a capability really belongs on the list (...) then governments have the obligation to protect and secure it, using law and public policy to achieve this end' (Nussbaum 2011a, 26). Going beyond this, she also thinks that there is a one-to-one relationship between the content of her list of capabilities and the content of what human rights lists actually *do* prescribe. For example, she states that 'the capabilities on my list cover the terrain covered by the so-called "first-generation rights" (political and civil liberties) and the so-called second-generation rights (economic and social rights)' (Nussbaum 2011a, 24). If we take these statements at face value, we are led to the conclusion that the full content of all capabilities is a requirement of justice, to be protected by the state.

Sometimes Nussbaum seems to acknowledge and accommodate concerns with this conclusion. For example, she indicates at several places what the protection of a specific capability would 'entail' (see formulations in Table A3.1). Apparently, Nussbaum doesn't think every capability can be straightforwardly interpreted as a political entitlement. This is due to a gap between what is aspired by the capability and what is socially influenceable (Sen 2004b, 329). She also remarks that some capabilities are 'natural goods' and that the entitlements of her list should only cover 'the *social basis* of these capabilities' (Nussbaum 2000b, 81). She gives the following example: 'Take women's health. Government cannot make all women emotionally healthy; but it can do quite a lot to influence emotional health, through suitable policies such as family law, rape law, and public safety' (Nussbaum 2000b, 82). Narrowing down capability entitlements along these lines (i.e. only to include their social basis) would mean to abandon the idea of a strict, literal, one-to-one relationship between a list of human characteristics and a list of capability-promoting rights. We would then get a *two-list structure*, with a second (much more modest) list giving us the rights protecting the social bases of the capabilities on the first list.

This seems like a good idea. However, now another problem emerges. For Nussbaum underestimates what governments could do to help foster the social bases of these capabilities, if only they wanted to. For example, when she adds that the capability of practical reason entails protection of the liberty of conscience and religious observance, she ignores that the government could also provide compulsory re-training camps for all those adults who walk around without a clear and critically reflected conception of the good, where philosophers would help them acquire the necessary skills. Similar retraining camps for affiliation and use of the senses seem to be required too (even keeping in mind the capability-not-functioning emphasis: having a capability requires actual training). The examples she mentions for the capability of emotional health are all accepted laws and policies, but these are only a drop in the ocean of what governments could do to improve the quality of our emotional life if they really were committed to. For large parts of Nussbaum's capabilities we normally do not turn to government but leave things to spontaneous processes of social life. If we take Nussbaum's list seriously, and would push for maximum government promotion of the social basis of these capabilities, we would get a massively intrusive state. People never playing any games would have to be trained in some games, people never cuddling dogs and cats would have be taught to do so, all of this to have the required capabilities. Only then would we really have a list of human rights that matches the social basis of the list of capabilities.

This shows how the restriction to the social basis of her capabilities is only a first step on the way to a non-intrusive, more human rights-like list. Ultimately, the problem is caused by the fact that Nussbaum's reliance on human nature as a normative criterion (a fully human flourishing life) tends to lead to an expansive list. To counteract this tendency, we may want to keep the anthropological starting-point but create two lists, one original list of human characteristics and a second one, of those rights which should protect the basis of these human characteristics. But then strong filtering devices need to be built in to get us from the natural (what is inescapably true of every human life) to the evaluative (what is good or makes us flourishing), from the evaluative to the moral (what deserves respect from others), and from the moral to the political (what deserves to be guaranteed through coercive means). But once we impose a filtering device, it will be that device which is doing the real normative work, not the account of humanity (Antony 2000; Claassen and Düwell 2013, 495–98).

These points can be generalized beyond Nussbaum's theory: they cast doubts on the viability of all enquiries into human nature as a strategy for founding human rights. There are two problems with respect to the fact that such theories lack explicit filtering devices.[1] First, they cannot make clear which elements of human life (functionings) can pass through to the next stages (into political theory, eventually) and why these and not

---

[1] To be fair: Nussbaum-I does have an explicit method of justification. We discuss its defects in (Claassen and Düwell 2013, 498–501). In that paper, the emphasis is on the lack of proof, here I would emphasize how it doesn't explicitly make the transitions discussed here (in the later Nussbaum there is the justificatory apparatus of political liberalism: see Section 1.3).

others. Call these the *content* of the filtering device. Second, they cannot explain the *formal* operations the filtering device is supposed to fulfil: the transitions from human characteristics to evaluative claims and finally to moral and political rights. These rights fall out of the air, so to speak. Why does the fact that human beings often (if not always) think, have emotions, have contact with other species, play, etc. generate a moral right to do so and a corresponding duty on others not to interfere? This is no small thing, if one considers that some other moral theories operate without a concept of rights (such as utilitarianism, moving directly from measurements of well-being to moral obligations). What needs to be shown is: (1) how we move from a concept of human nature to a concept of rights (i.e. how the latter comes into the picture in one's descriptive apparatus once one starts from human nature), and (2) how we move from a description of human nature to a normative justification of a set of basic rights. Both desiderata cannot be fulfilled by a theory of human nature, without importing external considerations.

This problem is an important motivation for my introduction, in Section 3.1, of a theory which shows how a deontic order of rights and duties is already part of our humanity, or better, of our practice-based agency. Such a theory does not suffer from a gap between human nature and rights claims to certain parts of that nature. We saw that this descriptive apparatus contains another gap within the social ontology (between participational and navigational agency) that forms its own challenge of justification (addressed in Sections 3.2 and 3.3). What is quite striking, however, is that theorists of social practices and institutions who have also defended some version of the deontic social ontology presented in Section 3.1, have – in strong contrast to my theory – reverted to an anthropological method of justification when they approach the subject of human rights. It is as if they forget to use their own social theories when the question of human rights comes on the table. Consider two examples.

The first example is from Searle. In a separate chapter on human rights, Searle sets himself the goal of answering the question whether there are any human rights. He then runs up against the problem that, in the framework of his social theory, 'being human' is not a status function like 'being president'. In contrast to the rest of social reality, there is no prior institution to which being human can easily be related, hence no status function which can define what the right contains (Searle 2010, 179–84). As a consequence, Searle argues that we need to defend a 'conception of human nature'. Here he says that: 'I think I can justify my conception of human nature biologically, and I can at least argue for my conception of what I think is valuable in human life' (Searle 2010, 192). However, this is followed by an immediate recognition that these arguments 'are not demonstrative, in the sense that any rational person is bound to accept them on pain of irrationality'. Later he concedes that 'the inventory of human rights will tend to be shaped by practical or pragmatic considerations' (Searle 2010, 195). Passages such as these indicate that Searle seems to have only half-hearted confidence in the recourse to human nature that he himself prescribes. This, in my view, is no coincidence since his use of a self-standing theory of human nature to ground human rights sits uneasily with the institutional grounding of all other rights in his theory. To be able to grasp the link between human rights and institutional life, he would have had to see how these rights are related to making certain free and autonomous moves within social life, i.e. accept something like the dual-level theory of agency that I endorse.

A strikingly similar pattern of reasoning can be found in Wenar's theory of rights. As noted in Section 3.1, he sees rights as derived from duties that define a social role. But when he comes to the issue of human rights, he faces similar difficulties as Searle. In modern times, in the absence of argumentative resort to a God to which we may owe duties, it is unclear how to construct human rights as arising out of duties connected to a role all humans have to fulfil. To solve this problem, he suggests that we need to switch from social roles to 'social kind norms', and interpret the kind norms attached to the human species. Here Wenar mentions Nussbaum's anthropological theory (!) of human nature as a way of filling this out.[2] At the same time, he admits that the prospect for this project of founding human rights on a kind norm remains highly uncertain and controversial (Wenar 2013, 223–5). Here again, a theorist who presents a general account of rights in terms of social roles, duties and institutions feels the need to make the jump to an asocial conception of human natural characteristics in order to understand the phenomenon of human rights.

This seems to be no accidental feature of Searle and Wenar's writings, if only because there are more examples.[3] The problem with these

---

[2] To be fair to Wenar, he also mentions a second strategy (within which he includes Griffin, Gewirth and the later Nussbaum) to flesh out kind norms, not by referring to human characteristics in an anthropological sense, but by referring to 'what all humans *have reason to want*' (Wenar 2013, 224). However, this strategy is still presented within the framework of his 'kind-desire' theory.

[3] Another example I found is Seumas Miller, who, despite his theory of social action, argues that human rights are prior to institutions, largely based on an account of universal human needs. See Miller (2010, 57, 66).

theories is that they do not take their own practice orientation seriously enough when it comes to human rights. We do not need a theory of human nature if we already have a theory of social action that includes a notion of rights and duties as essential elements of social life. Human rights can then be understood as an answer to a specific problem *within* social life: that social practices can be grossly *coercive*. Participational agency is compatible with structures of oppression. To escape these practices, we need a wider form of agency, which allows us freedom to navigate between practices. Human rights are the rights that make this wider form of agency possible; they allow one to be a role-chooser in addition to a role-bearer. Human rights are, therefore, better understood as a solution to a central problem in social life: coercion within practices. These rights are universal, because this is a universal problem for human beings (note however that my theory, while using the concept of social practices, has nothing to do with so-called 'political' or 'practice-based' theories of human rights[4]).

The reason why these social theorists do not take this route, it seems, is that while they do recognize the social embeddedness of action, they continue to work with a single-level theory of agency. If one does so, one is quickly thrown back to human nature for the justification of human rights, with all the problems diagnosed here. Only if one accepts a dual-level theory of agency, does the centrality of avoiding coercion open up in the way I have described it as the animating rationale behind a list of human rights. These remarks presuppose, but do not form a justification, of such rights, of course. For that we need to see if the gap identified earlier between participational and navigational agency can be closed; this was the task of Sections 3.2 and 3.3.

---

[4] It is now customary in the literature to make a distinction between 'naturalistic' or 'humanistic' theories of human rights (like Gewirth, Griffin or Nussbaum) and 'practice' or 'political' theories, like that of Charles Beitz (Beitz 2009). The point of the latter theories is to criticize the universalist normativity in the former theories and to call for a theory which is more closely linked to actually existing legal regimes of human rights. My theory, however, is as "moralistic" as the leading naturalistic ones, but gives a more socially oriented view of human life (or better, agential life).

Bibliography

Abizadeh, Arash. 2008. "Democratic Theory and Border Coercion. No Right to Unilaterally Control Your Own Borders." *Political Theory* 36 (1): 37–65.

2012. "On the Demos and Its Kin: Nationalism, Democracy, and the Boundary Problem." *American Political Science Review* 106 (4): 867–82.

Agné, Hans. 2010. "Why Democracy Must Be Global: Self-Founding and Democratic Intervention." *International Theory* 2 (3): 381–409.

Alexander, John. 2008. *Capabilities and Social Justice. The Political Philosophy of Amartya Sen and Martha Nussbaum.* Aldershot: Ashgate.

Alexander, Larry. 2008. "What Is Freedom of Association and What Is Its Denial?" *Social Philosophy and Policy* 25 (2): 1–21.

Alkire, Sabine. 2002. *Valuing Freedoms. Sen's Capability Approach and Poverty Reduction.* Oxford: Oxford University Press.

Anderson, Elizabeth. 1999. "What Is the Point of Equality?" *Ethics* 109 (2): 287–337.

2009. "Democracy: Instrumental vs. Non-Instrumental Value." In *Contemporary Debates in Political Philosophy,* edited by Thomas Christiano and John Christman, 213–27. Chichester, West Sussex: Wiley-Blackwell.

2010a. "Justifying the Capability Approach to Justice." In *Measuring Justice. Primary Goods and Capabilities,* edited by Harry Brighouse and Ingrid Robeyns, 81–100. Cambridge: Cambridge University Press.

2010b. "The Fundamental Disagreement between Luck Egalitarians and Relational Egalitarians." *Canadian Journal of Philosophy* Supplementary Volume 36: 1–24.

Anderson, Joel. 2008. "Disputing Autonomy. Second-Order Desires and the Dynamics of Ascribing Autonomy." *SATS – Nordic Journal of Philosophy* 9 (1): 7–26.

2014. "Regimes of Autonomy." *Ethical Theory and Moral Practice* 17 (3): 355–68.

Anderson, Joel, and John Christman. 2005. "Introduction." In *Autonomy and the Challenges to Liberalism. New Essays,* edited by John Christman and Joel Anderson, 1–23. Cambridge: Cambridge University Press.

Anderson, Joel, and Axel Honneth. 2005. "Autonomy, Vulnerability, Recognition, and Justice." In *Autonomy and the Challenges to Liberalism. New Essays,* edited by Joel Anderson and John Christman, 127–49. Cambridge: Cambridge University Press.

Antony, Louise. 2000. "Natures and Norms." *Ethics* 111: 8–36.

Arendt, Hannah. 1998. *The Human Condition*. 2nd edn. Chicago: The University of Chicago Press.

Aristotle. 1984. "Politics." In *The Complete Works of Aristotle: The Revised Oxford Translation. Volume II*, edited by Jonathan Barnes, 1986–2129. Princeton: Princeton University Press.

Arneson, Richard. 1989. "Equality and Equal Opportunity for Welfare." *Philosophical Studies* 56 (1): 77–93.

2000a. "Luck Egalitarianism and Prioritarianism." *Ethics* 110 (2): 339–49.

2000b. "Perfectionism and Politics." *Ethics* 111 (1): 37–63.

2003. "Liberal Neutrality on the Good: An Autopsy." In *Perfectionism and Neutrality. Essays in Liberal Theory*, edited by Steven Wall and George Klosko, 191–218. Lanham: Rowman & Littlefield.

2006. "Distributive Justice and Basic Capability Equality: 'Good Enough' Is Not Good Enough." In *Capabilities Equality. Basic Issues and Problems*, edited by Alexander Kaufman, 17–43. New York: Routledge.

2009. "The Supposed Right to a Democratic Say." In *Contemporary Debates in Political Philosophy*, edited by Thomas Christiano and John Christman, 197–212. Chichester, West Sussex: Wiley-Blackwell.

2010a. "Democratic Equality and Relating as Equals." *Canadian Journal of Philosophy* Supplementary Volume 36: 25–52.

2010b. "Two Cheers for Capabilities." In *Measuring Justice. Primary Goods and Capabilities*, edited by Harry Brighouse and Ingrid Robeyns, 101–27. Cambridge: Cambridge University Press.

Arrhenius, Gustaf. 2005. "The Boundary Problem in Democratic Theory." In *Democracy Unbound: Basic Explorations I*, edited by Folke Tersman, 14–29. Stockholm: Filosofiska Institutionen, Stockholms Universitet.

Atkinson, Anthony. 2015. *Inequality. What Can Be Done?* Cambridge: Harvard University Press.

Axelsen, David, and Lasse Nielsen. 2015. "Sufficiency as Freedom from Duress." *Journal of Political Philosophy* 13 (4): 406–26.

2017. "Capabilitarian Sufficiency: Capabilities and Social Justice." *Journal of Human Development and Capabilities* 18 (1): 46–59.

Baber, H. E. 2007. "Adaptive Preference." *Social Theory and Practice* 33 (1): 105–26.

Baderin, Alice. 2016a. "Political Theory and Public Opinion: Against Democratic Restraint." *Politics, Philosophy & Economics* 15 (3): 209–33.

2016b. "Two Forms of Realism in Political Theory." *European Journal of Political Theory* 13 (2): 132–53.

Bagnoli, Carla, ed. 2013. *Constructivism in Ethics*. Cambridge: Cambridge University Press.

2014. "Starting Points: Kantian Constructivism Reassessed." *Ratio Juris* 27 (3): 311–29.

Baldwin, Thomas. 2009. "Recognition: Personal and Political." *Politics, Philosophy, and Economics* 8 (3): 311–28.

Balint, Peter. 2015. "Identity Claims: Why Liberal Neutrality Is the Solution, Not the Problem." *Political Studies* 63 (2): 495–509.

Barclay, Linda. 2003. "What Kind of Liberal Is Martha Nussbaum?" *SATS – Nordic Journal of Philosophy* 4 (2): 5–24.

2012. "Natural Deficiency or Social Oppression? The Capabilities Approach to Justice for People with Disabilities." *Journal of Moral Philosophy* 9 (4): 500–20.

2016. "The Importance of Equal Respect: What the Capabilities Approach Can and Should Learn from Human Rights Law." *Political Studies* 64 (2): 385–400.

Barry, Brian. 2001. *Culture & Equality*. Cambridge: Polity.

Bartelson, Jens. 2008. "Globalizing the Democratic Community." *Ethics & Global Politics* 1 (4): 159–74.

Becker, Lawrence. 1980. "The Moral Basis of Property Rights." In *Nomos XXII: Property*, edited by J. Roland Pennock and John W. Chapman, 187–220. New York: New York University Press.

Beetham, David. 1995. "What Future for Economic and Social Rights?" *Political Studies* 43 (1): 41–60.

Begon, Jessica. 2015. "What Are Adaptive Preferences? Exclusion and Disability in the Capability Approach." *Journal of Applied Philosophy* 32 (3): 241–57.

2017. "Capabilities for All? From Capabilities to Function to Capabilities to Control." *Social Theory and Practice* 43 (1): 154–79.

Beitz, Charles. 2009. *The Idea of Human Rights*. Oxford: Oxford University Press.

Benbaji, Yitzak. 2005. "The Doctrine of Sufficiency: A Defense." *Utilitas* 17 (3): 301–32.

Benhabib, Seyla. 2012. "Is There a Human Right to Democracy? Beyond Interventionism and Indifference." In *Philosophical Dimensions of Human Rights*, edited by Claudio Corradetti, 191–214. Dordrecht/Heidelberg/New York/London: Springer.

Benkler, Yochai, and Helen Nissenbaum. 2006. "Commons-Based Peer Production and Virtue." *Journal of Political Philosophy* 14 (4): 394–419.

Benson, Paul. 1994. "Free Agency and Self-Worth." *The Journal of Philosophy* 91 (12): 650–68.

Berlin, Isaiah. 2002. *Liberty*. Oxford: Oxford University Press.

Bertea, Stefano. 2013. "Constitutivism and Normativity: A Qualified Defence." *Philosophical Explorations* 16 (1): 81–95.

Beyleveld, Deryck. 2015. "*Korsgaard* v. *Gewirth* on Universalization: Why Gewirthians Are Kantians and Kantians Ought to Be Gewirthians." *Journal of Moral Philosophy* 12 (5): 573–97.

Bilchitz, David. 2007. *Poverty and Fundamental Rights: The Justification and Enforcement of Socio-Economic Rights*. Oxford: Oxford University Press.

Biondo, Francesco. 2008. "Is Martha Nussbaum Really Political Liberal?" *Archiv Fur Rechts – Und Sozialphilosophie* 94 (3): 311–24.

Blake, Michael. 2002. "Distributive Justice, State Coercion, and Autonomy." *Philosophy & Public Affairs* 30 (3): 257–96.

Borchers, Dagmar. 2012. "Calculating on Identity? The Costs and Benefits of the Costs-of-Exit Debate." In *On Exit. Interdisciplinary Perspectives on the Right of Exit in Liberal Multicultural Societies*, edited by Annamari Vitikainen and Dagmar Borchers, 57–77. Berlin/Boston: De Gruyter.

Brennan, Geoffrey. 2012. "Political Liberty: Who Needs It?" *Social Philosophy & Policy* 29 (1): 1–27.

Brighouse, Harry, and Marc Fleurbaey. 2010. "Democracy and Proportionality." *Journal of Political Philosophy* 18 (2): 137–55.

Brighouse, Harry, and Ingrid Robeyns, eds. 2010. *Measuring Justice: Primary Goods and Capabilities*. Cambridge: Cambridge University Press.

Brighouse, Harry, and Adam Swift. 2006. "Equality, Priority, and Positional Goods." *Ethics* 116 (3): 471–97.

Brownlee, Kimberley. 2013. "A Human Right against Social Deprivation." *The Philosophical Quarterly* 63 (251): 199–222.

2015. "Freedom of Association: It's Not What You Think." *Oxford Journal of Legal Studies* 35 (2): 267–82.

Bruckner, Donald. 2009. "In Defense of Adaptive Preferences." *Philosophical Studies* 142 (3): 307–24.

Buchanan, Alan. 2010. "The Egalitarianism of Human Rights." *Ethics* 120 (4): 679–710.

2013. *The Heart of Human Rights*. Oxford: Oxford University Press.

Byskov, Morten. 2017. "Democracy, Philosophy, and the Selection of Capabilities." *Journal of Human Development and Capabilities* 18 (1): 1–16.

Carter, Ian. 1996. "The Concept of Freedom in the Work of Amartya Sen: An Alternative Analysis Consistent with Freedom's Independent Value." *Notizie Di Politeia* 43–4: 7–22.

1999. *A Measure of Freedom*. Oxford: Oxford University Press.

2011. "Respect and the Basis of Equality." *Ethics* 121 (3): 538–71.

2014. "Is the Capability Approach Paternalist?" *Economics & Philosophy* 30 (1): 75–98.

Casal, Paula. 2007. "Why Sufficiency Is Not Enough." *Ethics* 117 (2): 296–326.

Celikates, Robin. 2014. "Freedom as Non-Arbitrariness or as Democratic Self-Rule? A Critique of Contemporary Republicanism." In *To Be Unfree: Republicanism and Unfreedom in History, Literature, and Philosophy*, edited by Christian Dahl and Tue Andersen Nexo, 37–54. Bielefeld: Transcript.

Christiano, Thomas. 2008. *The Constitution of Equality. Democratic Authority and Its Limits*. Oxford: Oxford University Press.

2011. "An Instrumental Argument for a Human Right to Democracy." *Philosophy & Public Affairs* 39 (2): 142–76.

Christman, John. 1994. *The Myth of Property. Toward an Egalitarian Theory of Ownership*. New York/Oxford: Oxford University Press.

2004. "Relational Autonomy, Liberal Individualism, and the Social Constitution of Selves." *Philosophical Studies* 117 (1–2): 143–64.

2009. *The Politics of Persons. Individual Autonomy and Socio-Historical Selves*. Cambridge: Cambridge University Press.

2014. "Coping or Oppression: Autonomy and Adaptation to Circumstance." In *Autonomy, Oppression, and Gender*, edited by Andrea Veltman and Mark Piper, 201–26. Oxford: Oxford University Press.

Ciepley, David. 2013. "Beyond Public and Private: Toward a Political Theory of the Corporation." *American Political Science Review* 107 (1): 139–58.

Claassen, Rutger. 2007. "The Status Struggle. A Recognition-Based Interpretation of the Positional Economy." *Philosophy and Social Criticism* 34 (9): 1021–49.

2009a. "Institutional Pluralism and the Limits of the Market." *Politics, Philosophy, and Economics* 8 (4): 420–47.

2009b. "New Directions in Capability Theory: Republicanism and Deliberative Democracy (Book Review Essay)." *Res Publica* 15 (4): 421–28.

2011a. "Communication as Commodity. Should the Media Be on the Market?" *Journal of Applied Philosophy* 28 (1): 65–79.

2011b. "Making Capability Lists. Philosophy versus Democracy." *Political Studies* 59 (3): 491–508.

2011c. "The Commodification of Care." *Hypatia* 26 (1): 43–64.

2011d. "The Marketization of Security Services." *Public Reason* 3 (2): 124–45.

2013. "Public Goods, Mutual Benefits, and Majority Rule." *Journal of Social Philosophy* 44 (3): 270–90.

2014a. "Capability Paternalism." *Economics & Philosophy* 30 (1): 57–73.

2014b. "Human Dignity in the Capability Approach." In *The Cambridge Handbook of Human Dignity*, edited by Marcus Düwell, Jens Braarvig, Roger Brownsword, and Dietmar Mieth, 240–9. Cambridge: Cambridge University Press.

2015. "The Capability to Hold Property." *Journal of Human Development and Capabilities* 16 (2): 220–36.

2016. "Ecological Rights of Future Generations: A Capability Approach." In *Human Rights and Sustainability. Moral Responsibilities for the Future*, edited by Gerhard Bos and Marcus Duwell, 151–65. London: Routledge.

2017. "Capabilities and Financial Market Regulation." In *Just Financial Markets? Finance in a Just Society*, edited by Lisa Herzog, 56–77. Oxford: Oxford University Press.

2018a. "Justice as a Claim to (Social) Property." *Critical Review of International Social and Political Philosophy*. Available from https://www.tandfonline.com/doi/abs/10.1080/13698230.2017.1398867.

2018b. "Constructivism's Challenge: Justifying a Modern Self-Understanding." *Manscript in Preparation.*

2019a (forthcoming). "Selecting a List: The Capability Approach's Achilles Heel." In *Handbook on the Capability Approach*, edited by Enricca Chiappero, Siddiq Osmani, and Mozaffar Qizilbash. Cambridge: Cambridge University Press.

2019b (forthcoming). "European Duties of Social Justice: A Kantian Framework." *Journal of Common Market Studies.*

Claassen, Rutger, and Marcus Düwell. 2013. "The Foundations of Capability Theory: Comparing Nussbaum and Gewirth." *Ethical Theory and Moral Practice* 16 (3): 493–510.

Claassen, Rutger, and Anna Gerbrandy. 2016. "Rethinking Competition Law: From a Consumer Welfare to a Capability Approach." *Utrecht Law Review* 12 (1): 1–15.

Cohen, G.A. 1989. "On the Currency of Egalitarian Justice." *Ethics* 99 (4): 906–44.

Cohen, Joshua. 2003. "For a Democratic Society." In *The Cambridge Companion To Rawls*, edited by Samuel Freeman, 86–138. Cambridge: Cambridge University Press.

2006. "Is There a Human Right to Democracy?" In *The Egalitarian Conscience. Essays in Honour of G.A. Cohen*, edited by Christine Sypnowich, 226–48. Oxford: Oxford University Press.

Colburn, Ben. 2010a. "Anti-Perfectionisms and Autonomy." *Analysis* 70 (2): 247–56.

2010b. *Autonomy and Liberalism*. London: Routledge.

2011. "Autonomy and Adaptive Preferences." *Utilitas* 23 (1): 52–71.

Comim, Flavio, and Martha Nussbaum, eds. 2014. *Capabilities, Gender, Equality. Towards Fundamental Entitlements*. Cambridge: Cambridge University Press.

Conradie, Ina, and Ingrid Robeyns. 2013. "Aspirations and Human Development." *Journal of Human Development and Capabilities* 14 (4): 559–80.

Copp, David. 1992. "The Right to an Adequate Standard of Living: Justice, Autonomy, and the Basic Needs." *Social Philosophy & Policy* 9 (1): 231–61.

Crisp, Roger. 2003. "Equality, Priority, and Compassion." *Ethics* 113 (4): 745–63.

Crocker, David. 2008. *Ethics of Global Development. Agency, Capability, and Deliberative Democracy*. Cambridge: Cambridge University Press.

Crocker, David, and Ingrid Robeyns. 2010. "Capability and Agency." In *Amartya Sen*, edited by Christopher Morris, 60–90. Cambridge: Cambridge University Press.

Dagan, Hanoch, and Avihay Dorfman. 2017. "The Human Right to Property." *Theoretical Inquires in Law* 18 (2): 391–416.

Dagan, Hanoch, and Michael Heller. 2001. "The Liberal Commons." *Yale Law Journal* 110 (4): 549–623.

Dagger, Richard. 2005. "Autonomy, Domination, and the Republican Challenge to Liberalism." In *Autonomy and the Challenges to Liberalism. New Essays*, edited by John Christman and Joel Anderson, 177–203. Cambridge: Cambridge University Press.

Darwall, Stephen. 2006. *The Second-Person Standpoint. Morality, Respect and Accountability*. Cambridge: Harvard University Press.

De Maagt, Sem. 2016. *Constructing Morality: Transcendental Arguments in Ethics*. PhD Dissertation. Utrecht: OFR Institute for Philosophy. Available from: https://dspace.library.uu.nl/handle/1874/345118 (accessed on June 6, 2018).

2017. "Reflective Equilibrium and Moral Objectivity." *Inquiry* 60 (5): 443–65.

Deakin, Simon. 2006. "'Capacitas': Contract Law and the Institutional Preconditions of a Market Economy." *European Review of Contract Law* 2 (3): 317–41.

Deneulin, Séverine. 2002. "Perfectionism, Paternalism and Liberalism in Sen and Nussbaum's Capability Approach." *Review of Political Economy* 14 (4): 497–518.

2008. "Beyond Individual Freedom and Agency: Structures of Living Together in the Capability Approach." In *The Capability Approach. Concepts, Measures and Applications*, edited by Flavio Comim, Mozaffar Qizilbash, and Sabine Alkire, 105–24. Cambridge: Cambridge University Press.

2013. "Recovering Nussbaum's Aristotelian Roots." *International Journal of Social Economics* 40 (7): 624–32.

Deneulin, Séverine, and Lila Shahani, eds. 2009. *An Introduction to the Human Development and Capability Approach*. London: Earthscan.

Dorsey, Dale. 2008. "Toward a Theory of the Basic Minimum." *Politics, Philosophy & Economics* 7 (4): 423–45.

Dowding, Keith. 2006. "Can Capabilities Reconcile Freedom and Equality?" *The Journal of Political Philosophy* 14 (3): 323–36.

Drydyk, Jay. 2008. "Durable Empowerment." *Journal of Global Ethics* 4 (3): 231–45.

2011. "Responsible Pluralism, Capabilities, and Human Rights." *Journal of Human Development and Capabilities* 12 (1): 39–61.

2013. "Empowerment, Agency, and Power." *Journal of Global Ethics* 9 (3): 249–62.

Dworkin, Gerald. 1988. *The Theory and Practice of Autonomy*. Cambridge: Cambridge University Press.

Dworkin, Ronald. 1978. "Liberalism." In *Public and Private Morality*, edited by Stuart Hampshire, 113–43. Cambridge: Cambridge University Press.

Dworkin, Ronald. 2000. *Sovereign Virtue. The Theory and Practice of Equality*. Cambridge: Harvard University Press.

Dworkin, Ronald. 2002. "Sovereign Virtue Revisited." *Ethics* 113 (1): 106–43.

Ebels-Duggan, Kyla. 2011. "Critical Notice of Arthur Ripstein Force and Freedom: Kant's Legal and Political Philosophy." *Canadian Journal of Philosophy* 41 (4): 549–74.

Eggertsson, Thrainn. 2003. "Open Access versus Common Property." In *Property Rights. Cooperation, Conflict, and Law*, edited by Terry Anderson and Fred McChesney, 73–89. Princeton: Princeton University Press.

Elster, Jon. 1982. "Sour Grapes – Utilitarianism and the Genesis of Wants." In *Utilitarianism and Beyond*, edited by Amartya Sen and Bernard Williams, 219–38. Cambridge: Cambridge University Press.

Enoch, David. 2006. "Agency, Schmagency: Why Normativity Won't Come from What Is Constitutive of Action." *The Philosophical Review* 115 (2): 169–98.

Estlund, David. 1996. "The Survival of Egalitarian Justice in John Rawls's Political Liberalism." *Journal of Political Philosophy* 4 (1): 68–78.

2009. "Debate: On Christiano's *The Constitution of Equality.*" *Journal of Political Philosophy* 17 (2): 241–52.

Fabre, Cecile. 1998. "Constitutionalising Social Rights." *Journal of Political Philosophy* 6 (3): 263–84.

Feinberg, Joel. 1970. "The Nature and Value of Rights." *Journal of Value Inquiry* 4 (4): 243–57.

Feinberg, Joel. 1986. *Harm to Self.* Oxford: Oxford University Press.

Ferracioli, Luara, and Rosa Terlazzo. 2014. "Educating for Autonomy: Liberalism and Autonomy in the Capabilities Approach." *Ethical Theory and Moral Practice* 17 (3): 443–55.

Ferrero, Luca. 2009. "Constitutivism and the Inescapability of Agency." In *Oxford Studies in Metaethics*, edited by Russ Shafer-Landau, IV: 303–34. Oxford: Oxford University Press.

Fleurbaey, Marc. 2008. *Fairness, Responsibility, and Welfare.* Oxford: Oxford University Press.

Formosa, Paul, and Catriona Mackenzie. 2014. "Nussbaum, Kant, and the Capabilities Approach to Dignity." *Ethical Theory and Moral Practice* 17 (5): 875–92.

Frank, Robert. 1985. *Choosing the Right Pond. Human Behavior and the Quest for Status.* Oxford: Oxford University Press.

1999. *Luxury Fever. Why Money Fails to Satisfy in an Era of Excess.* Princeton: Princeton University Press.

2008. "Should Public Policy Respond to Positional Externalities?" *Journal of Public Economics* 92 (8–9): 1777–86.

Frankfurt, Harry. 1971. "The Freedom of the Will and the Concept of a Person." *Journal of Philosophy* 68: 5–20.

1987. "Equality as a Moral Ideal." *Ethics* 98 (1): 21–43.

1988. *The Importance of What We Care About.* Cambridge: Cambridge University Press.

Freeman, Samuel. 2011. "Capitalism in the Classical and High Liberal Traditions." *Social Philosophy & Policy* 28 (2): 19–55.

Garnett, Michael. 2016. "Value Neutrality and the Ranking of Opportunity Sets." *Economic and Philosophy* 32 (1): 99–119.

Gewirth, Alan. 1978. *Reason and Morality.* Chicago: The University of Chicago Press.

1996. *The Community of Rights.* Chicago: The University of Chicago Press.

2007. "Duties to Fulfill the Human Rights of the Poor." In *Freedom from Poverty as a Human Right*, edited by Thomas Pogge, 219–36. Oxford: Oxford University Press.

Giddens, Anthony. 1994. *The Constitution of Society.* Cambridge: Polity Press.

Gilabert, Paolo. 2013. "The Capability Approach and the Debate between Humanist and Political Perspectives on Human Rights. A Critical Survey." *Human Rights Review* 14 (4): 299–325.

Goodin, Robert. 2007. "Enfranchising All Affected Interests, and Its Alternatives." *Philosophy & Public Affairs* 35 (1): 40–68.

Gore, Charles. 1997. "Irreducibly Social Goods and the Informational Basis of Amartya Sen's Capability Approach." *Journal of International Development* 9 (2): 235–50.

Gough, Ian. 2014. "Lists and Thresholds: Comparing the Doyal–Gough Theory of Human Need with Nussbaum's Capabilities Approach." In *Capabilities, Gender, Equality. Towards Fundamental Entitlements*, edited by Flavio Comim and Martha Nussbaum, 357–81. Cambridge: Cambridge University Press.

Gould, Carol. 2004. *Globalizing Democracy and Human Rights*. Cambridge: Cambridge University Press.

2015. "A Social Ontology of Human Rights." In *Philosophical Foundations of Human Rights*, edited by Rowan Cruft, S. Matthew Liao, and Massimo Renzo, 177–95. Oxford: Oxford University Press.

Gourevitch, Alex. 2015. "Liberty and Its Economies." *Politics, Philosophy & Economics* 14 (4): 365–90.

Green, Jeffrey. 2016. "Liberalism and the Problem of Plutocracy." *Constellations* 23 (1): 84–95.

Green, Leslie. 1998. "Rights of Exit." *Legal Theory* 4 (2): 165–85.

Griffin, James. 2000. "Welfare Rights." *Journal of Ethics* 4 (1–2): 27–43.

2008. *On Human Rights*. Oxford: Oxford University Press.

2010. "Human Rights: Questions of Aim and Approach." *Ethics* 120 (4): 741–60.

Gutman, Amy. 2003. "Rawls on the Relationship between Liberalism and Democracy." In *The Cambridge Companion To Rawls*, edited by Samuel Freeman, 168–99. Cambridge: Cambridge University Press.

Habermas, Jürgen. 1990. "Discourse Ethics: Notes on a Program of Philosophical Justification." In *Moral Consciousness and Communicative Action*, 43–115. Cambridge: The MIT Press.

Hart, H.L.A. 1983. "Rawls on Liberty and It Priority." In *Essays in Jurisprudence and Philosophy*, 223–47. Oxford: Clarendon Press.

Hayward, Tim. 2013. "Human Rights versus Property Rights." JWI Working Paper 04.

Heath, Joseph. 2005. "Liberal Autonomy and Consumer Sovereignty." In *Autonomy and the Challenges to Liberalism. New Essays*, edited by John Christman and Joel Anderson, 204–25. Cambridge: Cambridge University Press.

2006. "Envy and Efficiency." *Revue de Philosophie Économique* 7 (2): 3–30.

2011. "Three Normative Models of the Welfare State." *Public Reason* 3 (2): 13–43.

Heller, Michael. 2001. "The Dynamic Analytics of Property Law." *Theoretical Inquires in Law* 2 (1): 79–95.

Hill, Thomas, Jr. 1991. "Servility and Self-Respect." In *Autonomy and Self-Respect*, 4–19. Cambridge: Cambridge University Press.

Hirsch, Fred. 1999. *Social Limits to Growth*. Lincoln: iUniverse.com.

Hirschman, Albert. 1970. *Exit, Voice, and Loyalty. Responses to Decline in Firms, Organizations, and States*. Cambridge: Harvard University Press.

Holland, Breena. 2008. "Ecology and the Limits of Justice: Establishing Capability Ceilings in Nussbaum's Capability Approach." *Journal of Human Development* 9 (3): 401–25.

Holmes, Stephen, and Cass Sunstein. 2000. *The Cost of Rights. Why Liberty Depends on Taxes*. New York: W.W. Norton & Company.

Holtug, Nils. 2007. "Prioritarianism." In *Egalitarianism. New Essays on the Nature and Value of Equality*, edited by Nils Holtug and Kasper Lippert-Rasmussen, 125–56. Oxford: Oxford University Press.

Honneth, Axel. 1995. *The Struggle for Recognition. The Moral Grammar of Social Conflicts*. Cambridge: The MIT Press.

2011. *Das Recht Der Freiheit. Grundriss Einer Demokratischen Sittlichkeit*.

Hübenthal, Christoph. 2006. *Grundlegung Der Christlichen Sozialethik*. Münster: Aschendorff Verlag.

Hume, David. 2000. *A Treatise of Human Nature*, edited by David Fate Norton and Mary J. Norton. Oxford: Oxford University Press.

Hurka, Thomas. 2002. "Capability, Functioning and Perfectionism." *Apeiron* 35 (4): 137–62.

Huseby, Robert. 2010. "Sufficiency: Restated and Defended." *Journal of Political Philosophy* 18 (2): 178–97.

Jackson, Ben. 2012. "Property-Owning Democracy: A Short History." In *Property-Owning Democracy. Rawls and Beyond*, edited by Martin O'Neill and Thad Williamson, 33–52. Malden, MA and Oxford: Wiley-Blackwell.

Jaggar, Alison. 2006. "Reasoning About Well-Being: Nussbaums Methods of Justifying the Capabilities." *Journal of Political Philosophy* 14 (3): 301–22.

Kant, Immanuel. 1996. "The Metaphysics of Morals." In *Practical Philosophy*, edited by Paul Guyer, 353–603. Cambridge: Cambridge University Press.

Katzer, Matthias. 2010. "The Basis of Universal Liberal Principles in Nussbaum's Political Philosophy." *Public Reason* 2 (2): 60–75.

Kelleher, J. Paul. 2015. "Capabilities versus Resources." *Journal of Moral Philosophy* 12 (2): 151–71.

Kelly, Thomas, and Sarah McGrath. 2010. "Is Reflective Equilibrium Enough?" *Philosophical Perspectives* 24 (1): 325–59.

Khader, Serene. 2011. *Adaptive Preferences and Women's Empowerment*. Oxford: Oxford University Press.

2012. "Must Theorising about Adaptive Preferences Deny Women's Agency?" *Journal of Applied Philosophy* 29 (4): 302–17.

Klosko, George. 1990. "The Obligation to Contribute to Discretionary Public Goods." *Political Studies* 38 (2): 196–214.

Kolodny, Niko. 2014a. "Rule over None 1: What Justifies Democracy?" *Philosophy and Public Affairs* 42 (3): 195–229.

2014b. "Rule over None 2: Social Equality and the Justification of Democracy." *Philosophy and Public Affairs* 42 (4): 287–336.

Korsgaard, Christine. 1996. *The Sources of Normativity*. Cambridge: Cambridge University Press.

2004. "Fellow Creatures: Kantian Ethics and Our Duties to Animals." The Tanner Lectures on Human Values.

2007. "Autonomy and the Second Person Within: A Commentary on Stephen Darwall's The Second Person Standpoint." *Ethics* 118 (1): 8–23.

2008. "Realism and Constructivism in Twentieth-Century Philosophy." In *The Constitution of Agency*, 302–26. Oxford: Oxford University Press.

2009. *Self-Constitution. Agency, Identity, and Integrity*. Oxford: Oxford University Press.

2011. "Interacting with Animals: A Kantian Account." In *The Oxford Handbook of Animal Ethics*, edited by Tom Beauchamp and R. G. Frey, 91–118. Oxford: Oxford University Press.

Kristinsson, Sigurdur. 2000. "The Limits of Neutrality: Toward a Weakly Substantive Account of Neutrality." *Canadian Journal of Philosophy* 30 (2): 257–86.

Kukathas, Chandran. 2003. *The Liberal Archipelago. A Theory of Diversity and Freedom*. Oxford: Oxford University Press.

Kymlicka, Will. 1989. *Liberalism, Community and Culture*. Oxford: Clarendon Press.

2002. *Contemporary Political Philosophy. An Introduction*. 2nd edn. Oxford: Oxford University Press.

Laitinen, Arto. 2007. "Sorting Out Aspects of Personhood. Capacities, Normativity and Recognition." *Journal of Consciousness Studies* 14 (5–7): 248–70.

Larmore, Charles. 1987. *Patterns of Moral Complexity*. Cambridge: Cambridge University Press.

Lehavi, Amnon. 2008. "Mixing Property." *Seton Hall Law Review* 38: 137–212.

Levey, Ann. 2005. "Liberalism, Adaptive Preferences, and Gender Equality." *Hypatia* 20 (4): 127–43.

Liao, S. Matthew. 2015. "Human Rights as Fundamental Conditions for a Good Life." In *Philosophical Foundations of Human Rights*, edited by Rowan Cruft, S. Matthew Liao, and Massimo Renzo, 79–100. Oxford/New York: Oxford University Press.

Locke, John. 1960. "Two Treatises of Government." In *Cambridge Texts in the History of Political Thought*, edited by Peter Laslett. Cambridge: Cambridge University Press.

Lomasky, Loren. 1987. *Persons, Rights, and the Moral Community*. Oxford: Oxford University Press.

2000. "Liberty and Welfare Goods: Reflections on Clashing Liberalisms." *The Journal of Ethics* 4 (1–2): 99–113.

Lovett, Frank. 2009. "Domination and Distributive Justice." *The Journal of Politics* 71 (3): 817–30.

MacIntyre, Alasdair. 1985. *After Virtue*. 2nd edn. London: Duckworth.

1999. "Social Structures and Their Threats to Moral Agency." *Philosophy* 74: 311–29.

Mackenzie, Catriona. 2008. "Relational Autonomy, Normative Authority, and Perfectionism." *Journal of Social Philosophy* 39 (4): 512–33.

Macpherson, C. B. 1978. "The Meaning of Property." In *Property. Mainstream and Critical Perspectives*, edited by Crawford Brough Macpherson, 1–14. Oxford: Basil Blackwell.

Marx, Karl. 1978. "Critique of the Gotha Program." In *The Marx-Engels Reader*, edited by Robert Tucker, 525–42. New York: W.W. Norton & Company.

Meade, James. 1964. *Efficiency, Equality, and the Ownership of Property*. London: George Allen and Unwin.

Menon, Nivedita. 2002. "Universalism without Foundations?" *Economy and Society* 51 (1): 152–69.

Meyer, Lukas, and Dominic Roser. 2009. "Enough for the Future." In *Intergenerational Justice*, edited by Axel Gosseries and Lukas Meyer, 219–48. Oxford: Oxford University Press.

Mill, John Stuart. 1991. "Considerations on Representative Government." In *On Liberty and Other Essays*, edited by John Gray. Oxford: Oxford University Press.

Miller, David. 1983. "Constraints on Freedom." *Ethics* 94 (1): 66–86.

Miller, David. 1999. *Principles of Social Justice*. Cambridge: Harvard University Press.

2004. "Justice, Democracy and Public Goods." In *Justice and Democracy. Essays for Brian Barry*, edited by Keith Dowding, Robert Goodin, and Carole Pateman, 127–49. Cambridge: Cambridge University Press.

2009. "Democracy's Domain." *Philosophy & Public Affairs* 37 (3): 201–28.

Miller, Seumas. 2001. *Social Action. A Teleological Account*. Cambridge: Cambridge University Press.

2010. *The Moral Foundations of Social Institutions*. Cambridge: Cambridge University Press.

Morriss, Peter. 2002. *Power. A Philosophical Analysis*. 2nd edn. Manchester: Manchester University Press.

Mulhall, Stephen, and Adam Swift. 1996. *Liberals and Communitarians*. 2nd edn. Oxford: Blackwell Publishing.

Munzer, Stephen. 1990. *A Theory of Property*. Cambridge: Cambridge University Press.

Näsström, Sofia. 2003. "What Globalization Overshadows." *Political Theory* 31 (6): 808–34.

2007. "The Legitimacy of the People." *Political Theory* 35 (5): 624–58.

2011. "The Challenge of the All-Affected Principle." *Political Studies* 59: 116–34.

Nelson, Eric. 2008. "From Primary Goods to Capabilities: Distributive Justice and the Problem of Neutrality." *Political Theory* 36 (1): 93–122.

Newman, Dwight. 2007. "Exit, Voice and 'Exile': Rights to Exit and Rights to Eject." *University of Toronto Law Journal* 57 (1): 43–79.

Nickel, James. 2005. "Poverty and Rights." *The Philosophical Quarterly* 55 (220): 385–402.

2007. *Making Sense of Human Rights.* 2nd edn. Malden and Oxford: Blackwell Publishing.

Nussbaum, Martha. 1988. "Nature, Function, and Capability: Aristotle on Political Distribution." *Oxford Studies in Ancient Philosophy* Supplementary Volume I: 145–84.

1990. "Aristotelian Social Democracy." In *Liberalism and the Good*, edited by R. Bruce Douglas, Gerald M. Mara, and Henry S. Richardson, 203–52. New York: Routledge.

1993. "Non-Relative Virtues: An Aristotelian Approach." In *The Quality of Life*, edited by Martha Nussbaum and Amartya Sen, 242–69. Oxford: Clarendon Press.

1995. "Aristotle on Human Nature and the Foundation of Ethics." In *World, Mind and Ethics: Essays on the Ethical Philosophy of Bernard Williams*, edited by J. E. J. Altham and Ross Harrison, 86–131. Cambridge: Cambridge University Press.

1997. "Capabilities and Human Rights." *Fordham Law Review* 66 (2): 273–300.

1998. "The Good as Discipline, The Good as Freedom." In *Ethics of Consumption. The Good Life, Justice, and Global Stewardship*, edited by David Crocker and Toby Linden, 312–41. Lanham: Rowman & Littlefield.

2000a. "Why Practice Needs Ethical Theory." In *The Path of the Law and Its Influence. The Legacy of Oliver Wendell Holmes, Jr.*, edited by Steven Burton, 50–86. Cambridge: Cambridge University Press.

2000b. *Women and Human Development. The Capabilities Approach.* Cambridge: Cambridge University Press.

2001. "Adaptive Preferences and Women's Options." *Economics & Philosophy* 17 (1): 67–88.

2003a. "Capabilities as Fundamental Entitlements: Sen and Social Justice." *Feminist Economics* 9 (2–3): 33–59.

2003b. "Political Liberalism and Respect: A Response to Linda Barclay." *SATS – Nordic Journal of Philosophy* 4 (2): 25–44.

2006. *Frontiers of Justice.* Cambridge: The Belknap Press.

2011a. "Capabilities, Entitlements, Rights: Supplementation and Critique." *Journal of Human Development and Capabilities* 12 (1): 23–37.

2011b. *Creating Capabilities. The Human Development Approach.* Cambridge: The Belknap Press.

2011c. "Perfectionist Liberalism and Political Liberalism." *Philosophy & Public Affairs* 39 (1): 3–45.

Okin, Susan Moller. 2002. "'Mistresses of Their Own Destiny': Group Rights, Gender, and Realistic Rights of Exit." *Ethics* 112 (2): 205–30.

2003. "Poverty, Well-Being and Gender: What Counts, Who's Heard?" *Philosophy and Public Affairs* 31 (3): 280–316.

Olsaretti, Serena. 2004. *Liberty, Desert and the Market. A Philosophical Study.* Cambridge: Cambridge University Press.

2005. "Endorsement and Freedom in Amartya Sen's Capability Approach." *Economics and Philosophy* 21 (1): 89–108.

Olson, Kevin. 2006. *Reflexive Democracy. Political Equality and the Welfare State.* Cambridge: The MIT Press.

O'Neill, Martin. 2008. "What Should Egalitarians Believe?" *Philosophy & Public Affairs* 36 (2): 119–56.

2012. "Free (and Fair) Markets without Capitalism." In *Property-Owning Democracy. Rawls and Beyond,* edited by Martin O'Neill and Thad Williamson, 75–100. Malden and Oxford: Wiley-Blackwell.

O'Neill, Martin, and Thad Williamson, eds. 2012. *Property-Owning Democracy. Rawls and Beyond.* Malden and Oxford: Wiley-Blackwell.

O'Neill, Onora. 1979. "The Most Extensive Liberty." *Proceedings of the Aristotelian Society* 80: 45–59.

1989. "Constructivisms in Ethics." In *Constructions of Reason,* 206–18. Cambridge: Cambridge University Press.

2001. "Practical Principles and Practical Judgment." *Hastings Center Report* July–August: 15–23.

2007. "Normativity and Practical Judgment." *Journal of Moral Philosophy* 4 (3): 393–405.

Oshana, Marina. 1998. "Personal Autonomy and Society." *Journal of Social Philosophy* 29 (1): 81–102.

Ostrom, Elinor. 1990. *Governing the Commons. The Evolution of Institutions for Collective Action.* Cambridge: Cambridge University Press.

Pallikkathayil, Japa. 2010. "Deriving Morality from Politics: Rethinking the Formula of Humanity." *Ethics* 121 (1): 116–47.

2016. "Neither Perfectionism nor Political Liberalism." *Philosophy & Public Affairs* 44 (3): 171–96.

Parfit, Derek. 2000. "Equality or Priority?" In *The Ideal of Equality,* edited by Matthew Clayton and Andrew Williams, 81–125. New York: St. Martin's Press.

Patten, Alan. 2012. "Liberal Neutrality: A Reinterpretation and Defense." *Journal of Political Philosophy* 20 (3): 249–72.

Peter, Fabienne. 2013. "The Human Right to Political Participation." *Journal of Ethics & Social Philosophy* 7 (2): 1–16.

Pettit, Philip. 1993. *The Common Mind.* New York/Oxford: Oxford University Press.

1997. *Republicanism. A Theory of Freedom and Government.* Oxford: Oxford University Press.

2001. "Capability and Freedom: A Defence of Sen." *Economics and Philosophy* 17 (1): 1–20.

2003. "Agency-Freedom and Option-Freedom." *Journal of Theoretical Politics* 15 (4): 387–403.

2008. "The Basic Liberties." In *The Legacy of HLA Hart,* edited by Matthew Kramer, 201–24. Oxford: Oxford University Press.

2010. "Freedom in the Spirit of Sen." In *Amartya Sen*, edited by Christopher Morris, 91–114. Cambridge: Cambridge University Press.

2012. *On the People's Terms. A Republican Theory and Model of Democracy.* Cambridge: Cambridge University Press.

2014. *Just Freedom*. New York/London: Norton.

Pierik, Roland, and Ingrid Robeyns. 2007. "Resources versus Capabilities: Social Endowments in Egalitarian Theory." *Political Studies* 55 (1): 133–52.

Piketty, Thomas. 2014. *Capital in the Twenty-First Century.* Cambridge: Belknap Press.

Platz, Jesse von. 2014. "Are Economic Liberties Basic Rights?" *Politics, Philosophy & Economics* 13 (1): 23–44.

Pogge, Thomas. 2002. "Can the Capability Approach Be Justified?" *Philosophical Topics* 30 (2): 167–228.

2007. "Severe Poverty as a Human Rights Violation." In *Freedom from Poverty as a Human Right: Who Owes What to the Very Poor?*, edited by Thomas Pogge, 11–54. Oxford: Oxford University Press.

2008. *World Poverty and Human Rights*. Cambridge: Polity Press.

Qizilbash, Mozaffar. 1998. "The Concept of Well-Being." *Economics & Philosophy* 14 (1): 51–73.

2011. "Sugden's Critique of the Capability Approach." *Utilitas* 23 (1): 25–51.

2016. "Some Reflections on Capability and Republican Freedom." *Journal of Human Development and Capabilities* 17 (1): 22–34.

Quong, Jonathan. 2011. *Liberalism Without Perfection*. Oxford: Oxford University Press.

Rawls, John. 1999a. *A Theory of Justice*. Revised edn. Oxford: Oxford University Press.

1999b. *The Law of Peoples*. Cambridge: Harvard University Press.

2001a. *Justice as Fairness. A Restatement*. Cambridge: The Belknap Press.

2001b. "Two Concepts of Rules." In *Collected Papers*, edited by John Rawls and Samuel Freeman, 20–46. Cambridge: Harvard University Press.

2005. *Political Liberalism*. Expanded edn. New York: Columbia Press.

Raz, Joseph. 1986. *The Morality of Freedom*. Oxford: Clarendon Press.

2010. "Human Rights Without Foundations." In *The Philosophy of International Law*, edited by Samantha Besson and John Tasioulas, 321–37. Oxford: Oxford University Press.

Reidy, David. 2012. "On the Human Right to Democracy: Searching for Sense without Stilts." *Journal of Social Philosophy* 43 (2): 177–203.

Reitman, Oonagh. 2004. "On Exit." In *Minorities within Minorities. Equality, Rights and Diversity*, edited by Avigail Eisenberg and Jeff Spinner-Halev, 189–208. Cambridge: Cambridge University Press.

Richardson, Henry. 1997. *Practical Reasoning About Final Ends*. Cambridge: Cambridge University Press.

2000. "Some Limitations of Nussbaum's Capabilities." *Quinnipiac Law Review* 19 (2): 309–32.

2001. "Autonomy's Many Normative Presuppositions." *American Philosophical Quarterly* 38 (3): 287–303.

2007. "The Social Background of Capabilities for Freedoms." *Journal of Human Development* 8 (3): 389–414.

Ripstein, Arthur. 2004. "Authority and Coercion." *Philosophy & Public Affairs* 32 (1): 2–35.

2009. *Force and Freedom. Kant's Legal and Political Philosophy*. Cambridge: Harvard University Press.

Robeyns, Ingrid. 2005a. "Selecting Capabilities for Quality of Life Measurement." *Social Indicators Research* 74 (1): 191–215.

Robeyns, Ingrid. 2005b. "The Capability Approach: A Theoretical Survey." *Journal of Human Development* 6 (1): 93–117.

Robeyns, Ingrid. 2006. "The Capability Approach in Practice." *Journal of Political Philosophy* 14 (3): 351–76.

2008. "Sen's Capability Approach and Feminist Concerns." In *The Capability Approach. Concepts, Measures and Applications*, edited by Flavio Comim, Mozaffar Qizilbash, and Sabine Alkire, 105–24. Cambridge: Cambridge University Press.

2016. "Capabilitarianism." *Journal of Human Development and Capabilities* 17 (3): 397–414.

2017a. "Having Too Much." In *Nomos LVIII: Wealth*, edited by Jack Knight and Melissa Schwartzberg, 1–44. New York: New York University Press.

Robeyns, Ingrid. 2017b. *Wellbeing, Freedom and Social Justice. The Capability Approach Re-Examined*. Cambridge: Open Book Publishers.

Ronzoni, Miriam. 2010. "Constructivism and Practical Reason: On Intersubjectivity, Abstraction and Judgment." *Journal of Moral Philosophy* 7 (1): 74–104.

Rose, Carol. 1998. "The Several Futures of Property: Of Cyberspace and Folk Tales, Emissions Trades and Ecosystems." *Minnesota Law Review* 83 (1): 129–82.

Rössler, Beate. 2004. *The Value of Privacy*. Cambridge: Polity Press.

Rostbøll, Christian. 2011. "Kantian Autonomy and Political Liberalism." *Social Theory and Practice* 37 (3): 341–64.

Rostbøll, Christian. 2015a. "Non-Domination and Democratic Legitimacy." *Critical Review of International Social and Political Philosophy* 18 (4): 424–39.

Rostbøll, Christian. 2015b. "The Non-Instrumental Value of Democracy: The Freedom Argument." *Constellations* 22 (2): 267–78.

2016. "Kant, Freedom as Independence, and Democracy." *The Journal of Politics* 78 (3): 792–805.

Rothstein, Bo. 1998. *Just Institutions Matter. The Moral and Political Logic of the Universal Welfare State*. Cambridge: Cambridge University Press.

Rousseau, Jean-Jacques. 1997. "The Social Contract." In *The Social Contract and Other Later Political Writings*, edited by Victor Gourevitch, 39–152. Cambridge: Cambridge University Press.

Sadurski, Wojciech. 1990. "Joseph Raz on Liberal Neutrality and the Harm Principle." *Oxford Journal of Legal Studies* 10 (1): 122–33.

Sangiovanni, Andrea. 2012. "Can the Innate Right to Freedom Alone Ground a System of Public and Private Rights?" *European Journal of Philosophy* 20 (3): 460–9.

Scanlon, Thomas. 1972. "A Theory of Freedom of Expression." *Philosophy & Public Affairs* 1 (2): 204–26.

2003a. "Rawls on Justification." In *The Cambridge Companion to Rawls,* edited by Samuel Freeman, 139–67. Cambridge: Cambridge University Press.

2003b. "The Diversity of Objections to Inequality." In *The Difficulty of Tolerance,* 202–18. Cambridge: Cambridge University Press.

Schemmel, Christian. 2011. "Why Relational Egalitarians Should Care About Distributions." *Social Theory and Practice* 37 (3): 365–90.

Schuppert, Fabian. 2014. *Freedom, Recognition and Non-Domination. A Republican Theory of (Global) Justice.* Dordrecht/Heidelberg/New York/ London: Springer.

Searle, John. 1995. *The Construction of Social Reality.* New York: The Free Press.

2004. "Social Ontology and Political Power." In *Freedom and Neurobiology. Reflections on Free Will, Language, and Political Power,* 79–110. New York: Columbia University Press.

2005. "What Is an Institution?" *Journal of Institutional Economics* 1 (1): 1–22.

2010. *Making the Social World. The Structure of Human Civilization.* Oxford: Oxford University Press.

Segall, Shlomi. 2007. "In Solidarity with the Imprudent: A Defense of Luck Egalitarianism." *Social Theory and Practice* 33 (2): 177–98.

Sen, Amartya. 1979. "Equality of What." The Tanner Lectures on Human Values.

1983. "Poverty, Relatively Speaking." *Oxford Economic Papers, New Series* 35 (2): 153–69.

1985a. *Commodities and Capabilities.* Oxford: Oxford University Press.

1985b. "Well-Being, Agency and Freedom: The Dewey Lectures 1984." *The Journal of Philosophy* 82 (4): 169–221.

1990. "Justice: Means versus Freedoms." *Philosophy and Public Affairs* 19 (2): 111–21.

1992. *Inequality Reexamined.* Cambridge: Harvard University Press.

1999a. "Democracy as a Universal Value." *Journal of Democracy* 10 (3): 3–17.

1999b. *Development as Freedom.* Oxford: Oxford University Press.

2001. "Reply." *Economics and Philosophy* 17 (1): 51–66.

2004a. "Capabilities, Lists, and Public Reason: Continuing the Conversation." *Feminist Economics* 10 (3): 77–80.

2004b. "Elements of a Theory of Human Rights." *Philosophy & Public Affairs* 32 (4): 315–56.

2005. "Human Rights and Capabilities." *Journal of Human Development* 6 (2): 151–66.

2009. *The Idea of Justice.* Cambridge: The Belknap Press.

2010. "The Place of Capability in a Theory of Justice." In *Measuring Justice. Primary Goods and Capabilities,* edited by Harry Brighouse and Ingrid Robeyns, 239–53. Cambridge: Cambridge University Press.

Sher, George. 1997. *Beyond Neutrality. Perfectionism & Politics*. Cambridge: Cambridge University Press.

Shields, Liam. 2012. "The Prospects for Sufficientarianism." *Utilitas* 24 (1): 101–17.

Shue, Henry. 1996. *Basic Rights. Subsistence, Affluence, and U.S. Foreign Policy*. 2nd edn. Princeton: Princeton University Press.

Siedentop, Larry. 2014. *Inventing the Individual. The Origins of Western Liberalism*. Cambridge: The Belknapp Press.

Simmons, A. John. 2013. "Democratic Authority and the Boundary Problem." *Ratio Juris* 26 (3): 326–57.

Smith, Matthew, and Carolina Seward. 2009. "The Relational Ontology of Amartya Sen's Capability Approach: Incorporating Social and Individual Causes." *Journal of Human Development and Capabilities* 10 (2): 213–35.

Song, Sarah. 2012. "The Boundary Problem in Democratic Theory: Why the Demos Should Be Bounded by the State." *International Theory* 4 (1): 39–68.

Srinivasan, Sharath. 2007. "No Democracy without Justice: Political Freedom in Amartya Sen's Capability Approach." *Journal of Human Development and Capabilities* 8 (3): 457–80.

Stark, Cynthia. 1997. "The Rationality of Valuing Oneself: A Critique of Kant on Self-Respect." *Journal of the History of Philosophy* 35 (1): 65–82.

2009. "Respecting Human Dignity: Contract versus Capabilities." *Metaphilosophy* 40 (3–4): 366–81.

Stein, Mark. 2009. "Nussbaum: A Utilitarian Critique." *Boston College Law Review* 50: 489–531.

Steiner, Hillel. 1994. *An Essay on Rights*. Oxford: Blackwell.

Stiglitz, Joseph. 2012. *The Price of Inequality*. London/New York: W.W. Norton & Company.

Stilz, Anna. 2009. *Liberal Loyalty. Freedom, Obligation, and the State*. Princeton: Princeton University Press.

Stoljar, Natalie. 2000. "Autonomy and the Feminist Intuition." In *Relational Autonomy. Feminist Perspectives on Autonomy, Agency, and the Social Self*, edited by Catriona Mackenzie and Natalie Stoljar, 94–111. New York/Oxford: Oxford University Press.

2014. "Autonomy and Adaptive Preference Formation." In *Autonomy, Oppression, and Gender*, edited by Andrea Veltman and Mark Piper, 227–52. Oxford: Oxford University Press.

Stout, Lynn. 2012. *The Shareholder Value Myth*. San Francisco: Berrett-Koehler Publishers.

Street, Sharon. 2010. "What Is Constructivism in Ethics and Metaethics?" *Philosophy Compass* 5 (5): 363–84.

Stroud, Barry. 1968. "Transcendental Arguments." *The Journal of Philosophy* 65 (9): 241–56.

Strudler, Alan. 2017. "What to Do with Corporate Wealth?" *Journal of Political Philosophy* 25 (1): 108–26.

Sugden, Robert. 2003. "Opportunity as a Space of Individuality: Its Value and the Impossibility of Measuring It." *Ethics* 113 (4): 783–809.

Sugden, Robert. 2006. "What We Desire, What We Have Reason to Desire, Whatever We Might Desire: Mill and Sen on the Value of Opportunity." *Utilitas* 18 (1): 33–51.

Sumner, L. W. 2006. "Utility and Capability." *Utilitas* 18 (1): 1–19.

Talbott, William. 2005. *Which Rights Should Be Universal?* Oxford: Oxford University Press.

Tan, Kok-Chor. 2008. "A Defense of Luck Egalitarianism." *The Journal of Philosophy* 55 (11): 665–90.

Tasioulas, John. 2002. "Human Rights, Universality, and the Values of Personhood." *European Journal of Philosophy* 10 (1): 79–100.

2010. "Taking Rights out of Human Rights." *Ethics* 120 (4): 647–78.

Taylor, Charles. 1985. "Atomism." In *Philosophy and the Human Sciences*, 187–210. Cambridge: Cambridge University Press.

Temkin, Larry. 2003a. "Egalitarianism Defended." *Ethics* 113 (4): 764–82.

2003b. "Equality, Priority or What?" *Economics and Philosophy* 19 (1): 61–87.

Terlazzo, Rosa. 2014. "The Perfectionism of Nussbaum's Adaptive Preferences." *Journal of Global Ethics* 10 (2): 183–98.

2016. "Conceptualizing Adaptive Preferences Respectfully: An Indirectly Substantive Account." *Journal of Political Philosophy* 24 (2): 206–26.

Teschl, Miriam, and Flavio Comim. 2005. "Adaptive Preferences and Capabilities: Some Preliminary Conceptual Explorations." *Review of Social Economy* 63 (2): 229–47.

Tierney, Brian. 1997. *The Idea of Natural Rights. Studies on Natural Rights, Natural Law and Church Law 1150–1625*. Atlanta: Scholars Press.

Tomasi, John. 2012. *Free Market Fairness*. Princeton: Princeton University Press.

Tuck, Richard. 1979. *Natural Rights Theories. Their Origin and Development*. Cambridge: Cambridge University Press.

Valentini, Laura. 2012. "Kant, Ripstein and the Circle of Freedom: A Critical Note." *European Journal of Philosophy* 20 (3): 450–9.

2013. "Justice, Disagreement and Democracy." *British Journal of Political Science* 43 (1): 177–99.

Van Duffel, Siegfried. 2013. "Natural Rights to Welfare." *European Journal of Philosophy* 21 (4): 641–64.

Van Hees, Martin. 2012. "Rights, Goals and Capabilities." *Politics, Philosophy & Economics* 12 (3): 247–59.

Van Parijs, Philippe. 1995. *Real Freedom for All. What (If Anything) Can Justify Capitalism?* Oxford: Oxford University Press.

Vizard, Poly. 2007. "Specifying and Justifying a Basic Capability Set: Should the International Human Rights Framework Be given a More Direct Role?" *Oxford Development Studies* 35 (3): 225–50.

Waldron, Jeremy. 1988. *The Right to Private Property*. Oxford: Clarendon Press.

1989. "Autonomy and Perfectionism in Raz's Morality of Freedom." *Southern California Law Review* 62: 1097–1152.

1999. *Law and Disagreement*. Oxford: Oxford University Press.

2004. "Liberalism, Political and Comprehensive." In *Handbook of Political Theory*, edited by Gerald F. Gaus and Chandran Kukathas, 89–99. London: Sage.

Wall, Steven. 1998. *Liberalism, Perfectionism and Restraint*. Cambridge: Cambridge University Press.

2006. "Rawls and the Status of Political Liberty." *Pacific Philosophical Quarterly* 87 (2): 245–70.

Wall, Steven, and George Klosko. 2003. "Introduction." In *Perfectionism and Neutrality. Essays in Liberal Theory*, edited by Steven Wall and George Klosko, 1–27. Lanham: Rowman & Littlefield.

Weinstock, Daniel. 2004. "Beyond Exit Rights: Reframing the Debate." In *Minorities within Minorities. Equality, Rights and Diversity*, edited by Avigail Eisenberg, 227–46. Cambridge: Cambridge University Press.

Wenar, Leif. 2005. "The Nature of Rights." *Philosophy & Public Affairs* 33 (3): 223–52.

Wenar, Leif. 2013. "The Nature of Claim-Rights." *Ethics* 123 (2): 202–29.

Westlund, Andrea. 2003. "Selflessness and Responsibility for Self: Is Deference Compatible With Autonomy?" *The Philosophical Review* 112 (4): 483–523.

Whelan, Frederick. 1983. "Prologue: Democratic Theory and the Boundary Problem." In *Liberal Democracy*, edited by J. Roland Pennock and John W. Chapman, 13–47. New York: New York University Press.

White, Michael. 2012. *Political Philosophy. A Historical Introduction*. 2nd edn. Oxford: Oxford University Press.

White, Stuart. 1997. "Freedom of Association and the Right to Exclude." *Journal of Political Philosophy* 5 (4): 373–91.

2003. *The Civic Minimum. On the Rights and Obligations of Economic Citizenship*. Oxford: Oxford University Press.

2013. "Freedom of Association." In *The International Encyclopedia of Ethics*, edited by Hugh LaFollette, 373–82. London: Blackwell Publishing.

Wilkinson, Richard, and Kate Pickett. 2010. *The Spirit Level. Why Equality Is Better for Everyone*. London: Penguin Books.

Williamson, Thad. 2012. "Realizing Property-Owning Democracy." In *Property-Owning Democracy. Rawls and Beyond*, edited by Martin O'Neill and Thad Williamson, 225–48. Malden and Oxford: Wiley-Blackwell.

Winch, Peter. 1990. *The Idea of a Social Science and Its Relation to Philosophy*. 2nd edn. London: Routledge.

Wolff, Jonathan, and Avner De-Shalit. 2007. *Disadvantage*. Oxford: Oxford University Press.

Young, Iris Marion. 2011. *Responsibility for Justice*. Oxford: Oxford University Press.

Ypi, Lea. 2008. "Statist Cosmopolitanism." *Journal of Political Philosophy* 16 (1): 48–71.

Zale, Kellen. 2016. "Sharing Property." *University of Colorado Law Review* 87: 501–79.

Index